Arabic Thought

and Its Place in History

De Lacy O'Leary

DOVER PUBLICATIONS, INC.
Mineola, New York

Bibliographical Note

This Dover edition, first published in 2003, is an unabridged republication of the 1939 revision of the work first published by Routledge & Kegan Paul Ltd., London, in 1922.

Library of Congress Cataloging-in-Publication Data

O'Leary, De Lacy, b. 1872
    Arabic thought and its place in history / De Lacy OLeary.
       p. cm.
    Includes bibliographical references (p.) and index.
    ISBN 0-486-42762-5 (pbk.)
     1. Philosophy, Arab. I. Title.

B741 .04 2003
181'.92—dc21

2002041310

Manufactured in the United States of America
Dover Publications, Inc., 31 East 2nd Street, Mineola, N.Y. 11501

FOREWORD

History traces the evolution of the social structure in which the community exists to-day. There are three chief factors at work in this evolution; racial descent, culture drift, and transmission of language: the first of these physiological and not necessarily connected with the other two, whilst those two are not always associated with each other. In the evolution of the social structure the factor of first importance is the transmission of culture, which is not a matter of heredity but due to contact, for culture is learned and reproduced by imitation and not inherited. Culture must be taken in the widest sense to include political, social, and legal institutions, the arts and crafts, religion, and the various forms of intellectual life which show their presence in literature, philosophy, and otherwise, all more or less connected, and all having the common characteristic that they cannot be passed on by physical descent but must be learned in after life. But race, culture, and language resemble one another in so far as it is true that all are multiplex and perpetually interwoven, so that in each the lines of transmission seem rather like a tangled skein than an ordered pattern; results proceed from a conflicting group of causes amongst which it is often difficult to apportion the relative influences.

The culture of modern Europe derives from that of the Roman Empire, itself the multiple resultant

of many forces, amongst which the intellectual life
of Hellenism was most effective, but worked into a
coherent system by the wonderful power of organization, which was one of the most salient characteristics
of that Empire.   The whole cultural life of mediæval
Europe shows this Hellenistic-Roman culture passed
on, developed, and modified by circumstances.   As
the Empire fell to pieces the body of culture became
subject to varying conditions in different localities,
of which the divergence between the Greek-speaking
East and the Latin-speaking West is the most striking
example.   The introduction of Muslim influence
through Spain is the one instance in which we seem
to get an alien culture entering into this Roman
tradition and exercising a disturbing influence.   In
fact, this Muslim culture was at bottom essentially a
part of the Hellenistic-Roman material, even the
theology of Islam being formulated and developed
from Hellenistic sources, but Islam had so long lived
apart from Christendom and its development had
taken place in surroundings so different that it seems
a strange and alien thing.   Its greatest power lay in
the fact that it presented the old material in an
entirely fresh form.

It is the effort of the following pages to trace the
transmission of Hellenistic thought through the
medium of Muslim philosophers and Jewish thinkers
who lived in Muslim surroundings, to show how this
thought, modified as it passed through a period of
development in the Muslim community and itself
modifying Islamic ideas, was brought to bear upon
the culture of mediæval Latin Christendom.   So
greatly had it altered in external form during the
centuries of its life apart, that it seemed a new type of

intellectual life and became a disturbing factor which diverted Christian philosophy into new lines and tended to disintegrate the traditional theology of the Church, directly leading up to the Renascence which gave the death-blow to mediæval culture : so little had it altered in real substance that it used the same text-books and treated very much the same problems already current in the earlier scholasticism which had developed independently in Latin Christendom. It will be our effort so to trace the history of mediæval Muslim thought as to show the elements which it had in common with Christian teaching and to account for the points of divergence.

DE L. O'L.

CONTENTS

CHAPTER I

THE SYRIAC VERSION OF HELLENISM

The subject proposed in the following pages is the history of the cultural transmission by which Greek philosophy and science were passed from Hellenistic surroundings to the Syriac speaking community, thence to the Arabic speaking world of Islam, and so finally to the Latin Schoolmen of Western Europe. That such a transmission did take place is known even to the beginner in mediæval history, but how it happened, and the influences which promoted it, and the modifications which took place *en route*, appear to be less generally known, and it does not seem that the details, scattered through works of very diverse types, are easily accessible to the English reader. Many historians seem content to give only a casual reference to its course, sometimes even with strange chronological confusions which show that the sources used are still the mediæval writers who had very imperfect information about the development of intellectual life amongst the Muslims. Following mediæval usage we sometimes find the Arabic writers referred to as " Arabs " or " Moors," although in fact there was only one philosopher of any importance who was an Arab by race, and com-

paratively little is known about his work. These
writers belonged to an Arabic speaking community,
but very few of them were actually Arabs.

After the later Hellenistic development Greek
culture spread outward into the oriental fringe of
people who used Syriac, Coptic, Aramaic, or Persian
as their vernacular speech, and in these alien surroundings it took a somewhat narrower development and
even what we may describe as a provincial tone.
There is no question of race in this. Culture is not
inherited as a part of the physiological heritage
transmitted from parent to child ; it is learned by
contact due to intercourse, imitation, education, and
such like things, and such contact between social
groups as well as between individuals is much helped
by the use of a common language and hindered by
difference of language. As soon as Hellenism over-
flowed into the vernacular speaking communities
outside the Greek speaking world it began to suffer
some modification. It so happened also that these
vernacular speaking communities wanted to be cut
off from close contact with the Greek world because
very bitter theological divisions had arisen and had
produced feelings of great hostility on the part of
those who were officially described as heretics against
the state church in the Byzantine Empire.

In this present chapter we have to consider three
points ; in the first place the particular stage of
development reached by Greek thought at the time
when these divisions took place ; secondly the cause

of these divisions and their tendencies ; and thirdly
the particular line of development taken by Hellenistic culture in its oriental atmosphere.

First stands the question of the stage of development reached by Hellenism, and we may test this by
its intellectual life as represented by science and
philosophy, at the time when the oriental offshoot
shows a definite line of separation. English education, largely dominated by the principles learned at
the renascence, is inclined to treat philosophy as
coming to an end with Aristotle and beginning
again with Descartes after a long blank during which
there lived and worked some degenerate descendants
of the ancients who hardly need serious consideration.
But this position violates the primary canon of
history which postulates that all life is continuous,
the life of the social community as well as the physical
life of an organic body : and life must be a perpetual
series of causes and results, so that each event can
only be explained by the cause which went before,
and can only be fully understood in the light of the
result which follows after. What we call the " middle ages " had an important place in the evolution
of our own cultural condition, and owed much to
the transmitted culture which came round from
ancient Hellenism through Syriac, Arabic, and Hebrew
media. But this culture came as a living thing
with an unbroken and continuous development
from what we call the " classic " age. As the
philosophy of the great classic schools passes down

to these later periods it shows great modifications, but this alteration is itself a proof of life. Philosophy, like religion, in so far as it has a real vitality, must change and adapt itself to altered conditions and new requirements : it can remain pure and true to its past only in so far as its life is artificial and unreal, lived in an academic atmosphere far removed from the life of the community at large. In such an unnatural atmosphere no doubt, it is possible for a religion or a philosophy to live perfectly pure and uncorrupt, but it is certainly not an ideal life : in real life there are bound to be introduced many unworthy elements and some which can only be described as actually corrupt. So it is inevitable that as a religion or a philosophy lives and really fulfils its proper functions it has to pass through many changes. Of course the same holds good for all other forms of culture : it may be true that a country is happy if it has no history, but it is the placid happiness of vegetable life, not the enjoyment of the higher functions of rational being.

In considering the transmission of Greek philosophy to the Arabs we see that philosophy still as a living force, adapting itself to changed conditions but without a break in the continuity of its life. It was not, as now, an academic study sought only by a group of specialists, but a living influence which guided men in their ideas about the universe in which they lived and dominated all theology, law, and social ideas. For many centuries it pervaded the

atmosphere in which Western Asia was educated
and in which it lived. Men became Christians, for
a time the new religious interest filled their minds,
but later on it was inevitable that philosophy should
re-assert its power, and then Christian doctrine had
to be re-cast to conform to it : the descendants of
these people became Muslims and then again, after an
interval, religion had to conform itself to current
philosophy. We have no such dominant philosophical system in force to-day, but we have a certain
mass of scientific facts and theories which form an
intellectual background to modern European life
and the defenders of traditional religion find it
necessary to adjust their teaching to the principles
implied in those facts and theories.

But the important point is that then Christian
teachers began to put themselves into touch with
current philosophy, and so when the Muslims later
on did the same, they had to reckon with philosophy
as they found it actually living in their own days :
they did not become Platonists or Aristotelians in
the sense in which we should understand the terms.
The current philosophy had changed from the older
standards, not because the degenerate people of those
days could not understand the pure doctrines of
Plato and Aristotle, but because they took philosophy
so seriously and earnestly as an explanation of the
universe and of man's place in it that they were bound
to re-adjust their views in the light of what they regarded as later information, and the views had altered

to adjust themselves with the course of human experience.

From Plato onwards philosophy had been very largely concerned with theories which more or less directly concerned the structure of society : it was perceived that a very large part of man's life, duties, and general welfare, was intimately concerned with his relations to the community in which he lived. But soon after the time of Aristotle the general conditions of the social order were seen to be undergoing a profound modification : great empires with highly organised administrations replaced the self-governing city states of the older period, and social life had to adjust itself to the new conditions. A man who was a citizen of the Roman Empire was a citizen in quite a different sense from that in which one was a citizen of the Athenian Republic. The Stoic philosophy, which is of this later age, already presupposes these new conditions and in course of time the other schools orientated themselves similarly. One of the first results is a tendency to eclecticism and to combination of the tenets of several schools. The new outlook, broader in its horizon, perhaps shallower in other respects, impelled men to take what was an imperialist attitude instead of a local or national one. Precisely similar changes were forced upon the Jewish religion. Hellenistic Judaism, at the beginning of the Christian era, is concerned with the human species and the race of Israel is considered chiefly as a means of bringing illumination to mankind at

large. It was this Hellenistic Judaism which cul-
minated in St. Paul and the expansion of the Christian
Church, whilst orthodox Judaism, that is to say the
provincial Jewery of Palestine reverted to its racial
attitude under the pressure of circumstances partly
reactionary against the too rapid progress of Hellenism
and partly political in character.

The old pagan religions showed many local varieties,
and from these a world-wide religion could only be
evolved by some speculative doctrines which reconciled their divergences. Never has a religion of any
extension been formed from local cults otherwise
than by the ministry of some kind of speculative
theology : sometimes the fusion of cults has spon-
taneously produced such a theology, as was the case
in the Nile valley and in Mesopotamia in early times,
and when the theology was produced it brought its
solvent power to bear rapidly and effectively on
other surrounding cults. As many races and states
were associated together in the Greek Empire which,
though apparently separated into several kingdoms,
yet had an intellectual coherence and a common
civilization, and this was still more definitely the case
when the closer federation of the Roman Empire
followed, philosophy was forced more and more in
the direction of speculative theology : it assumed
those ethical and doctrinal functions which we
generally associate with religion, the contemporary
local cults concerning themselves only with ritual
duties. Thus in the early centuries of the Christian

era. Hellenistic philosophy was evolving a kind of
religion, of a high moral tone and definitely monotheistic in doctrine. This theological philosophy
was eclectic, but rested upon a basis of Platonism.

Whilst the philosophers were developing a monotheistic and moral system which they hoped to make a
world religion, the Christians were attempting a
similar task on somewhat different lines. The
earlier converts to the Christian religion were not as
a rule drawn from the educated classes and shewed
a marked suspicion and dislike towards those superior
persons, such as the Gnostics, or at least the pre-
Marcionite Gnostics, who were disposed to patronise
them. Gradually however this attitude changed and
we begin to find men like Justin Martyr who had
received a philosophical education and yet found it
quite possible to co-ordinate contemporary science
and Christian doctrine. In Rome, in Africa, and in
Greece the Christians were a despised minority,
chiefly drawn from the unlettered class, and osten-
tatiously ignored by the writers of the day. Like
the Jew of the Ghetto they were forced to live an
isolated life and thrown back upon their internal
resources. But in Alexandria and, to a lesser
degree in Syria, they were more in the position of the
modern Jew in Anglo Saxon lands, though bitterly
hated and occasionally persecuted, and were brought
under the intellectual influences of the surrounding
community and thus experienced a solvent force
in their own ideas. When at last Christianity

appears in the ascendant it has been largely re-cast by Hellenistic influences, its theology is re-stated in philosophical terms, and thus in the guise of theology a large amount of philosophical material was transmitted to the vernacular speaking hinterland of Western Asia.

The Arabic writer Masûdi informs us that Greek philosophy originally flourished at Athens, but the Emperor Augustus transferred it from Athens to Alexandria and Rome, and Theodosius afterwards closed the schools at Rome and made Alexandria the educational centre of the Greek world (Masûdi : *Livre de l'avertissement*, trad. B.Carra de Vaux, Paris, 1896, p. 170). Although grotesquely expressed this statement contains an element of truth in so far as it represents Alexandria as gradually becoming the principal home of Greek philosophy. It had begun to take a leading place even in the days of the Ptolemies, and in scientific, as distinguished from purely literary work, it had assumed a position of primary importance early in the Christian era. The schools of Athens remained open until A.D. 529, but had long been out of touch with progressive scholarship. Rome also shows great philosophers, most often of oriental birth, down to a late age, but although these were given a kindly welcome and a hearing, Roman education was more interested in jurisprudence, indeed the purely Roman philosophical speculation is that embedded in Justinian's code. Antioch also had its philosophy, but this was never of more than secondary importance.

In the course of what we may term the Alexandrian period the Platonic school had steadily taken the first place. It was indeed considerably changed from the ancient Academic standards, chiefly by the introduction of semi-mystical elements which were attributed to Pythagoras, and later by fusion with the neo-Aristotelian school. The Pythagorean elements probably can be traced ultimately to an Indian source, at least in such instances as the doctrine of the un-reality of matter and phenomena which appears in Indian philosophy as *māyā*, and the re-incarnation of souls which is *avatar*. The tendency of native Greek thought, as seen in Democritus and other genuinely Greek thinkers, was distinctly material-istic, but Plato apparently incorporates some alien matter, probably Indian, perhaps some Eygptian ideas as well. We know there was a transmission of oriental thought influencing Hellenism, but very little is known of the details. Certainly Plotinus and the neo-Platonists were eclectic thinkers and drew freely from oriental sources, some disguised as Pytha-gorean, by a long sojourn in Greek lands.

In the 3rd century A.D. we find the beginnings of what is known as neo-Platonism. A very typical passage in Gibbon's *Decline and Fall* (ch. xiii) refers to the neo-Platonists as " men of profound thought and intense application ; but, by mistaking the true object of philosophy, their labours contributed much less to improve than to corrupt the human understanding. The knowledge that is suited to our situation and powers, the whole compass of moral, natural, and mathematical science, was neglected by the new Plantonists ; whilst they exhausted their strength in the verbal disputes of metaphysics, attempted to explore the secrets of the invisible world, and studied to reconcile Aristotle with Plato, on subjects of which both these philosophers were as ignorant as the rest of mankind." Although this passage is coloured by some of the peculiar prejudices of Gibbon it fairly represents a common attitude towards neo-Platonism and might equally apply to every religious movement the world has ever seen.

The neo-Platonists were the result, we may say the inevitable result, of tendencies which had been at work ever since the age of Alexander and the widening of the mental horizon and the decay of interest in the old civic life. The older philosophers had endeavoured to produce efficient citizens ; but under imperialist conditions efficient citizens were not so much wanted as obedient subjects. Through all this period there are very clear indications of the new trend of thought which assumes a more theological and philanthropic character, aiming at producing good men rather than useful citizens. The specu- lations of Philo the Jewish Platonist give very plain indications of these new tendencies as they appeared in Alexandria. He shows the monotheistic tendency which was indeed present in the older philosophers but now begins to be more strongly emphasized as philosophy becomes more theological in its speculations, though no doubt in his case this was largely due to the religion he professed. He expressed the doctrine of a One God, eternal, unchanging, and passionless, far removed above the world of phenomena, as the First Cause of all that exists, a philosophical monotheism which can be fitted in with the Old Testament but does not naturally proceed from it. The doctrine of an Absolute Reality as the necessary cause of all that is variable, something like the fulcrum which Archimedes needed to move the world, was one to which all philosophy, and especially the Plantonic school, was tending. But, as causation to some extent implies change, this First Cause could not be regarded as directly creating the world, but only as the eternal source of an eternally proceeding emanation by means of which the power of the First Cause is projected so as to produce the universe and all it contains. The essential features of this teaching are, the absolute unity of the First Cause, its absolute reality, its eternity, and its invariability, all of which necessarily removes it above the plane of things knowable to man ; and the operative emanation ceaselessly issuing forth, eternal like its source, yet acting in time and space, an emanation which Philo terms the *Logos* or " Word." Although these theories are to a large extent only an expression of logical conclusions towards which the Platonists were then advancing, Philo had curiously little influence. No doubt there was a tendency to regard his teaching as mainly an attempt to read a Platonic meaning into Jewish doctrine, and certainly the large amount of attention he devoted to exegesis of the Old Testament and to Jewish apologetics would prevent his works from receiving serious attention from non-Jewish readers. Again, although his ideas about monotheism and the nature of God were those to which Platonism was tending, they represent also a Jewish attitude which, starting from a monotheistic standpoint was then, under Hellenistic influence, making towards a supra-sensual idea of God, explaining away the anthropomorphisms of the Old Testament and postulating an emanation, the *Hochma* or " wisdom " of God as the intermediary in creation and revelation. Undoubtedly Philo, or the Philonic school of Hellenistic Judaism, was responsible for the Logos doctrine which appears in the portions of the New Testament bearing the name of St. John. He had an influence also on Jewish thought as appears in the Targums where the operative emanation which proceeds from the First Cause is no longer the " wisdom " of God but the " Word." He seems to have had no influence at all on the course of Alexandrian philosophy generally.

The tendencies which were at work in Philo were also leavening Greek thought outside Jewish circles and all schools of philosophy show a growing definiteness in their assertion of One God eternal and invariable, as the source and First Cause of the universe. It is a recognition of the principal of uniformity in nature and of the necessity of accounting for the cause of this uniformity. The Gnostic sects, which were of philosophical origin, simply show the definite accept- ance of this First Cause and, having accepted it as on a plane far removed above imperfection and variation, suggest intermediary emanations as explaining the production of an imperfect and variable universe from a primary source which is itself perfect and un- changing. The descriptive accounts of the successive emanations, each less perfect than that from which it proceeds, which ultimately produced the world in which we perceive phenomena, are different in different Gnostic systems, often crude enough and grotesque in our eyes, and frequently drawing from Christianity or Judaism or some other of the oriental religions which were then attracting the attention of the Roman world. But these details are of minor importance. All Gnostic theories bear witness to the belief that there is a First Cause, absolutely real, perfect, eternal, and far removed above this world of time and space, and that some emanation or emanations must have intervened to connect the resultant world, such as we know it, with this sublime Cause: and such belief indicates in crude form a general conviction which was getting hold of all current thought in the early centuries of the Christian era.

Complementary to this was the psychological teaching represented by the Aristotelian commentator Alexander of Aphrodisias who taught at Athens, A.D. 198-211. His extant works include commentaries

on the first book of the Analytica Priora, on the
Topica, Meterology, *de sensu,* the first five books of the
Metaphysics and an abridgment of the other books
of the Metaphysics, as well as treatises on the soul, etc.
Over and over again his treatise on the soul and his
commentaries are translated into Arabic, paraphrased,
and made the subject of further commentaries, until
it seems that his psychology is the very nucleus of all
Arabic philosophy, and it is this which forms the main
point of the Arabic influence on Latin scholasticism.
It becomes indeed absolutely essential that we understand the Alexandrian interpretation of the Aristotelian psychology if we are to follow the oriental
development of Greek science.

The first point is to understand what is to be
implied in the term " soul." Plato was really a
dualist in that he regards the soul as a separate
entity which animates the body and compares it to a
rider directing and controlling the horse he rides.
But Aristotle makes a more careful analysis of
psychological phenomena. In the treatise *de anima*
he says " there is no need to enquire whether soul and
body are one, any more than whether the wax and
the imprint are one ; or, in general, whether the
matter of a thing is the same with that of which it is
the matter." (Aristot : *de anima.* II. i. 412. b. 6.)
Aristotle defines the soul as " the first actuality of a
natural body having in it the capacity of life " (id. 412.
b. 5), in which " first " denotes that the soul is the
primary form by which the substance of the body is

actualized, and " actuality " refers to the actualizing principle by which form is given to the body which otherwise would be only a collection of separate parts each having its own form but the aggregate being without corporate unity until the soul gives it form ; in this sense the soul is the realization of the body (cf. Aristot : *Metaph*. iii. 1043. a. 35). A dead body lacks this actualizing and centralizing force and is only a collection of limbs and organs, yet even so it is not an artificial collection such as a man might put together, but " a natural body having in it the capacity of life," that is to say, an organic structure designed for a soul which is the cause or reason of its existence and which alone enables the body to realize its object.

The soul contains four different faculties or powers which are not strictly to be taken as " parts " though in the passage cited above Aristotle uses the term " parts." These are, (1) the nutritive, the power of life whereby the body performs such functions as absorbing nourishment, propagating its species, and other functions common to all living beings, whether animal or vegetable : (ii) the sensible, by which the body obtains knowledge through the medium of the special senses of sight, hearing, touch, etc., and also the " common sense " by means of which these perceptions are combined, compared, and contrasted so that general ideas are obtained which ultimately rest on the sense perceptions : (iii) the locomotive, which prompts to action, as desire, appetite, will, etc., also

based, though indirectly, on sense perception, being
suggested by memories of senses already in action :
(iv) the intellect or pure reason, which is concerned
with abstract thought and is not based on sense perception. All these, embracing life in its widest
application, are classed together as soul, but the last,
the intellect, *nous*, or rational soul, is peculiar to man
alone. It does not depend on the senses, directly
or indirectly, and so, whilst the other three faculties
necessarily cease to function when the bodily organs
of sense cease, it does not necessarily follow that this
rational soul will cease as it is apparently independent
of the organ sense. This *nous* or " spirit " is reduced by
Aristotle to a much more restricted range than is
usual in the older philosophers and is taken to mean
that which has the capacity of abstract knowledge,
independent of the information due, directly or
indirectly, to sense perception. It would seem, however, to be a distinct species of faculty for Aristotle
says : " As regards intellect and the speculative
faculty the case is not yet clear. It would seem,
however, to be a distinct species of soul, and it alone is
capable of separation from the body, as that which is
eternal from that which is perishable. The remaining
parts of the soul are, as the foregoing consideration
shows, not separable in the way that some allege
them to be : at the same time it is clear that they are
logically distinct." (Arist. *de anima*. II. ii. 413. b. 9).
It is suggested that (i) the rational soul is of a distinct
species and so presumably derived from a different

source than the other faculties of the soul, but nothing is said as to whence it is derived : (ii) it is capable of existence independently of the body, that is to say its activity does not depend on the operation of the bodily organs, but it is not stated that it does so exist ; (iii) it is eternal on the ground that it can exist apart from the perishable.

The obscurity of this statement has led to a great divergence in its treatment by commentators. Theophrastus offers cautious suggestions and evidently regards the rational soul as differing only in degree of evolution from the lower forms of soul faculty. It was Alexander of Aphrodisias who opened up new fields of speculation, distinguishing between a material intellect and an active intellect. The former is a faculty of the individual soul and this it is which is the form of the body, but it means no more than the capacity for thinking and is of the same source as the other faculties of the human soul. The active intellect is not a part of the soul but is a power which enters it from outside and arouses the material intellect to activity ; it is not only different in source from the material soul, but different in character in that it is eternal and so always has been and always will be, its rational power existing quite apart from the soul in which the thinking takes place ; there is but one such substance and this must be identified with the deity who is the First Cause of all motion and activity, so that the active intellect is pictured as an emanation from the deity entering the human soul, arousing it to the exercise of its higher functions, and then returning to its divine source. This theistic interpretation of Aristotle was strongly opposed by the commentator Themistius who considers that Alexander forces the statement of the text out of its natural meaning and draws an unwarrantable deduction from the two sentences " these differences must be present in the soul," and " this alone is immortal and eternal." It seems, however, that Alexander's interpretation played an important part in the formation of neo-Plantonic theory, and it certainly is the key to the history of Muslim philosophy, and is not without its importance in the development of Christian mysticism.

The neo-Platonic school was founded by Ammonius Saccas, but really takes its definite form under *Plotinus* (d. 269 A.D.). In sketching in brief outline the leading principles of this system we shall confine ourselves to the last three books of the *Enneads* (iv-vi) as these, in the abridged form known as the " Theology of Aristotle " formed the main statement of neo-Platonic doctrine known to the Muslim world. In the teaching of Plotinus God is the Absolute, the First Potency (*Enn.* 5. 4. 1.), beyond the sphere of existence (id. 5. 4. 2.), and beyond reality, that is to say, all that we know as existence and being is inapplicable to him, and he is therefore unknowable, because on a plane which is altogether beyond our thought. He is unlimited and infinite (id. 6. 5. 9.) and consequently One, as infinity excludes the possibility of any other than himself on the same plane of being. Yet Plotinus does not allow the numeral " one " to be applied to God as numerals are understandable and refer to the plane of existence in which we have our being, so that " one " as a mere number is not attributed to God, but rather singularity in the sense of an exclusion of all comparison or of any other than himself. As Absolute God implies a compelling necessity so that all which proceeds from him is not enforced but is necessarily so in the sense that nothing else is possible ; thus, for example, it results from him that two sides of a triangle are greater than the third side, they are not forced into greater length, but in the nature of things must be so, and this necessary nature has its compelling source in the First Cause. Yet Plotinus will not allow us to say that God " wills " anything, for will implies a desire for what is not possessed or is not yet present (id. 5. 3. 12) ; will operates in time and space, but necessity has for ever proceeded from the Eternal One who does not act in time. Nor can we conceive God as knowing, conscious, or thinking, all terms which describe our mental activities in the world of variable phenomena ; he is all-knowing by immediate apprehension ('αθρόα 'επιβολή) which in no way resembles the operation of thought but is superconscious, a condition which Plotinus describes as " wakefulness " ('εγρήγορσις), a perpetual being aware without the need of obtaining information.

From the true God, the eternal Absolute, proceeds

the *nous*, a term which has been variously rendered as
Reason, Intellect, Intelligence, or Spirit, this last
being the term which Dr. Inge regards as the best
expression (Inge : *Plotinus*. ii. p. 38), and this *nous*
is fairly equivalent to the Philonic and Christian
Logos. An external emanation is necessitated in
order that the First Cause may remain unchanged
which would not be the case if it had once not been a
source and then had become the source of emanation ;
there can be no " becoming " in the First Cause. The
emanation is of the same nature as its cause, but is
projected into the world of phenomena. It is self-
existent, eternal, and perfect, and comprehends
within itself the " spirit world," the objects of abstract reason, the whole of the reality which
lies behind the world of phenomena ; the things
perceived are only the shadows of these real
ones. It perceives, not as seeking and finding,
but as already possessing (id. 5. 1. 4.), and the things
perceived are not separate or external but as included
and apprehended by immediate intuition (id. 5. 2. 2.)

From the *nous* proceeds the *psyche*, the principle of
life and motion, the world soul which is in the universe
and which is shared by every living creature. It also
knows, but only through the processes of reasoning,
by means of separating, distributing, and combining
the data obtained by sense perception, so that it
corresponds in function to the " common sense " of
Aristotle, whilst the *nous* shows the functions which are
attributed to it by Aristotle and has the character
which Alexander reads into Aristotle.

The work of Plotinus was continued by his pupil Porphyry (d. 300 A.D.) who taught at Rome, and is chiefly noteworthy as the one who completed the fusion of Platonic and Aristotelian elements in the neo-Platonic system, and especially as introducing the scientific methods of Aristotle. Plotinus had criticized adversely the Aristotelian categories (*Enn.* vi.), but Porphyry and all the later neo-Platonists returned to Aristotle. Indeed, he is best known to posterity as the author of the *Isagoge*, long current as the regular introduction to the logical Organon of Aristotle. Then came *Jamblichus* (d. 330), the pupil of Porphyry who used neo-Platonism as the basis of a pagan theology ; and finally Proklus (d. 485) its last great pagan adherent who was even more definitely a theologian.

Neo-Platonism was the system just coming to the fore-front when the Christians of Alexandria began to be in contact with philosophy. The first prominent Alexandrian Christian who endeavoured to reconcile philosophy and Christian theology was *Clement of Alexandria* who, like Justin Martyr, was a Platonist of the older type. Clement's *Stromateis* is a very striking work which shows the general body of Christian doctrine adapted to the theories of Platonic philosophy. It does not tamper with the traditional Christian doctrine, but it is evidently the work of one who sincerely believed that Plato had partially foreseen what the Gospels taught, and that he had used a clear and efficient terminology which was in all respects suitable for the expression of profound truths, and so Clement uses this terminology, incidentally assuming the Platonic metaphysics, and so unconsciously modifies the contents of Christianity. If we ask whether this results in a fair presentation of Christian teaching we shall perhaps be inclined to admit that, in spite of modification and in view of the scientific attitude of the times it substantially does so : when truths already expressed by those who have not received a scientific training are repeated by those who have and who are careful to cast their expression into logical and consistent form, some modification is inevitable. Whether the scientific assumptions and philosophy generally of Clement were correct is, of course, another matter ; modern opinion would say it was incorrect. But, so far as contemporary science went, it was obviously an honest effort. It has not been appreciated by all Clement's successors and he is one of the few Christian leaders who has been formally deprived of the honorific title of " saint " which was at one time prefixed to his name. Within the next few centuries the re-formulation of Christianity proceeded steadily until at last it appears as essentially Hellenistic, but with the Platonic element now modified by the more spiritualistic influences of neo-Platonism. Undoubtedly this was a gain for Christianity, for when we read the *Didache* and other early non-Hellenistic Christian material we cannot help feeling that it shows a narrower and more cramped outlook and one far less suited to satisfy the needs and aspirations of humanity at large. It is curious to compare Clement of Alexandria with Tertullian, one of the greatest, if not the greatest, of the literary lights of Latin Christianity, but severe, puritanically rigid, and suspicious and hostile in his attitude towards philosophy which he regards as essentially pagan.

The next great leader of Alexandrian Christian thought was Origen himself a pupil of Plotinus, and one who found little difficulty in adapting contemporary philosophy to Christian doctrine, although this adaptation was by no means received with approval in all parts of the Christian community. Under Clement and Origen the catechetical instruction which was regularly given in all churches to candidates for baptism was expanded and developed on the lines of the lectures given by the philosophers in the Museum, and so a Christian school of philosophical theology was formed. This development was not regarded favourably by the older fashioned churches nor by the philosophers of the Museum, and even amongst the Alexandrian Christians there was a section which viewed it with disapproval, especially evident when the school became so prominent that it tended to overshadow the ordinary diocesan organization.

This is not the place to consider the various intrigues which ultimately compelled Origen to leave Alexandria and retire to Palestine. There, at Caesarea, he founded a school on the model of that at Alexandria. This second foundation did not attain the same eminence as its proto-type, perhaps because Origen's influence turned its activities into a direction too highly specialised in textual criticism, but it prompted a development which ultimately played an important part in the history of the Syrian church where, for some time to come, theological activity mainly centered in these schools which had their imitators amongst the Zoroastrians and the Muslims. The first such school in Syria was founded at Antioch by Malchion about 270 A.D. and deliberately copied the pattern set at Alexandria and ultimately became its rival.

About fifty years later a school was established at Nisibis, the modern Nasibin on the Mygdonius river, in the midst of a Syriac speaking community. The church had spread inland from the Mediterranean shores and had by this time many converts in the hinterland who were accustomed to use Syriac and not Greek. For the benefit of these the work at Nisibis was done in Syriac, Syriac versions were prepared of the theological works studied at Antioch, and the Greek language was taught so that the Syriac speaking Christians were brought into closer touch with the life of the Church at large.

The acquiescence of the Church in the Alexandrian philosophy had far-reaching consequences. The Church did not officially adopt the neo-Platonic philosophy in its entirety, but it had to adjust itself to an atmosphere in which the neo-Platonic system was accepted as the last word in scientific enquiry and

where the Aristotelian metaphysics and phychology
were assumed as an established and unquestionable
basis of knowledge.   It was impossible for churchmen,
educated in this atmosphere, to do otherwise than
accept these principles, just as it is impossible for us
to admit that the body of a saint can be in two places
at once, our whole education training us to assume
certain limitations of time and space, although a
devout Muslim of Morocco can believe it and honours
two shrines as each containing the body of the same
saint who, he believes, in his life time had power of
over-passing the limitations of space.   The general
postulates of the later Platonic and Aristotelian
philosophy were firmly established in the fourth
century in Alexandria and its circle, and were no more
open to question than the law of gravity or the
rotundity of the earth would be to us.   It was known
that there were people who questioned these things,
but it could only be accounted for by blind ignorance
in those who had not received the benefits of an
enlightened education.   The Christians were no more
able to dispute these principles than anyone else.
They were perfectly sincere in their religion, many
articles of faith which present considerable difficulty
to the modern mind presented no difficulty to them ;
but it was perfectly obvious that the statements of
Christian doctrine must be brought into line with the
current theory of philosophy, or with self evident
truth as they would have termed it.   It shows a
strange lack of historical imagination when we talk

slightingly about how Christians quarrelled over
words, forgetting what these words represented and
how they stood for the established conclusions of
philosophy as then understood.

This comes out very plainly in the Arian controversy. Both sides agreed that Christ was the Son of
God, the relation of Father and Son being, of course,
not that of human parentage but rather by way of
emanation : both agreed that Christ was God, as the
emanation necessarily had the same nature as the
source from which it proceeded : both agreed that the
Son proceeded from the Father in eternity and before
the worlds were created, the Son or Logos being the
intermediary of creation. But some, and these, it
would seem, mainly associated with the school of
Antioch, so spoke of the Son proceeding from the
Father as an event which had taken place far before
all time in the remoteness of eternity, it is true, but
so that there was when the Father had not yet be-
gotten the Son, for, they argued, the Father must have
preceded the Son as the cause precedes the effect, and
so the Son was, as it were, less eternal than the Father.
At once the Alexandrians corrected them.   To begin
with there are no degrees in eternity : but, most
serious error of all, this idea made God liable to
variation, at one period of eternity he had been alone,
and then he had become a father : philosophy taught
that the First Cause, the True God, is liable to no
change, if he is Father now, he must have been so
from all eternity : we must understand the Son as

the Logos for ever eternally issuing forth from the
Father as source. The actual merits of the controversy do not at present concern us : we simply notice
the fact that the current Greek philosophy entirely
dominated the theology of the Church and it was
imperative for that theology to be expressed in terms
which fitted in with the philosophy. The result of
the Arian struggle was that the Eastern church came
to recognise the Alexandrian philosophy as the
exponent of orthodoxy, and in this it was followed
by the greater part of the Western Church, though
the West Goths still remained attached to the Arian
views which they had learned from their first teachers.

By the fifth century Arian doctrine had been
completely eliminated from the state church and
Alexandrian philosophy which had been the chief
means of bringing about this result, was dominant,
although there are indications that it was viewed with
suspicion in some quarters. Amongst the controversies which took place in the post-Nicene age the
most prominent are those which concerned the person
of the incarnate Christ, and these are largely questions
of psychology. It was generally admitted that man
has a *psyche* or animal soul which he shares with the
rest of the sentient creatures, and in addition to this a
spirit or rational soul which, under the influence of
the neo-Platonists or of Alexander of Aphrodisias,
was regarded as an emanation from the creative
spirit, the Logos or " Agent Intellect," a belief which
Christian theologians supported by the statement in

Genesis that God breathed into man the breath of life and so man became a living soul. In fact St. Paul had already distinguished between the two elements, the animal soul and the immortal spirit, in accordance with the psychology which had been developed in his time. But Christian theology supposed that in Christ was also present the eternal Logos which had been the creative Spirit and of which the spirit or rational soul was itself an emanation. What, therefore, would be the relation between the Logos and its own emanation when they came together in the same person? If the Alexandrian philosophy and the Christian religion were both true the problem was capable of reasonable solution : if its only answer was a manifest absurdity then either the psychology or Christianity was in error, and then, as always, it was assumed that contemporary science was sure and religion had to be tested by its standard. To this particular problem two solutions were proposed. The one, especially maintained at Alexandria, was that the Logos and the rational soul or spirit, being in the relation of source and emanation, necessarily fused together when simultaneously present in the same body, the point being of course that the Logos was the agent of creation, the True God not acting therein as it was an activity in time, but through the intermediary of the Logos, whilst the animal soul dispersed through creation was ultimately derived from the Logos, but the spirit was directly proceeding from it, all of which represents the philosophical theory formulated by Alexander of Aphrodisias and the neo-Platonists and then accepted as unassailable. The other solution, which found its chief advocates at Antioch, laid stress on the completeness of the humanity of Christ so that the body, animal soul, and spirit were necessarily complete in the humanity and the Logos dwelt in the human frame without subtracting the spirit which was one of the essentials of humanity, and so there could have been no fusion because this would have implied the return of the spirit to its source and consequently its subtraction from the humanity of Christ. This solution, it will be observed, postulates the same psychology as the other, and whichever view prevailed the Church would be irrevocably committed to the current psychology by this definition of its doctrine.

Both solutions offered perfectly logical deductions from the postulates assumed and it only wanted the advocates of one or the other to over-state the case so as to transgress against the teachings of philosophy or of traditional religion. The first false move came from Antioch. Laying great stress on the completeness of the humanity of Christ so that body, soul, and spirit were necessarily connected in the human frame, the view was so expressed as to describe the Virgin Mary as the mother of the human Christ, body, soul, and spirit alone, which implied, or seemed to imply, that at birth Christ was man only and afterwards became God by the Logos entering into the human body, a conclusion possibly not intended by those who expressed their views but pressed by their opponents. This had been the teaching of Diodorus and of Theodore of Mopseustia both associated with the school of Antioch, and defended in its extremer form by Nestorius, a monk of Antioch, who was made bishop of Constantinople in A.D. 428. Violent controversies ensued which resulted in a general council at Ephesus in 431, where the Alexandrian party succeeded in getting Nestorius and his followers condemned as heretics. Two years later the Nestorians, absolutely confident that their opponents were utterly illogical in supposing that the rational soul and the Logos in Christ were fused or united together, repudiated the official church and organised themselves as the Church which had no part with the heretics of Ephesus. The state Church, however, had the weight of the temporal authority behind it, and the heavy hand of persecution fell severely upon the Nestorians. In Antioch and Greek speaking Syria persecution did its work effectually and the Nestorians were reduced to the position of a fugitive sect, in Egypt, as might be expected, they had no footing, and the westerns as usual agreed with the dominant state church : only amongst the Syriac speaking Christians the Nestorian teaching had a free course, and that section for the most part adhered to it.

Some time before this the school at Nisibis had been closed, or rather removed to Edessa. In A.D. 363

the city of Nisibis had been handed over to the
Persians as one of the conditions of the peace which
closed the unfortunate war commenced by Julian,
and the members of the school, retiring into Christian
territory, had re-assembled at Edessa, where a school
was opened in 373, and thus Edessa in a Syriac
speaking district but within the Byzantine Empire,
became the centre of the vernacular speaking Syriac
church.

At the Nestorian schism the school at Edessa was
the rallying place of those who did not accept the
decisions of Ephesus, but in 439 it was closed by the
Emperor Zeno on account of its strong Nestorian
character, and the ejected members led by Barsuma, a
pupil of Ibas (d. 457), who had been the great
luminary of Edessa, migrated across the Persian
border.   Barsuma was able to persuade the Persian
king Piruz that the orthodox, that is to say the state,
Church was pro-Greek, but that the Nestorians were
entirely alienated from the Byzantine Empire by the
harsh treatment they had received.   On this understanding they were favourably received and remained
loyal to the Persian monarchy in the subsequent
wars with the Empire.   The Nestorians re-opened
the school at Nisibis and this became the focus of
Nestorian activity by which an orientalised phase of
Christianity was produced.   Gradually the Nestorian missionaries spread through all central Asia and
down into Arabia so that the races outside the Greek
Empire came to know Christianity first in a Nestorian

form. It seems probable that Muhammad had contact with Nestorian teachers (Hirschfeld: *New
Researches*. p. 23), and certainly Nestorian monks and
missionaries had much intercourse with the earlier
Muslims. These Nestorians were not only anxious
to teach Christianity but very naturally attached the
utmost importance to their own explanations of the
person of Christ. This could only be made clear by the
help of theories drawn from Greek philosophy, and so
every Nestorian missionary became to some extent
a propagandist of that philosophy : they translated
into Syriac not only the great theologians such as
Theodore of Mopseustia who explained their views,
but also Greek authorities such as Aristotle and his
commentators because some knowledge of these was
necessary to understand the theology. Much of this
work of translation shows a real desire to explain
their teaching, but it shows also a strong resentment
against the Emperor and his state church ; as that
church used the Greek language in its liturgy and
teaching, the Nestorians were anxious to discard
Greek, they celebrated the sacraments only in Syriac
and set themselves to promote a distinctly native
theology and philosophy by means of translated
material and Syriac commentaries. These became the
medium by which Aristotle and the neo-Platonic
commentators were transmitted to Asia outside the
Empire, and so later on as we shall see it was a group
of Nestorian translators who, by making Arabic versions from the Syriac, first brought Hellenistic philos-

ophy to the Arabic world.   But there was also a weak side, for the Nestorian Church, cut off from the wider life of Hellenism, became distinctly provincial.   Its philosophy plays round and round that prevalent at the schism, it spreads this philosophy to new countries, it produces an extensive educational system, and elaborates its material, but it shows no development. If we regard the main test of educational efficiency as being in its research product and not simply the promulgation of material already attained, then Nestorianism was not an educational success : and it seems that this should be the supreme test, for knowledge is progressive, and so the smallest contribution towards further progress must be of more real value than the most efficient teaching of results already achieved.   Yet it would be difficult to overestimate the importance of Nestorianism in preparing an oriental version of Hellenistic culture in the pre-Muslim world.   Its main importance lies in its being preparatory to Islam which brought forward Arabic as a cosmopolitan medium for the interchange of thought and so enabled the Syriac material to be used in a wider and more fruitful field.

Although Nestorius had been condemned, the Church was left with a problem.   The objection was true that, if the Logos and the rational soul in Christ were fused together so that the rational soul or spirit lost itself in its source, the Logos dwelt in an animal body and the full humanity of Christ disappeared.

The Nestorian view of a temporary " connection " was now condemned as heretical, but was it necessary to go to the other extreme of " fusion " which was the logical result of the Alexandrian teaching ? The Church wished to be philosophically correct and yet to avoid the conclusions which might be drawn from either view in its extreme form. In fact philosophy ruthlessly pressed home was the danger of which the Church was most afraid, feeling in some dim realm of sub-consciousness that the deposit of faith did not quite fall into line with science, or at least with the science then in fashion ; and the Church's real enemies were the enthusiasts who were confident that doctrine and philosophy were both absolutely true. Nor have we, even in these days, altogether learned the lesson that both are still partial and progressive. Islam had to go through exactly the same experience in her day and came out of it with very similar results, that is to say both the Christian and Muslim churches finally chose the *via media* adopting the philosophical statement of doctrine but condemning as heretical the logical conclusions which might be deduced. The Alexandrian school, elated perhaps at its victory over Nestorius, became rather intemperate in the statement of its views and pressed them home to an extreme conclusion. At once the warning prediction of the Nestorians was justified : the teaching of a " fusion " between the Logos and the rational soul in Christ entirely undermined his humanity. Another controversy ensued

and in this, as in the former one, neither side suggested
any doubt as to the psychology or metaphysics
borrowed from the Aristotelian and neo-Platonic
philosophies, that was throughout assumed as certain,
the problem was to make Christian doctrine fit in
with it.   Now those who opposed the Alexandrian
conclusions maintained the theory of a " union "
between the Logos and the rational soul in Christ,
so that the complete humanity was preserved as well
as the deity, and the union was such as to be inseparable and so safeguarded from the Nestorian theory.
In fact this was simply admitting the philosophical
statement and forbidding its being pressed home to
its   possible   conclusions.   This   is   described   as
" orthodox " doctrine and rightly so in the sense that
it expresses, though in philosophical terms, a doctrine
as it was held before the Church had learned any
philosophy, and excluded possible deductions which
came within range as soon as a philosophical statement was made.   This is the normal result when
doctrine originally expressed by those ignorant of
philosophy has to be put into logical and scientific
terms :   the only orthodox representation of the
traditional belief must be a compromise.

This second controversy resulted in the Council of
Chalcedon in A.D. 448, at which the advocates of the
theory of " fusion " were expelled from the state
church, and thus a third body was formed, each of
the three claiming to represent the true faith.   Practically the whole of the Egyptian Church followed the

" fusionists " or Monophysites or Jacobites, as they were called after Jacob of Serugh, who was mainly instrumental in organizing them as a church : in Syria also they had a strong following. Like the Nestorians they were persecuted by the Emperor and the state church, but unlike them they did not migrate outside the Byzantine Empire, but remained an important though strongly disaffected body within its limits, though later on they sent out off-shoots into other lands. Like the Nestorians they tended to discard the language of their persecutors and to use the vernacular Coptic and Syriac : it is rightly claimed that the golden age of Syriac literature and philosophy begins with the Monophysite schism. A curious line of demarcation however, is observed in Syriac between the Jacobites in the West and the Nestorians in the East : they used different dialects, which is probably the result of their geographical distribution, and they used different scripts in writing which was partly due to deliberate intension, though partly also to the use of slightly different implements for writing.

When we consider the results of the Monophysite and Nestorian schisms we begin to understand why so much Greek philosophical material was translated into Syriac, whilst the Nestorian movement was the effective reason why Syriac gradually became the medium for transmitting Hellenistic culture into the parts of Asia which lay beyond the confines of the Byzantine Empire during the centuries immediately

preceding the outspread of Islam. It is obvious that
the late Aristotelian and neo-Platonic philosophers
were of vital importance to everyone engaged in the
theological controversies of the day, and the Aristotelian logic was of equal importance as on it de-
pended the way in which terms were used. After
their separation from the Greek Church the Nestorians
and Monophysites turned to the vernacular speaking
Christians, and so a large body of philosophical as well
as theological matter was translated into Syriac ;
very much less into Coptic, for the Egyptian Monophysites were not called upon to face so much controversy as their brethren in Syria.

The period between the schisms and the beginning
of Muslim interest in philosophy was one of prolific
translation, commenting, and exposition. Whilst
there is much interest in tracing the literary history
of a nation, there is comparatively little in following
the history of a literature which is confined to activities
of this sort, for it cannot be much more than a list of
names. Commentary and essay might indeed open up
a field of originality, but nothing of the sort appears
in this type of Syriac work : it seems as though the
provincialism which followed severance from the
Greek world brought in narrowing restrictions so
that, although we get able and diligent workers, they
never seem able to advance beyond re-state-
ment, more or less accurate, of results already
achieved.

Besides philosophy and theology we find a con-

siderable interest in medicine and the two sciences of
chemistry and astronomy which were treated as
allied to it, for astronomy, regarded from the astrological point of view, was supposed to be closely
associated with the conditions of life and death, of
health and disease. Medical studies were especially
attached to the school of Alexandria. Philosophy
proper had been so largely taken over by theology
that the secular investigators were rather impelled to
turn to the natural sciences and as a centre of medical
and allied studies the ancient school of Alexandria
continued its development without loss of continuity,
but under changed conditions. John Philoponus, or
John the Grammarian, as he was called, was one of
the later commentators on Aristotle and also one of
the early lights of this medical school. The date of
his death is not known, but he was teaching at
Alexandria at the time when Justinian closed the
schools at Athens in A.D. 529. The next great leader
of this school was Paul of Aegina who flourished at the
time of the Muslim conquest, and whose works long
served as popular manuals of medicine. The founders
of the medical school at Alexandria established a
regular course of education for the training of medical
practitioners, and for this purpose selected sixteen
works of Galen, some of which were re-edited in an
abridged form, and were made the subject of regular
explanatory lectures. At the same time the school
became a centre of original research, not only in
medicine, but also in chemistry and other branches of

natural science. Thus, on the eve of the Muslim
conquest Alexandria had become a great home of
scientific enquiry. To some extent this was unfortunate as the existing traditions in Egypt directed
those investigations very much into obscurantist lines
and tended to the use of magical forms, talismans, etc.,
and to introduce an astrological bias. This afterwards became the great defect of Arabic medicine as
appears later even in mediæval Padua, but it was not
the fault of Islam, it was an inheritance from Alexandria. Such material as remains of Syriac research
shows us a saner and sounder method in vogue there,
but Alexandria had eclipsed the Syrian scientists at
the time of the Muslim invasion, at least in popular
esteem, and this was a determining factor in directing
Arabic research into these astrological by-paths.

Amongst the famous products of this school was
Paul of Aegina, whose medical works formed the
basis of much of the mediæval Arabic and Latin
teaching, and the priest Ahrun (Aaron) who composed
a manual of medicine which was afterwards translated into Syriac and became a popular authority,
Alexandria was the centre also of chemical science.
and as such was the parent of later Arabic alchemy.
It appears from M. Berthelot's exhaustive study of
Arabic chemistry (*La chimie au moyen age*: Paris.
1893) that the Arabic material may be divided into
two classes, the one based upon, and mainly
translated from, the Greek writers current in Alexandria, the other representing a later school of

independent investigation. Of the former class Berthelot gives three specimens, the Books of Crates, of al-Habid, and of Ostanes, all representing the Greek tradition which flourished at Alexandria on the eve of the Muslim invasion.

Whilst the Alexandrians kept alive an interest in medical and the allied sciences the separated branches of the vernacular speaking churches of Asia were more interested in logic and speculative philosophy. It was perhaps natural that the Monophysites with their strong Egyptian connection should adopt the commentaries of John Philoponus, himself a Monophysit of a type, but both they and the Nestorians invariably used Porphyry's *Isagoge* as an introductory manual. In the general treatment of metaphysics and psychology as applied to theology, and in the treatment of theology itself, the Monophysites inclined more towards neo-Platonism and mysticism than the Nestorians, and their life centered more in the monasteries, whilst the Nestorians adhered rather to the older system of local schools, although they too had monasteries, and in course of time the schools adopted the discipline and methods of the convent.

The oldest and greatest of the Nestorian schools was that of Nisibis, but in A.D. 550 Mar Ahba, a convert from Zoroastrianism, who had become *catholicos* or patriarch of the Nestorians, established a school at Seleucia on the model of Nisibis. A little later the Persian king, Kusraw Anushirwan (Nushirwan, flor. 531-578 A.D.) who had been greatly impressed by the

view of Hellenistic culture which he had obtained
during his war with Syria, and had offered hospitality
to the ejected Greek philosophers when Justinian
closed the schools at Athens, founded a Zoroastrian
school at Junde-Shapur, in Khuzistan, where not only
Greek and Syriac works, but also philosophical and
scientific writings brought from India, were translated into Pahlawi, or Old Persian, and there the
study of medicine taught by Greek and Indian
physicians was developed more fully than in the
theological atmosphere of the Christian schools,
although some of the most distinguished medical
teachers in this school were themselves Nestorian
Christians.   Amongst the alumni of Junde-Shapur
were the Arab Hares b. Kalada, who afterwards
became famous as a practitioner, and his son Ennadr,
cited in the 5th canon of Ibn Sina (Avicenna), an
enemy of the Prophet Muhammad who was amongst
those defeated at the battle of Badr and was put to
death by 'Ali.   Several Indian medical writers are
cited by Razes and others, notably Sharak and
Qolhoman, whilst the treatise on poisons by the
Indian Shanak was, at a later date, translated into
Persian by Manka for Yahya b. Khalid the Barmecide
and afterwards into Arabic for the 'Abbasid Khalif
al-Ma'mun.   Manka, who was medical attendant to
Harunu r-Rashid, translated from Sanskrit various
medical and other works.   Besides the Christian and
Zoroastrian schools there was also a pagan school at
Harran, of whose foundation we have no further

information. Harran had been a centre of Hellenic influence from the time of Alexander the Great and remained a refuge for the old Greek religion when the Greek world at large had become Christian. Although it would appear that Harran had an inheritance from the ancient Babylonian religion, which had a late revival during the first centuries of the Christian era, this had been entirely overlaid with the developments of paganism as revised by the neo-Platonists. Indeed Harran shows the last stand of Greek paganism and neo-Platonism as the two had been formulated by Porphyry and they continued there to live out a vigorous though secluded life.

There were thus several agencies at work developing and extending Hellenistic influence in Persia and Mesopotamia which later on became a Persian province, and besides these established schools there were many secondary forces. The Persian armies returning from the invasion of Syria brought back many items of Hellenic culture, amongst them the Greek system of baths which was copied in Persia and continued by the Muslims who spread this refinement throughout the Islamic world, so that what we call the Turkish bath is a lineal decendant of the old Greek bath passed through the Persians of pre-Muslim times, and then spread more widely by the Muslims. These armies brought home also a great admiration for Greek architecture and engineering, and Greek architects, engineers, and craftsmen being amongst the most valued plunder brought back

from Syria, by their help Persia endeavoured to start
building in the Greek style. Thus the centuries
immediately before the outspread of Islam show a
wide and steady extension of Hellenistic influences in
all the different forms of culture, in science, philosophy,
art, architecture, and in the luxuries of life : and
even before this, ever since the days of Alexander the
Great, there had been a percolation of Greek influence,
so that Western Asia was steeped in Hellenistic art,
in many cases very crudely represented and combined
with native elements. When the oppressive control
of the Umayyads was lifted and the native population
came again to its own, we can hardly wonder that
this meant a revival of Hellenism.

We have already mentioned *Ibas* (d. 457) as the
teacher of Barsuma who led the Nestorian migration
into Persia and re-opened the school of Nisibis. This
Ibas had been the great luminary of the school of
Edessa in its last days and seems to have been the first
to make a Syriac translation of Porphyry's *Isagoge*,
the recognised manual of logic preparatory to Aristotle's Organon. This shows that logic had been
taken as the chief material of education amongst the
Nestorians and very much the same seems to have
been the case amongst the Monophysites.

About the same time flourished *Probus*, who is
said to have been a presbyter of Antioch, and produced commentaries upon Porphyry's *Isagoge*, and
on Aristotle's *Hermeneutica*, *Soph. Elench.*, and
Analytica Priora, these commentaries becoming

favourite manuals amongst the Syriac speaking
students of logic. Hoffman's *De Hermeneuticis apud
Syros* (Leipzic, 1873) gives the text of the commentary
on the *Hermeneutica* followed by a Latin translation.
The method employed here and in all Syriac commentaries is to take a short passage, often no more than a
few words, of the Text of Aristotle translated into
Syriac and then give an explanation of the meaning
sometimes extending to several pages, sometimes
only a brief remark, according to the difficulty of the
text, very much as if a teacher were reading aloud and
explaining passages by passage as he read. This
became the usual method of commenting and was
afterwards copied by the Muslims in their commentaries on the Qur'an. The commentary on the
Isagoge has been published by Baumstark (*Aris-
totles bei den Syrern*, Leipzic, 1900), and that on the
Analytica Priora by the great Louvain scholar Prof.
Hoonacker in the *Journal Asiatique* for July-August,
1900.

The greatest of the Monophysite scholars was
Sergius of Ras al-'Ayn (d. 536), who was both a
translator and the author of original treatises on
philosophy, medicine, and astronomy. His medical
work was his chief interest and he left a permanent
mark as a translator into Syriac of a considerable
part of Galen. He spent some time in Alexandria
where he perfected himself in a knowledge of Greek and
learned chemistry and medicine in the Alexandrian
medical school then just beginning its career. Some

of his translation of Galen is preserved in the British Mus. MSS. Addit. 14661 and 17156 : in the latter are fragments of the " Medical art " and " Faculties of the aliments " which have been edited by Sachau (Inedita Syriaca, Vienna, 1870). Of his philosophical work Sachau has given us the versions which he made of the *Isagoge* and *Table* of Porphyry, and Aristotle's *Categories* and the dubious *de mundo*, as well as a treatise on " the soul " which is not the *de anima* of Aristotle. He wrote original treatises on logic in seven books (incomplete—Brit. Mus. Add. 14660 contains that on the categories), on " negation and affirmation," on " genus, species, and individual," on " the causes of the universe according to Aristotle " and minor essays. In astronomy he has left a tract " on the influence of the moon " which is based on the work of Galen (cf. Sachau, op. cit.) The writings of Sergius circulated amongst both Nestorians and Monophysites, all regarding him as a leading authority on medicine and logic, and in medicine it seems that he was the founder of a Syriac school which became the parent of Arabic medicine, certainly that school owed its impetus to him. Bar Hebraeus refers to him as " a man eloquent and greatly skilled in the books of the Greeks and Syrians and a most learned physician of men's bodies. He was indeed orthodox in his opinions, as the " Prologue " bears witness, but in morals corrupt, depraved, and stained with lust and avarice " (Bar Hebraeus. ed. Abbeloos et Lamy. i. 205-7)·

In the same century lived *Ahudemmeh* who became bishop of Tagrit in A.D. 559, and introduced the commentary of John Philoponus as the regular manual of instruction amongst the Syriac speaking Monophysites. He is said to have composed treatises on the definitions of logic, on the freedom of the will, on the soul, on man considered as a microcosm, and on the composition of man as of soul and body, this last in part preserved in MS. Brit. Mus. Addit. 14620.

Amongst the Nestorian scholars of the sixth century was *Paul the Persian* who produced a treatise on logic which he dedicated to King Khusraw and has been published in M. Land's *Analecta Syriaca* (iv).

This has brought us to the period of the Muslim invasion. In 638 Syria was conquered, and the conquest of Mesopotamia followed in the course of the same year, that of Persia four years later. In 661 the Umayyad dynasty of Arab rulers was established in Damascus ; but all this did not greatly affect the internal life of the Christian communities who lived on in perfect liberty, subject only to the payment of the poll tax.

About 650 the Nestorian Henanieshu' wrote a treatise on logic (cf. Budge : *Thomas of Marga.* i. 79) and commented on John Philoponus.

The Monophysites had no great schools like the Nestorians, but their convent at Qensherin, on the left bank of the Euphrates, was a great centre of Greek studies. Its most famous product was *Severus Sebokt* who flourished on the eve of the Muslim conquest. He was the author of a commentary on Aristotle's *Hermeneutica* of which only fragments survive, of a treatise on the syllogisms of the *Analytica Priora*, and of epistles dealing with terms used in the *Hermeneutica* and on the difficult points in Aristotle's *Rhetoric* (cf. Brit. Mus. Add. 14660, 17156). In astronomy he wrote on " the Figures of the Zodiac " and on " the Astrolabe," the former of these is preserved in Br. Mus. Add. 14538 and has been published by Sachau (op. cit.), the latter in Berlin MS. Sachau 186 and published by Nau in the *Journal Asiatique* of 1899.

Athanasius of Balad who became Monophysite patriarch in 684 was a pupil of Severus Sekobt, and is chiefly known as the translator of a new Syriac version of Porphyry's *Isagoge* (Vatican Ms. Syr. 158. cf. Bar Hebraeus *Chron. Eccles.* ed. Abbeloos et Lamy. i. 287).

James of Edessa (d. 708 A.D.) also was a pupil of Severus Sebokt at the same convent, was made bishop of Edessa about 684 and abandoned this see in 688 as the result of his failure to carry out the reformation of the monasteries in his diocese : he retired to the monastery of St. James at Kaishun, between Aleppo and Edessa, but left this to become lecturer at the monastery of Eusebona, in the diocese of Antioch where " for eleven years he taught the psalms and the reading of the scriptures in Greek and revived the Greek language which had fallen into disuse " (Bar Hebr. *Chron. Eccles.* i. 291). Attacked

by the brethren who disapproved of the study of
Greek, he migrated to the monastery of Tel'eda where
he prepared a revised version of the Peshitta or
Syriac Vulgate of the Old Testament, finally returning
to Edessa about four months before his death.   His
Enchiridion, a treatise on the terms used in philosophy,
is preserved in the Brit. Mus. MS. Addit. 12154.

George, who became " bishop of the Arabs " in
686, was himself a pupil of Athanasius of Balad and
translated the whole logical Organon of Aristotle, of
which his versions of the *Catagories*, *Hermeneutica*,
and *Analytica Priora* appear in Brit. Mus. Addit.
14659, each furnished with an introduction and
commentary.

These names cover the whole period between the
two schisms and the Muslim invasion and suffice
to show that the Syriac speaking community continued diligent in the study of the Aristotelian logic
and metaphysics, and also gave attention to medical
and scientific studies.   It is not exactly a brilliant
or original form of cultural activity, for the most part
it was only the transmission of received texts with the
preparation of new translations, commentaries, and
explanatory treatises, but this itself fulfilled an important function.   The Muslim invasion made no
change in the course of these studies : the Umayyads
did not interfere with the schools and the Syriac
students went their own way living a life quite apart
from that of their Arab rulers.   Now and then un-
scrupulous or angry clergy appealed to the Khalif

against their fellow clergy and this was the commonest
cause of interference which the historians describe as
persecution. Such was the experience of *Henany-
eshu'* who became Nestorian Catholicos in A.D. 686.
The bishop of Nisibis made complaints against him
to the Khalif 'Abdul-Malik in consequence of which
he was deposed, imprisoned, and then thrown over a
cliff. He was not killed by his fall, though severely
lamed ; by the kindness of some shepherds he was
sheltered and nursed back to health, and then retired
to the monastery of Yannan near Mosul, resuming
his patriarchal office after the death of the bishop of
Nisibis, and holding it until his own death in 701
(Bar Heb. *Chron. Eccles.* Abbeloos et Lamy. ii. 135-
140). Besides sermons, letters, and a biography of
Dewada, he wrote an educational treatise on " the
twofold duty of the school " as a place of religious and
moral influence on the one hand, and of an academy of
the humanities on the other (cf. Assemsan BO.)
iii. part I. 154 and also an " Explanation of the
Analytica " (id).

Mar Abha III. became Nestorian Catholicos
somewhere about 740 (133 A.H.) and produced a
commentary on Aristotle's logic (cf. Bar Heb. ii. 153).

This brings us down to the period when the Muslim
world began to take an interest in these philosophical
and scientific studies, and translations and commentaries began to appear in Arabic. But Syriac studies
did not at once disappear and it will be convenient
to enumerate briefly some of those who appeared in

later times down to the age of Bar Hebraeus (d. A.D.
1286), with whom the literary history of Syriac comes
to an end. In the latter part of the eighth century we
find *Jeshudcna* bishop of Basra writing an " introduction to logic." Shortly afterwards *Jeshubokt*
metropolitan of Persia wrote on the Categories (cf.
Journ. Asiat. May-June. 1906). Hunayn b. Ishaq,
his son Ishaq, and his nephew Hubaysh, with some
other companions, formed the college of translators
established at Baghdad by the Khalif al-Ma'mun to
render the Greek and other philosophical and scientific
texts into Arabic, a work to which we shall refer again ;
but Hunayn, who was a Nestorian Christian, was
also occupied in making translations from the Greek
into Syriac : he prepared, or revised, Syriac versions of
Porphyry's *Isagoge*, Aristotle's *Hermeneutica*, part of
the *Analytica*, the *de generatione et corruptione*, the
de anima, part of the *Metaphysics*, the *Summa* of
Nicolas of Damascus, the Commentary of Alexander
of Aphrodisias, and the greater part of the works of
Galen, Dioscorus, Paul of Aegina, and Hippocrates.
His son Ishaq also made a translation of Aristotle's
de anima, and it is significant that this treatise and the
commentary of Alexander Aphr. now begins to take
the most prominent place in philosophical study ;
the centre of interest is moving from logic to psychology. About the same time the physician *John Bar
Maswai* (d. A.D. 857) composed various medical
works in Syriac and Arabic. He, like Hunayn, was
one of the intellectual group which the 'Abbasids

gathered together in their new capital city of Baghdad.
Contemporary also were the Syriac writers *Denha* (or
Ibas) who compiled a commentary on the Aristotelian
logical Organon : *Abzud*, the author of a poetical
essay on the divisions of philosophy, and then, after
a series of minor writers on logic, *Dionysius Bar
Salibi* in the twelfth century A.D., who composed
commentaries on the *Isagoge*, the *Categories*, *Hermeneutica*, and *Analytica* ; and in the early part of
the following century *Yaqub Bar Shakako*, author of a
collection of " Dialogues " of which the second book
deals with philosophical questions of logic, physics,
mathematics, and metaphysics.

The series of Syriac philosophical writers closes
with *Gregory Bar Hebraeus*, or *Abu l-Faraj* in the
thirteenth century A.D. whose " Book of the Pupils of
the Eyes " is a compendium of logic summarising and
explaining the Isagoge, and Aristotle's Categories, Hermeneutica, Analytica, Topica, and Sophistica Elenchi ;
his " Book of the Upholding of Wisdom " being a
summary introduction to logic, physics, metaphysics,
and theology.   A third work " The Cream of Science "
is an encyclopædia of the Aristotelian philosophy,
and this work appears also in an abridged form as the
" Business of Businesses."   He was also the translator into Syriac of Dioscorus on simples, and author
of a treatise on the medical *Questions* of Hunayn b.
Ishaq, and of a work on geography called " the Ascent
of the Spirit."   Although esteemed as one of the
greatest Syriac authorities and for centuries holding a

place of primary importance, he was in reality no more than a compiler who produced encyclopædic works dealing with the researches of his predecessors.

The great importance of the Syriac speaking Christian communities was as the medium whereby Hellenistic philosophy and science was transmitted to the Arabic world. There was no independent development in its Syriac atmosphere, and even the choice of material had already been made by the Hellenists before it passed into Syriac hands. It was now definitely established that the basis of the " humanities " was the Aristotelian logic, and that this as well as all other studies in the work of Aristotle was to be interpreted according to the neo-Platonic commentators. In medicine and chemistry the curriculum of the school of Alexandria was recognised as authoritative and this, in so far as it was based upon Galen and Hippocrates, and upon the teaching of Paul of Aegina in obstetrical medicine, was to the good : but there was a mystical side of Alexandrian science mixed up with astrology, so that particular drugs had to be taken where certain planets were in the ascendant, and such like ideas, which gave a magical tone to Alexandrian and Arabic medicine which was not for its advantage, although it must be remembered that the ready contempt formerly poured upon Arabic science as mere charlatanism is now expressed more cautiously : we are prepared to admit that very much real and valuable work was done in medicine and chemistry,

although it is probable that the Egyptian obscurantism
did rather tend to hinder the steady development of
the sounder tradition derived from Galen and the
Greek physicians.

We are thus able to understand that " Muslim
theology, philosophy, and science put forth their first
luxurant shoots on a soil which was saturated with
Hellenistic culture." (Nicholson : *Mystics of
Islam*. London. 1914 .p. 9.)   The passage of Hellenism
took place through five channels :—

(i) The Nestorians who hold the first place as the
earliest teachers of the Muslims and the most important transmittors of medicine.

(ii) The Jacobites or Monophysites who were the
chief influences in introducing neo-Platonic speculations and mysticism.

(iii) The Zoroastrians of Persia and especially the
school of Junde-Shapur, although this had a strong
Nestorian element.

(iv) The Pagans of Harran who came forward at
a later stage.

(v) The Jews who, in this connection, occupy a
somewhat peculiar position : they had no contact
with the tradition of Aristotelian philosophy, their
academies at Sora and Pumbaditha were concerned
with their own traditional law and Bible exegesis
only.   Jewish philosophical studies began later and
were themselves derived from the Arabic philosophers.
But they shared with the Nestorians an inclination
towards medical studies so that Jewish physicians

appear in the early days of Baghdad.   Yet they come
distinctly second to the Nestorians.   Thus amongst
the medical writers mentioned by Dr. Leclerq in his
Histoire de la médicine arabe (Paris, 1876) we find
amongst the names cited for the tenth cent. A.D.
that there are 29 Christians, 3 Jews, and 4 pagans of
Harran, though in the next century only 3 Christians
appear, as against 7 Jews, the work then passing very
largely into Muslim hands.

CHAPTER II

THE ARAB PERIOD

Islam in its earlier form was entirely an Arab religion. The temporal side of the Prophet Muhammad's mission shows him engaged in an effort to unite the tribes of the Hijaz in a fraternal union, to limit the custom of the *razzia* (*ghazza*) or marauding foray, and to form an orderly community. These temporal aims were due to the influence of Madina on the Prophet and to the conviction that it was only in such a community that his religious teaching could obtain a serious attention. In Mecca he had been faced with constant opposition chiefly due to the tribal jealousies and strife which formed the normal condition of a Bedwin community. Madina was a city in a sense quite different from that in which the term could be applied to Mecca. It had developed a civic life, rudimentary no doubt but very far in advance of the Meccan conditions, and had inherited a constitutional tradition from Aramaean and Jewish colonists. At Madina the Prophet began to perceive the difference produced by the association of men in an ordered communal life as contrasted with the incoherence of the older tribal conditions, and the accompanying difference of attitude towards religion.

This last was not really due to civic life but more directly to Jewish influence, although no doubt the conditions of city life were more favourable to the evolution of speculative theology than those of the wilder tribes. The older Arabs seem to have accepted the idea of one supreme God, but speculated little about him : they did not regard the supreme deity as at all entering into their personal interests, which were concerned only with the minor tribal deities who were expected to attend diligently to tribal affairs and were sharply censured when they appeared to be negligent about the interests of their clients. The desert man had no tendency to the sublime thoughts about God with which he is sometimes credited, nor had he any great reverence towards the minor members of his pantheon. The Prophet found it one of his most difficult tasks to introduce the observance of prayer amongst the Arabs, and they do not appear very much attached to it at the present day. In Madina the Prophet was in contact with men whose attitude towards religion was very different and who were more in sympathy with the principles which he had learned from very much the same sources as themselves.

In Madina, therefore, the Prophet added a temporal side to the spiritual work in which he had been previously engaged. It was not consciously a change of attitude, but simply the adoption of a subsidiary task which seemed to provide a most useful accessory to the work which he had already been doing. Its

keynote is given in the Madinian Sura 49.10, " Only
the faithful are brethren, wherefore make peace
between your brethren." It was a call to his fellow
Arabs of the Hijaz to cease their strife and to unite
in the bonds of brotherhood. Such a union on the
part of those whose habits and ideals were warlike
and who were disinclined to the arts of peace, necessarily produced an attitude of hostility towards persons outside their community. Was this militant
attitude any part of Muhammad's plans ? The
answer must certainly be in the negative. The military enterprises of early Islam were no part of its
original programme. In those enterprises the Prophet and his immediate successors show a hesitating
and dubious attitude ; obviously their hands were
forced and they take the lead reluctantly. As Fr.
Lammens says :—

Le Qoran travailla à réunir les tribus du Higaz.
La prédication de Mahomet réussit à mettre sur
pied une armée, la plus nombreuse, la plus dis-
ciplinée qu'on eût vue jusque-là dans la Péninsule.
Cette force ne pouvait longtemps demeurer sans
emploi. Par ailleurs l-islam, en imposant la paix
entre les tribus, ralliées à la nouvelle religion ou
simplement à l'état médinois en formation,—le *ta'līf
al-qoloūb* poursuivait ce dernier objectif—l'islam
allait fermer tout issue à l'inquiète activité des
nomades. Il prétendait supprimer à tout le moins
limiter, le droit de razzia, placé à la base de cette
société patriarcalement anarchique. Il fallait s'at-

tendre à voir le torrent ; momentanément endigué, déborder sur les régions frontiéres.

" Que Mahomet ait assigné ce but à leurs efforts ? Il devient difficile de défendre cette thèse, trop facilement acceptée jusqu'ici."

(Lammens : *Le berceau de l'islam.* Rome, 1914, i. p. 175.)

In the expedition against Mecca a militant attitude was the inevitable result of compelling circumstances. The Meccans were actively hostile and had adopted a persecuting attitude towards those who accepted the new religion. At the time the Quraysh tribe, to which Muhammad belonged, was so far in the ascendant that its adhesion was necessary for the progress of Islam in the Hijaz : the championship of some prominent tribe was essential, and Muhammad himself was deeply attached to the traditional " House of God " at Mecca, to which his own family was bound by many associations ; besides he desired the adherence of his own tribe as his mission was to it in the first place. Had the Meccan opposition not been broken down the Muslim religion could have been no more than the local cult of Madina, and even as such would have had to be perpetually on the defensive. No doubt the " holy war " as an institution was based on the traditions of this expedition, but such a war is related to the later enterprises for the conquest of non-Arab nations by a line of development which the Prophet himself could hardly have anticipated. The challenge to Heraclius is on a

similar footing.   Although we may not be disposed to
accept the traditional account given by Bukhari,
there no doubt was some such challenge.   But
Heraclius had only recently re-conquered Syria for
the Byzantine Empire, the land he had acquired
included a considerable portion of the Syrian desert
which formed a geographical unity with Arabia, and
amongst his subjects were Arab tribes closely akin
to those of the Hijaz.

Islam became a militant religion because it spread
amongst the Arabs at a time when they were beginning to enter upon a career of expansion and conquest,
and this career had already commenced before Muhammad had got beyond the first—the purely
spiritual—stage of his work. The only reason why the
earlier Arab efforts were not followed up immediately
seems to have been that the Arabs were so surprised
at their success that they were unprepared to take
advantage of it.   For some time previously Arab
settlements had been formed in the debateable land
where the Persian and Byzantine Empires met, but
this encroachment had been more or less veiled by
the nominal suzerainty of one or other of the great
states.   The Quda, a tribe of Himyaritic Arabs, had
settled in Syria and become Christian, and was
charged by the Byzantine Emperor with the general
control of the Arabs of Syria (Masudi : iii., 214–5);
that tribe was superseded by the tribe of Salih
(id. 216), and that by the Arab kingdom of Ghasan
which acknowledged the Emperor of Byzantium as

its overlord, whilst the Arab kingdom of Hira acknowledged the Persian king. Somewhere between A.D.
604 and 610, when the first beginnings of persecution
were falling on the Prophet in Mecca, the Arabs led
by al-Mondir inflicted a crushing defeat upon the
Persian army under King Khusraw Parwiz, who, a
few years before, had led a victorious force to the
invasion of the Byzantine province of Syria. This
victory showed the Arabs that, in spite of its imposing
appearance, the Persian Empire, and presumably the
Byzantine also, were vulnerable, and a determined
effort might easily place the wealth of both at the
disposal of the Arabs.

The Muslim conquests of the 7th century A.D.
form the last of a series of great Semitic outspreads
of which the earliest recorded in history resulted in
the formation of the empire of Babylon some 2225
years before the Christian era. In all these the
motive power lay in the Arabs who represent the
parent Semitic stock, the more or less nomadic inhabitants of the barren highlands of Western Asia,
who have always tended to prey upon the more
cultured and settled dwellers in the river valleys and
on the lower slopes of the hills.

" The belts between mountain and desert, the banks
of the great rivers, the lower hills near the sea, these
are the lines of civilization (actual or potential) in
Western Asia. The consequence of these conditions
is that through all the history of Western Asia there
runs the eternal distinction between the civilized

cultivators of the plains and lower hills and the wild
peoples of mountain and desert.   The great monarch-
ies which have arisen here have rarely been effective
beyond the limits of cultivation ; mountain and desert
are another world in which they can get, at best,
only precarious footing.   And to the monarchical
settled peoples the near neighbourhood of this unsub-
jugated world has been a continual menace.   It is a
chaotic region out of which may pour upon them at
any weakening of the dam hordes of devastators.
At the best of times it hampers the government by
offering a refuge and recruiting ground to all the
enemies of order." (Bevan : *House of Seleucus*, i.,
p. 22.)

Scornful of agriculture and with a strong distaste
for settled and especially for urban life, the Bedwin
are those who have remained nomads by preference,
and like all races at that stage of evolution, find the
most congenial outlet for their vigour in tribal
warfare and plundering expeditions.   From the
earliest dawn of history they have always been strongly tempted by the wealth of the settled communities
within reach, and appear in the oldest records as
robber bands.   Sometimes predatory excursions were
followed by settlement, and the invading tribes
learned the culture of those amongst whom they
settled : all the Semitic groups other than the Arabs
had formed such settlements before the 7th century
A.D., and these groups are distinguished one from
another, and all from the parent stock, simply by

the cultural influences due to the earlier inhabitants of the lands they entered ; the Arab stock itself remained high and dry, the stranded relic of more primitive conditions, though itself not absolutely free from a reacting influence. The only thing that ever has restrained the incursions of these nomadic tribes into such neighbouring lands as offer hope of plunder is the military power of those who endeavour to place a barrier for the protection of the settled community of the cultivated area, and every Arab outspread has been due, not to the pressure of hunger resulting from the desiccation of Arabia, nor to religious enthusiasm, but simply to the weakness of the power which tried to maintain a dam against them.

In the 7th century A.D. the two powers bordering on the Arab area were the Byzantine and Persian empires. Both of these were, to all appearance, flourishing and stable, but both alike were in reality greatly weakened by external and internal causes which were closely parallel in the two. Externally, both had been severely shaken by some centuries of warfare in which they had disputed the supremacy of Western Asia, and both had suffered from rear attacks by more barbarous foes. Internally, both alike had a thoroughly unsatisfactory social structure, though the details differ : in the Byzantine Empire almost the whole burden of a very heavy taxation fell upon the middle classes, the *curiales*, and the armies were mainly composed of foreign mercenaries, whilst in the Persian Empire a rigid caste system

stifled natural development. In both we see a state
church engaged in active persecution and thereby
alienating a large section of the subject population.

The career of Muslim conquest came with great
suddenness. Between the years 14 and 21 A.H.
(A.D. 635–641) the Arabs obtained possession of
Syria, Iraq, Egypt, and Persia. They owed to Islam
the united action which made these conquests possible, but the older Muslims who had shared the ideals
and labours of the Prophet, though put at the head,
were carried forward reluctantly and yet irresistibly
by the expanding force behind them. Many of them
viewed these large accessions with very real anxiety.
When the second Khalif Umar saw the large number of
prisoners and captives from Jalûlâ (Persia) flocking
into Arabia, he exclaimed, " O, God, I take refuge
with thee from the children of these captives of
Jalûlâ."

Already the community of Islam contained three
distinct strata. (i) The " old believers," i.e., the
sahibs or companions of the Prophet and the early
converts who placed the religion of Islam first and
desired that religion to produce a real brotherhood
of all believers, whether Arab or not. Important by
their prestige they were numerically in the minority.
(ii) The Arab party, consisting of those who had embraced Islam only when Muhammad had shown his
power by the capture of Mecca. They accepted
Muslim leadership because Muhammad and the first
two Khalifs were at the moment in the ascendancy,

but they had no attachment to the religion of Islam.
They were those who would have gone forward to
conquest under any efficient leader as soon as it was
clear that Persia and the Greek Empire were vulnerable, and to them it was a detriment that union
under a leader incidentally involved adherence to a
new religion. At the head of these purely secular
Arabs was the Umayyad clan of the tribe of Quraysh,
and the main thing which gained their continued
adherence to Islam was that the Prophet himself
had belonged to that tribe and so the prestige of
Islam involved that of the Quraysh who thereby
became a kind of aristocracy. Although the Umayyads were thus able to gratify their personal pride,
always a strong factor in semi-civilised psychology,
and even to obtain a considerable measure of control
over the other tribes, this only served to perpetuate
the pre-Islamic conditions of tribal jealousy, for the
primacy of the Quraysh was bitterly resented by many
rivals. For the most part the true Arab party was,
and still is, indifferent towards religion.

" The genuine Arab of the desert is, and remains
at heart, a sceptic and a materialist ; his hard, clear,
keen, but somewhat narrow intelligence, ever alert
in its own domain, was neither curious nor credulous
in respect to immaterial and supra-sensual things ;
his egotistical and self-reliant nature found no place
and felt no need for a God who, if powerful to protect,
was exacting of service and self-denial." (Browne :
Literary Hist. of Persia, i., pp. 189–190.)

The Arab certainly was not disposed to regard the conquered alien, even if he embraced Islam, as a brother. To him the conquest of foreign lands meant only the acquisition of vast estates, of great wealth and unlimited power : to him the conquered were simply serfs to be used as a means of rendering the conquered lands more productive. The conquered were allowed the choice either to embrace Islam or to pay the poll tax, but the 'Umayyads discouraged conversion as damaging to the revenue, although the cruel and hated Hajjaj b. Yusuf (d. 95) forced even converts to pay the tax from which they were legally exempt. (iii) The third stratum consisted of the " clients " (mawla, plur. mawâlî), the non-Arab converts, theoretically received as brethren and actually so treated by the " old believers," but regarded as serfs by Arabs of the Umayyad type. Owing to the wide expansion of Islam these rapidly increased in number until, in the 2nd century of the Hijra, they formed the vast majority of the Muslim world.

The two first Khalifs were " old believers " who had been companions of the Prophet in his flight from Mecca. The third, 'Uthman, had also been one of the Prophet's companions, but he was a weak man and moreover, belonged to the 'Umayyad clan, which, as the aristocratic element in Mecca, was then in the ascendant and, unable to free himself from the nepotism which is an Arab failing, allowed the rich conquests of Syria, Egypt, Iraq, and Persia to become the prey of ambitious members of the clan and thus

suffered the complete secularising of the Islamic state.
When, in 35 A.H., he fell a victim to the assassin, he
was succeeded by 'Ali, one of the older Muslims and
the Prophet's cousin and son-in-law. But at 'Ali's
accession the internal division appears as an accom-
plished fact. The purely secular Arabs, led by the
'Umayyad Mu'awiya, who was governor of Syria,
entirely refused to recognise 'Ali, affecting to regard
him as implicated in the murder of 'Uthman, or at
least as protecting his murderers. On the other hand,
the Kharijite sect, claiming to represent the older
Muslim type, but in reality mainly composed of the
Arabs of Arabia and of the military colonies, who
were envious of the power and wealth of the Umayyad
faction, at first supported him, then turned against
him, and in 41 were responsible for his assassination.

At 'Ali's death Mu'awiya became Khalif and
founded the Umayyad dynasty which ruled from 41
to 132 A.H. During the whole of this period the
official Khalifate was Arab first and Muslim only in
the second place. This forms the second period of
the history of Islam when the religion of the Prophet
was allowed to sink into the background and the Arab
regarded himself as the conqueror ruling over a
subject population. There was no forcible conversion
of a subject population, indeed, save in the reign of
'Umar II (A.H. 99–101) conversions were rather
discouraged as detrimental to the poll tax levied on
non-Muslims. There was no attempt to force the
Arabic language : until the reign of 'Abdu l-Mâlik

(65–86), who started an Arabic coinage, the public records were kept and official business transacted in Greek, Persian, or Coptic, as local requirements demanded, and the change to Arabic seems to have been suggested by the non-Muslim clerks. When Arabic became the official medium of public business then, of course, motives of convenience and self-interest caused its general adoption. Hitherto it had been used in prayer by those who had become Muslim, but now it had to be learned more accurately by all who had to do with the collection of the revenue or the administration of justice. Incidentally this became a matter of great importance, as it provided a common medium for the exchange of thought throughout the whole Muslim world.

As rulers in Syria, the Arabs were in contact with a fully developed culture which was brought to bear upon them in various ways, in the structure of society and in social order generally, in the arts and crafts, and in intellectual life. The Greek influence was nearest at hand, but there was also a very strong Persian element in close contact with them. The provincial officials of Syria, all trained in the methods of the Byzantine Empire, continued in their employ, and, as Syria was the seat of the 'Umayyad government, the state came under Greek influence. Yet, for all this, even in 'Umayyad times, the Persian influence seems to have been very strong in political organization. The governments already existing in Egypt and Syria were provincial, dependent upon

and subordinate to, the central government at Byzantium, and constantly recruited by Byzantine officials,
at least in their upper grades. The Persian government, on the other hand, was a self-contained one,
fully organised throughout and including the supreme
and central authority. Until the fall of the 'Umayyads, after which Persian influence became supreme,
the political structure of the Muslim state was somewhat experimental; apparently the rulers left the details
altogether to the subordinate officials who adapted
to the needs of the state such elements as they
could use from the old provincial administration.

In the matter of taxation the early Khalifate continued the system already in vogue and employed
existing methods for the collection of the newly
imposed poll tax. It was on this side that the
'Umayyad rule was most unsatisfactory. Like many
who have been bred in poverty and have afterwards
suddenly come into great wealth, the Arabs behaved
as though their wealth was inexhaustible : each
governor bought his appointment from the state and
it became a recognised custom for him to exact a
cash payment from the outgoing governor, and then
he was free to raise what he could from his defenceless
subjects to prepare for the day when his opportunities
of exaction came to an end. The thoroughly unsatisfactory condition of the 'Umayyad financial system
was one of the leading causes of their fall. One of the
'Umayyad sheikhs, named Minkari, when asked the
reason of their fall, replied :—

" We gave to pleasure the time which should have been devoted to business. Our subjects, harshly treated by us and despairing of obtaining justice, longed to be delivered from us : the tax payers, over-burdened with exactions, were estranged from us : our lands were neglected, our resources wasted. We left business to our ministers who sacrificed our interests to their own advantage, and transacted our affairs as they pleased and without our knowledge. The army, with its pay always in arrear, ceased to obey us. And so the small number of our supporters left us without defence against our enemies, and the ignorance of how we stood was one of the chief causes of our fall." (Masudi : vi., 35–36.)

It will not be unfair to say, therefore, that during the 'Umayyad period the Arabs learned practically nothing of the art of government and of the work of administration. They were in the position of prodigal young heirs who leave all details to their men of business and content themselves with squandering the proceeds.

In the case of civil law matters were rather different. The civil law is necessarily based on the social and economic structure of the community, and in the acquired provinces this was so different from that prevailing in Arabia that it was necessarily forced on the attention of the Arabs. Moreover, in primitive Islam, the line was not clearly drawn between the canon law and the civil law. Inheritance, the taking of pledges, and such like matters, were to the Arabs

subject to the direction and sanction of the law of
God as revealed by his Prophet. Thus, for example,
Sura 4, one of the later Madinian revelations, contains a statement of the law relating to guardianship,
inheritance, marriage, and kindred topics, according
to the social conditions prevailing at Madina. But
in the Greek and Persian dominions the conquering
Arab had to deal with more complex conditions for
which the revealed law made no provision, although
what it did contain so far touched the subject that
it could not be treated regardless of revelation. It
seemed impossible to disregard the revealed precepts
and substitute an alien legislation, although this has
been done in the modern Ottoman Empire, but not
without many and grave protests ; in the first century it would have been intolerable, for every disaffected faction would have used it to break up the
Muslim state which was only held together by the
prestige of the Prophetical tradition. We may well
suppose that the 'Umayyads would have had no reluc-
tance to try the experiment, but it was too dangerous.
The only alternative was to expand the sacred law
so as to include new requirements, and in the 'Umayyad period this was done by the addition of a vast
number of fictitious traditions professing to relate
what the Prophet had said and done in conditions in
which he had never been placed. In describing these
traditions as " fictitious," it is not necessarily implied
that they were fraudulent, although many were so,
showing an obvious motive in increasing the privi-

leges and rights of the dominant faction or asserting
the tribal pre-eminence of the Quraysh, etc. But
more often they are " fictitious " in the sense of legal
fictions rightly correcting the actual law in the interests of equity. When entirely new conditions arose, the
question would be asked, " How would the Prophet
have acted in this case ? " The early companions
of the Prophet, educated in the same environment
as he had been educated, and confident that their
outlook was essentially the same as his, had no
hesitation in stating what he would have done or
said, and their statement was almost certainly correct : but they worded their evidence, or it was afterwards worded for them, as a statement of what the
Prophet actually had done or said. And, later again,
in a subsequent generation, when new problems arose,
no difficulty was felt in accepting the supposition that
the Prophet would have admitted the reasonable and
just solution which the Roman jurists proposed. Thus
it finally came to pass that a considerable portion of
the Roman civil law was embodied in the traditions
of Islam (cf. Santillana : *Code civil et commerciel
tunisien.* Tunis, 1899, etc.) It is not to be supposed
that Arab governors and judges studied the Roman
code, they simply accepted its provisions as they
found them in force in Syria and Egypt, and thus
learned its general principles from the usage of the
civil courts already existing. In many places material is found in the traditions which can be traced to
Zoroastrian, Jewish, and even Buddhist sources,

though these deal rather with ritual and the description of the unseen world and serve to show how readily Islam absorbed elements with which it was in contact. So far as the actual needs of the civil law are concerned, the chief source was the Roman law, and these needs fill a very large part of the traditions.

It was not until the close of the 'Umayyad period that the Muslims began to develop a scientific jurisprudence and to make a critical examination and codification of the traditions. In the case of jurisprudence there were at first two schools, a Syrian and a Persian. The Syrian school formulated its system under the leadership of *al-Awza'i* (d. 157), and for some time it prevailed over all parts of the Muslim world which had been parts of the Byzantine Empire. The Persian school owed its origin to *Abu Hanifa* (d. 150) and, as the seat of government was removed to Iraq by the 'Abbasids and Abu Hanifa's system was enforced by his pupil Abu Yusuf (d. 182) who was chief Qadi under the Khalif Harunu r-Rashid, it had a tremendous advantage over the Syrian school. It became the official system of the 'Abbasid courts and still holds its own through Central Asia, North India, and wherever the Turkish element prevails, whilst the Syrian system has become extinct. Abu Hanifa's system represents a serious and moderate revision of the methods which had already come into use as extending the discipline of Islam to the needs of a complex and advanced civilization. Under the 'Umayyads the jurists had supplemented any deficiencies in the law by their own opinion (*ra'y*) which meant the application of the judgment of a man trained under the Roman law as to what was just and fair. In that early period no derogatory sense was attached to "opinion" which rested on the theory that the intellect could intuitively perceive what is right and just, thus assuming that there is an objective standard of right and wrong capable of apprehension by philosophical enquiry, a theory which shows the influence of Greek ideas embodied in the Civil Code. But the 'Abbasid period experienced an orthodox reaction which tended to limit freedom in using speculative opinion, and Abu Hanifa shows this limitation. In his system weight was attached to every positive statement of the Qur'an which could be taken as bearing upon the civil law, only to a slight extent did he avail himself of the evidence of tradition, to a much larger extent he employs *qiyas* or "analogy," which means that a new condition is judged by comparison with some older one already treated in the Qur'an, and he also employed what he called *istihsan*, "the preferable," that is to say, what seemed to be equitable and right even when it diverged from the logical conclusion which could be deduced from the revealed law. Only in this latter case did he admit what can be described as "opinion," and this is strictly limited to the adoption of a course necessary to avoid an obvious injustice. As thus stated, Abu Hanifa's system was broader, milder, and more reasonable than any other treatment of the Islamic law : but it is a mistake to suppose that it still is mild and reasonable, for in the course of time the decisions pronounced as to " the preferable " have become hardened into precedents and the Hanifite code expresses only those fixed decisions of early mediæval Islam without flexibility. The case is parallel with the English treatment of equity. In older times equity shows us the philosophical principles of justice correcting the defects of common law ; but modern practice displays these principles fossilized as precedents and as rigid and formal in their application as the common law itself. As first conceived, " the preferable " shows the influence of Roman law and Greek philosophy, both of which contemplated an objective standard of right and wrong which could be discovered by investigation, the Stoic teaching, predominant in Roman law, tending to treat this discovery as intuitive. Unsupported by other evidence, we might hesitate to suggest that *istihsan* necessarily had a Hellenistic basis, but when we compare the ideas of Abu Hanifa with the contemporary teaching of Wasil b. 'Ata (d. 131) in theology, we are forced to the conclusion that the same influences are at work in both, and in Wasil these are certainly derived from Greek philosophy. We are not justified in supposing that Abu Hanifa ever read the Greek philosophers or the Roman law, but he lived at a period when the general principles deduced from these sources were beginning to permeate Muslim thought, though in fact his teaching

tends to limit and define the application of the general
principles according to a system. The older Muslims
supposed that good and evil depend simply on the
arbitrary will of God, who commands and forbids as
he sees fit : it was the influence of the Greek philosophy which brought in the idea that these distinctions
are not arbitrary but due to some natural difference
existing in nature between good and evil and that
God is just in that his decrees conform to this standard.

In orthodox Islam there are now four schools of
jurisprudence showing allowable differences in the
treatment of the canon law. Most absurdly they are
sometimes described as " sects " : this they are not
as the differences of opinion are fully recognised as
all equally orthodox. The followers of Abu Hanifa
form the most numerous of these schools, the other
three being all more or less reactionary as compared
with it. The contemporary Malik b. Anas (d. 179)
was openly actuated by dislike of the admission of
istihsan and the recognition thereby given to " opinion "   for this he substituted what he called *istislah*
or " public expediency," allowing analogy to be set
aside only when its logical conclusion would be
detrimental to the community. The difference seems
to be more a verbal correction than a material change,
but the under ying motive is clear and indicates an
orthodox reaction. At the same time he attached
much greater weight to the evidence of tradition,
adding to it also the principle of *ijma* or " consensus,"

which in his system meant the common usage of Madina. Undoubtedly Ibn Malik's position was theoretically sound : the Islamic state had taken form at Madina and nothing could give so clear light on the policy of the Prophet and his companions as the local customary law of the mother city. At the same time Ibn Malik took tradition quite seriously, indeed, the critical and scientific treatment of tradition begins with his manual known as the *Muwatta*. To-day Ibn Malik's school prevails in Upper Egypt and North Africa west of Egypt. The third authority *ash-Shafi'i* (d. 204) takes an intermediate position between Abu Hanifa and Ibn Malik, interpreting *ijma* as the general usage of Islam, and not of the city of Madina alone. The fourth authority, *Ahmad b. Hanbal* (d. 241), shows an entirely reactionary position which reverted to a close adherence to Qur'an and tradition ; it carried great weight amongst the orthodox, especially in Baghdad, but now survives only in remote parts of Arabia.

In the sphere of the arts and crafts, our best evidence lies in architecture and engineering. In these the Arabs had no skill and were conscious of their incapacity. The earliest mosques were simply enclosures surrounded by a plain wall, but a new type was developed under the first 'Umayyad Khalif Mu'awiya, who employed Persian non-Muslim builders in the construction of the mosque at Kufa, and they worked on the lines of the architecture already used by the Sasanid kings. In this mosque the traditional square enclosure was retained, but the quadrangle was surrounded by a cloister in the form of a collonade with pillars 30 cubits high of stone drums held together by iron clamps and lead beddings. From this the cloistered quadrangle became the general type of the congregational mosque and remained so until late Turkish times, when it was partly superseded by the Byzantine domed church. The dome had been used in earlier times only as the covering of a tomb, standing alone or attached to a mosque.

The same Khalif Mu'awiya employed bricks and mortar in restorations which he made at Mecca, and introduced Persian workmen to execute the repairs. In 124 A.H. (A.D. 700) the fifth 'Umayyad Khalif found it necessary to repair the damage caused at Mecca by flood, and for this purpose employed a Christian architect from Syria.

In the time of the next Khalif al-Walid, the " Old Mosque " of Fustat (Cairo), that now known as the " Mosque of 'Amr," was rebuilt by the architect Yahya b. Hanzala, who probably was a Persian. The earlier mosque had been a simple enclosure. The next oldest mosque of Cairo, that of Ibn Tulun (A.H. 283) also had a non-Muslim architect, the Christian Ibn Katib al-Fargani.

Not only in the earlier period, but also in the days of the Abbasids, the Muslims relied exclusively upon Greek and Persian, to a less degree on Coptic, architects, engineers, and craftsmen for building and decoration. In Spain of the 2nd century (8th century A.D.) we find the Byzantine Emperor sending a mosaic worker and 320 quintals of tessarae for the adorning of the great mosque at Cordova.

In origin all Muslim art had a Byzantine beginning, but the traditions of Byzantine art received a peculiar direction by passing through a Persian medium, and this medium colours all work done after the close of the 'Umayyad period. Only in the west, in Spain, and to a less degree in North Africa, do we find traces of direct Byzantine influence in later times. But Persian art, as developed under the later Sasanids, was itself derived from Byzantine models, and mainly from models and by craftsmen introduced by Khusraw I. (circ. A.D. 528) ; but even at that early stage there were also some Indian influences apparent in Persian and East-Byzantine work, as, for example, in the use of the horse-shoe arch which first appears in Western Asia in the church of Dana on the Euphrates, circ. A.D. 540. But the horse-shoe arch in pre-Muslim times, as in India, is purely decorative and is not employed in construction.

Thus it appears that the real work of Islam in art and architecture lay in connecting the various portions of the Muslim world in one common life, so that Syria, Persia, Iraq, North Africa, and Spain shared the same influences, which were ultimately Greek or Graeco-Persian, the Indian element, of quite secondary importance, entering directly through Persia. Already before the outspread of Islam, Byzantine art had entirely replaced native models in Egypt, and this was largely the case in Persia as well. At most we can say that Islam evolved a quasi-Byzantine style which owed its distinctive features to the limitations of the Persian artists, but which occasionally attained a better level by the importation of Byzantine craftsmen. Exactly the same general conclusions hold good in the history of the ceramic arts and in the illumination of manuscripts, though here the observance of the Qur'anic prohibition of the portrayal of animal figures, strictly observed only in some quarters and least regarded in Persia and Spain, caused a greater emphasis to be laid on vegetable forms in decoration, and on geometrical patterns.

In the field of science and philosophy, where we get such abundant evidence in the 'Abbasid period, we are left with very little material under the 'Umayyads. We know that the medical school at Alexandria continued to flourish, and we read of one Adfar, a Christian, who was distinguished as a student of the books of Hermes, the occult authority which did most to divert Egyptian science into a magical direction, and we are informed that he was sought out by a young Roman named Morienus (Marianos) who became his pupil and at his master's death retired to a hermitage near Jerusalem. Later on the prince Khalid b. Yazid, of the 'Umayyad family (d. 85 A.H.—704 A.D.) is said to have become the pupil of Marianos and to have studied with him chemistry, medicine, and astronomy. He was the author of three epistles, in one of which he narrated his conversations with

Marianos, another relates the manner in which he studied chemistry, and a third explains the enigmatical allusions employed by his teachers. Long before this medical and scientific studies had passed over to Persia, but Alexandria retained its reputation as the chief centre of such work throughout the 'Umayyad period.

Towards the end of the 'Umayyad age the influence of Hellenistic thought begins to appear in the nature of criticism upon accepted views of Muslim theology. As in jurisprudence, we have no ground for supposing that Muslims at this stage were directly acquainted with Greek material, but general ideas were obtained by intercourse with those who had been long under Hellenistic influences, and especially by intercourse with Christians amongst whom the premises of psychology, metaphysics, and logic had encroached very largely upon the field of theology by the nature of the subjects debated in the Arian, Nestorian, and Monophysite controversies which turned mainly upon psychological and metaphysical problems. The ideas with which the Muslims were brought into contact suggested difficulties in their own theology, as yet only partially formulated, and in religious theories which had taken form in a community entirely ignorant of philosophy. Some of the older fashioned believers met these questions with a plain negative, simply refusing to admit that there was a difficulty or any question for consideration : reason ('aql), they said, could not be applied to the revelation of God, and it was alike an innovation to dispute that revelation or to defend it.   But others felt the pressure of the questions proposed and, whilst strictly faithful to the statements of the Qur'an, endeavoured to bring their expression into conformity with the principles of philosophy.

The questions first proposed were concerned with (a) the revelation of the Word of God, and (b) the problem of free will.

(a) The Prophet speaks of revelation as " coming down " (*nazala*) from God and refers to the " mother of the book " which seems to designate the unrevealed source from which the revealed words are derived.   It may be that this refers to the idea of which the word is the expression, and that in this the Prophet was influenced by Christian or Jewish theories which had originally a Platonic colouring, but it seems probable that he had no very clear theory as to the " mother of the book."   At an early date the view arose that the Qur'an had existed, though not expressed in words, that the substance and meaning were eternal as part of the wisdom of God, though it had been put into words in time and then communicated to the Prophet, which is now the orthodox teaching on the basis of Qur. 80. 15. that it was written " by the hands of scribes honoured and righteous," this being taken to mean that it was written at God's dictation by supernatural beings in paradise and afterwards sent down to the Prophet. That is not the necessary meaning of the verse, which may refer to the previous revelations made to the Jews and Christians which the Prophet regarded as true but afterwards corrupted, so that the Qur'an is simply the pure transcription of Divine Truth imperfectly represented by those earlier revelations. Under the 'Umayyads, when a rigid orthodoxy was taking form in quarters not sympathetic towards the official Khalif, a view arose that the actual words expressed in the Qur'an were co-eternal with God, and it was only the writing down of these words which had taken place in time. It seems probable that this theory of an eternal " word " was suggested by the Christian doctrine of the " Logos." It can be traced primarily to the teaching of St. John Damascene (d. circ. 160 A.H. = A.D. 776) who served as secretary of state under one of the 'Umayyads, either Yazid II. or Hijam, and his pupil Theodore Abucara (d. 217 =832), who express the relation of the Christian Logos to the Eternal Father in terms very closely resembling those employed in Muslim theology to denote the relation between the Qur'an or revealed word and God. (cf. Von Kremer : *Streifzuege.* pp. 7-9). We know from the extant works of these two Christian writers that theological discussions between Muslims and Christians were by no means uncommon at the time.

The *Mu'tazilites* of whom *Wasil b. 'Ata* (d. 131) is generally regarded as the founder, were a sect of rationalistic tendencies, and they were opposed to the doctrine of the eternity of the Qur'an and the

claim that it was uncreated because the conclusions to
be drawn seemed to them to introduce distinct
personalities corresponding to the persons of the
Christian Trinity, and in these views they were undoubtedly influenced by the form in which St. John
Damascene presented the doctrine of the Trinity.
As it was implied that there was an attribute of wisdom
possessed by God which was not a thing created by
God but eternally with him, and this wisdom may be
conceived as not absolutely identical with God but
possessed by him, the Mu'tazilites argued that it was
something co-eternal with God but other than God,
and so an eternal Qur'an was a second person of the
Godhead and God was not absolutely one. Al-
Muzdar, a Mu'tazilite greatly revered as an
ascetic, expressly denounces those who believe in an
eternal Qur'an as ditheists. The Mu'tazilites
called themselves *Ahlu t-Tawhid wa-l-'Adl* " the
people of unity and justice," the first part of this
title implying that they alone were consistent defenders of the doctrine of the Divine Unity.

(b) As to the freedom or otherwise of the human
will, the Qur'an is perfectly definite in its assertion
of God's omnipotence and omniscience : all things
are known to him and ruled by him, and so human
acts and the rewards and punishments due to men
must be included : " no misfortune happens either
on earth or in yourselves but we made it,—it was in
the book " (Qur. 57. 22) ; " everything have We set
down in the clear book of our decrees " (Qur. 36) ;

" had We pleased We had certainly given to every soul
its guidance, but true is the word which hath gone
forth from me,—I shall surely fill hell with jinn and
men together." (Qur. 32. 13). Yet the appeal for
moral conduct implies a certain responsibility, and
consequently freedom, on man's part. In the mind
of the Prophet, no doubt, the inconsistency between
moral obligations and reponsibility on the one hand,
and the unlimited power of God on the other, had not
been perceived, but towards the end of the 'Umayyad
period these were pressed to their logical conclusions.
On the one side were the *Qadarites* (*qadr* " power "),
the advocates of free will. This doctrine first appears
in the teaching of *Ma'bad al-Yuhani* (d. 80 A.H.) who
is said to have been the pupil of the Persian Sinbuya
and taught in Damascus. Very little is known of the
early Qadarites, but it is stated that Sinbuya was put
to death by the Khalif 'Abdu l-Malik, and that the
Khalif Yazid II. (102-106 A.H.) favoured their views.
On the other side were the *Jabarites* (*jabr*, " com-
pulsion ") who preached strict determinism and were
founded by the Persian *Jahm b. Safwan* (d. circ. 130).
It is baseless to argue that either free will or determinism were necessarily due to Persian pre-Islamic
beliefs, it is evident that the logical deduction of
doctrinal theology in either direction was done by
Persians ; they were, indeed, the theologians of
early Islam. It must be noted that the full development of fatalism was not reached until a full
eentury after the foundation of Islam and that

its first exponent was put to death as a heretic.

The earlier Qadarites had a Persian origin, but the reaction against the Jabarites was led by Wasil b. 'Ata whose teaching clearly shows the solvent force of Hellenistic philosophy acting on Muslim theology. Wasil was the pupil of the Qadarite Hasan ibn Abi l-Hasan (d. 110) but he " seceded " from his teacher and this is given as the traditional reason for calling him and his followers the *Mu'tazila* or " secession," and did so on the ground of the apparant injustice imputed to God in his apportionment of rewards and penalties.   The details of the controversy are quite secondary, the important point is that the Mu'tazilites claimed to be " the people of Unity and Justice," this latter meaning that God conformed to an objective standard of just and right action so that he could not be conceived as acting arbitrarily and in disregard of justice, an idea borrowed from Hellenistic philosophy for the older Muslim conception regarded God as acting as he willed and the standard of right and wrong merely a dependent on his will.

Throughout the whole 'Umayyad period we see the conquering Arabs, so far the rulers of the Muslim world, in contact with those who, though treated with arrogant contempt as serfs, were really in possession of a much fuller culture than their rulers.   In spite of the haughty attitude of the Arab there was a considerable exchange of thought, and the community of Islam began to absorb Hellenistic influences in several directions, and so the canon law and theology

of the Muslims was beginning, at the end of the
'Umayyad period, to be leavened by Greek thought.
It was, however, a period of indirect influence;
there is no indication, save in a few instances in the
study of natural science and medicine, of Muslim
teachers or students availing themselves directly of
Greek material, but only that they were in contact
with those who were familiar with the work of Greek
philosophers and jurists. It was a period of su-
pended animation, to some extent, during which a new
language and a new religion were being assimilated by
the very diverse elements now comprised in the
Khalifate, and those elements were being welded
together in a common life. However great were the
sectarian and political differences of later times, the
church of Islam long remained, and to a great extent
still remains, possessed with a common life in the
sense that there is a mutual understanding between
the several parts and that thus an intellectual or
religious influence has been able to pass rapidly from
one extreme to the other, and the religious duty of
pilgrimage to Mecca has done much to foster this
community of life and to promote intercourse between
the several parts. Such an understanding has by no
means always produced sympathy or friendliness, and
the various movements as they have passed from one
part to the other have often been considerably
modified in the passage; but the motive power
behind a movement in Persia has been intelligible in
Muslim Spain—though perhaps intensely disliked

there—and most often a movement beginning in any one district has sooner or later had some contact with every other district. There is no such division in Islam as that which prevents the average English churchman from knowing about and appreciating a religious movement at work in the Coptic or Serbian church. The common life of Islam is largely based on the use of the Arabic language as the medium of daily life, or at least of prayer and the medium of scholarship, and this was extremely effective before the inclusion of large Turkish and Indian elements which have never really become Arabic speaking. It was this which made the Arabic speaking community of Islam so favourable a medium of cultural transmission. The 'Umayyad period was a marking time during which this common life was being evolved, and with it was evolved necessarily the bitterness of sectarian and faction divisions which always result when divergent types are in too close contact with one another.

CHAPTER III

THE COMING OF THE 'ABBASIDS

The rule of the 'Umayyads had been a period of tyrannical oppression on the part of the Arab rulers upon their non-Arab subjects and especially upon the *mawali* or converts drawn from the native population of the conquered provinces who not only were not admitted to equality, as was the professed principle of the religion of Islam, but were treated simply as serfs. This was in no sense due to religious persecution, for it was the converts who were the most aggrieved, nor was it due to a racial antipathy as between a Semitic and an Aryan people, nor yet to anything that could be described as a " national " feeling on the part of the Persians and other conquered races, but simply a species of " class " feeling due to the contempt felt by the Arabs for those whom they had conquered and hatred on the part of the conquered towards their arrogant masters, a hatred intensified by disgust at their misgovernment and ignorance of the traditions of civilization. There were other causes also which helped to intensify this feeling of hatred especially in the case of the Persians. Amongst these was a semi-religious feeling, even amongst those who had become converts to Islam. It had been the

old usage of the Persians to regard the Sasanid
kings, the descendants of the legendary *kayani*
dynasty of heroes who had first established a settled
community in Persia, as *bagh* not quite perhaps what
we should understand as " gods," but rather as
incarnations of deity, the divine spirit passing on by
transmigration from one ruler to another, and so they
ascribed to the king miraculous powers and worshipped
him as the shrine of a divine presence. At the Muslim
conquest the Sasanid kings had not only ceased to
rule, but the dynasty had become extinct. Many of
the Persians who, in spite of adopting Islam, still
clung to their old ideas, were quite ready to treat the
Khalif with the same adoration as their kings, but felt
a distinct distaste for the theory of the Khalifate
according to which the Khalif was no more than a
chieftain elected in the democratic fashion of the
desert tribes, a thing which seemed to them like
reversion to primitive barbarism. Our own experience
in dealing with oriental races has shown us that there
is a great deal which must be taken seriously in ideas of
this kind. Of course those who had been subjects of
the Roman Empire had no inclination towards
deifying their rulers, unless perhaps some who had
been only recently incorporated from more oriental
elements : but those who had been under Persian rule
craved a deified prince. In A.H. 141-142 this took
the form of an attempt to deify the Khalif by a
fanatical sect of Persian origin known as the Rawan-
diyya which broke out into open revolt when the

Khalif refused to be treated as a god and cast their leaders into prison : the members of the sect, and many other of their fellow-countrymen, considered that a Khalif was no valid sovereign who refused to be recognised as a deity. From the second century of the Hijra down to modern times there has been a continuous stream of pseudo-prophets who have claimed to be gods, or successful leaders who have been deified by their followers. The latest of these appears in the earlier phases of the Babi movement, A.D. 1844-1852, though the doctrines of re-incarnation and of the presence of the divine spirit in the leader seem to be less emphasized in present day Babism, at least in this country and America.

The most prevalent form of these ideas occurs in the essentially Persian movement known as the *Shiʻa* or " schismatics." These are divided into two types, both alike holding that the succession of the Prophet is confined to the hereditary descendants of 'Ali the cousin and son-in-law of the Prophet to whom alone was given the divine right of the *Imamate* or leadership. The two types differ in the meaning of this Imamate, the one group contenting itself with maintaining that 'Ali and his descendants have a divine authority whereby the Imams are the only legitimate rulers of Islam and its infallible guides ; of this moderate type of Shiʻa is the religion of Morocco and the form prevalent about San'a in South Arabia. The other group presses the claim that the Imam is the incarnation of a divine spirit, sometimes asserting that it was only by fraud that the prophet Muhammad interposed and acted as spokesman for the divine Imam 'Ali. Of this type is the Shi'a which forms the state religion of modern Persia, spreading westwards into Mesopotamia and eastwards into India. The commonest belief, prevalent in the modern Shi'a, is that there were twelve Imams of whom 'Ali was the first, and Muhammad al-Muntazar, who succeeded at the death of his father the eleventh Imam al-Hasan al-Askari in 260 A.H. (=A.D. 873) was the last. Soon after his accession Muhammad Al-Muntazar " vanished " at Samárrá, the town which served as the 'Abbasid capital from A.H. 222 to 279. The mosque at Samárrá is said to cover an underground vault into which he disappeared and from which he will emerge again to resume his office when the propitious time has arrived, and the place whence he is to issue forth is one of the sacred spots visited by Shi'ite pilgrims. Meanwhile the Shahs and princes are ruling the faithful only as deputies of the concealed Imam. The disappearance of Muhammad al-Muntazar took place more than a century after the fall of the 'Umayyads but we have anticipated in order to show the general tendency of the Shi'ite ideas which were prevalent even in 'Umayyad times, especially in Northern Persia, and did much to promote the revolt against the secularised 'Umayyad rule.

A curious importance also is attached to the date. The disaffection of the *mawali* came to a head towards the end of the first century of the Muslim era. There was a general belief that the completion of the century would see the end of existing conditions, just as in Western Europe the year 1000 A.D. was expected to mark the dawn of a new world. Dissatisfaction was at its height, especially in Khurasan, and the disaffected for the most part rallied round the 'Alids.

The 'Alid claims which did so much to overthrow the 'Umayyad dynasty and indirectly led to the bringing forward of the Persian element by which the transmission of Hellenistic culture was most furthered, are best understood by the help of a genealogical table.

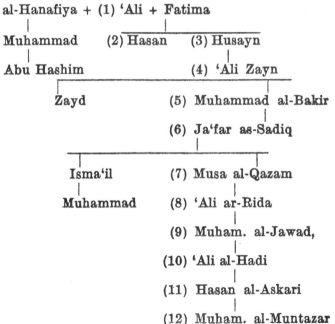

al-Hanafiya + (1) 'Ali + Fatima

Muhammad	(2) Hasan	(3) Husayn
Abu Hashim		(4) 'Ali Zayn

Zayd		(5) Muhammad al-Bakir
		(6) Ja'far as-Sadiq

Isma'il		(7) Musa al-Qazam
Muhammad		(8) 'Ali ar-Rida
		(9) Muham. al-Jawad,
		(10) 'Ali al-Hadi
		(11) Hasan al-Askari
		(12) Muham. al-Muntazar

'Ali had two wives, (i) al-Hanafiya, by whom he had a
son Muhammad, and (ii) Fatima, the daughter of the
Prophet Muhammad, by whom he had two sons,
Hasan and Husayn. All the 'Alid party believed that
'Ali should have succeeded the Prophet by divine
right and regarded the first three Khalifs as usurpers.
Already under the third Khalif Uthman the dis-
satisfied *mawla* element had begun to look to 'Ali as
their champion, and he in the true spirit of early
Islam supported their claim to the rights of brotherhood as fellow Muslims. This partisanship received
its extreme expression in the preaching of the Jewish
convert 'Abdu b. Saba, who declared the divine right
of 'Ali to the Khalifate as early as A.H. 32. 'Ali
himself apparently did not take so pronounced a
view, but certainly regarded himself as in some degree
injured by his exclusion. In 35 'Ali was appointed
Khalif and Ibn Saba then declared that he was not
only Khalif by divine right, but that a divine spirit
had passed from the Prophet to him, so that he was
raised to a supernatural level. This theory 'Ali himself repudiated. When he was assassinated in 40
'Abdu declared that his martyred soul had passed to
heaven and would in due course descend to earth
again : his spirit was in the clouds, his voice was
heard in the thunder, the lightning was his rod.

The Umayyad party led by Mu'awiya never submitted to 'Ali, although they did not question the
legitimacy of his appointment. At his death Mu-
'awiya became the fifth Khalif, but had to face the

claims of al-Hasan, 'Ali's son. Al-Hasan made terms with Mu'awiya and died in 49, poisoned, it was commonly stated. The other son, al-Husayn, tried to enforce his claim, but met a tragic death at Kerbela. After al-Husayn's death some of the 'Alid partisans recognised Muhammad the son of 'Ali and al-Hanafiya as the fourth Imam ; he, it is true, disowned these supporters, but that was a detail to which they paid no attention. His supporters were known as Kaysanites, and owed their origin to Kaysan, a freedman of 'Ali, who formed a society for the purpose of avenging the deaths of al-Hasan and al-Husayn. When this Muhammad died in 81 his followers divided into two sections, some accepting the fact of his death, others supposing that he had simply passed into concealment to appear again in due course. This idea of a " concealed " Imam was a heritage from the older religious theories of Persia and recurs again and again in Shi'a history. The important point is that both sections of this party continued to exist all through the 'Umayyad period, steadily refusing to recognise the official Khalifa as more than usurpers, and looking forward to the day when they could avenge the martyrdom of 'Ali and his sons.

We need not linger over the family of al-Hasan and his descendants. They were involved in 'Alid risings at Madinna, and after the suppression of one of these in 169, long after the fall of the 'Umayyads, Idris the great-grandson of al-Hasan escaped to the far West and established a " moderate " Shi'ite

Dynasty in what is now Morocco, so that the subsequent history of that house concerns the history of the West.

Most of the Shi‘ites regard the third Imam al-Husayn as being succeeded by his son ‘Ali Zayn. Al-Husayn, like al-Hasan, was not only the son of ‘Ali, but also of the Prophet's daughter, Fatima. In al-Husayn's case moreover there was another heritage which ultimately proved more important than descent from either ‘Ali or Fatima : he was generally supposed to have married the daughter of the last of the Persian kings, the " mother of the Imams," and this traditional marriage with the Persian princess, —its historical evidence is very dubious—has been regarded by the Persian Shi‘ites as the most important factor in the Imamate, although this, of course, has nothing whatever to do with the religion of Islam. That so great weight could be attached to such a consideration serves to show how really foreign and non-Muslim a thing the Shi‘a is. ‘Ali Zayn had two sons, Zayd and Muhammad al-Bakir. Of these Zayd was a pupil of Wasil b. ‘Ata and associated with the Mu‘tazilite movement : he is generally regarded as a rationalist. Indeed, as we shall now see frequently, the heretical Shi‘ite party was very generally mixed up with free thought and frequently shows adherence to Greek philosophy : it seems as though its inspiring spirit was hostility towards orthodox Islam, and a readiness to ally itself with anything which tended to criticize unfavourably the orthodox doctrines.

Zayd had a body of followers who established themselves in North Persia where they held their own for
some time, and a branch of their party still exists in
South Arabia, still suspected of rationalist pro-
clivities. Most of the Shi'ites, however, recognised
Muhammad al-Bakir as the fifth Imam, and Ja'far
as-Sadiq as the sixth. This latter also was a devoted
follower of the " new learning," that is to say, of
Hellenistic philosophy, and is generally regarded as the
founder, or at least the chief exponent, of what are
known as *batinite* views, that is to say the allegorical
interpretation of the Qur'an, so that revelation is made
to mean, not the literal statement, but an inner
meaning, and this inner meaning generally shows a
strong influence of Hellenistic philosophy. It is only
the divinely directed Imam who can expound the true
meaning of the Qur'an which remains a sealed book to
the uninitiated. Ja'far was, it would appear, the
first of the 'Alids who openly asserted that he was a
divine incarnation as well as an inspired teacher :
his predecessors had done no more than acquiesce in
such claims when made by their followers, and very
often had repudiated them.

Abu Hashim, the son of Muhammad b. al-Hanafiya,
died in 98 A.H. poisoned, it was generally believed, by
the Khalif Sulayman, and bequeathed his rights to
Muhammad b. 'Ali b. 'Abdullah, a descendant of the
house of Hashim, to which the Prophet and 'Ali had
belonged, the rival clan of the Quraysh tribe opposed
to the clan of the 'Umayyads. Abu Hashim assumed

that the Imamate was his to be passed on to whom he saw fit, a view of the Imamate which was not accepted by the stricter Shi'ites who were legitimists, but the partisans of Abu Hashim do not seem to have been extremists in spite of their Kaysanite origin. In 99 the Khalifate passed to Umar II. the one 'Umayyad who showed 'Alid sympathies, putting an end to the public cursing of 'Ali which had formed part of the public ritual in the mosques of Damascus since the days of Mu'awiya and who represented a type of personal piety to which the 'Umayyad Khalifs had hitherto been strangers. His brief reign of less than three years did not, however, remove the evils of tyranny and misgovernment, and he was followed by other rulers more in conformity with the old bad type.

About the time of Umar's death a deputation of Shi'ites waited upon Muhammad b. 'Ali the Hashimite, a man of noted piety and the one who had now become, as legatee of Abu Hashim the son of Muhammad b. al-Hanafiya, the recognised head of an important wing of the Shi'ites, and swore to support him in an endeavour to obtain the Khalifate " that God may quicken justice and destroy oppression " (Dinwari : *Akhbaru t-Tiwal*. ed. Guirgass, Leiden. p. 334): and Muhammad had answered that " this is the season of what we hope and desire, because one hundred years of the calendar are completed " (id.)

The supporters of the family of Muhammad b. al-Hanafiya, who had now transferred their allegiance to

Muhammad b. 'Ali, were extremely important, not so much by reason of their numbers as by their excellent organisation. They had developed a regular system of missionaries (*da'i*, plur. *du'at*) who travelled under the guise of merchants and confined their teaching to private instructions and informal intercourse, a method which has become the standard type of Muslim missionary propaganda. By Abu Hashim's death and legacy Muhammad b. 'Ali found this very fully organised missionary work at his service, and its emissaries were fully confident that his acceptance of the overtures of the Shi'ite deputation meant that he stood as the champion of Shi'ite claims. The stricter Shi'ites who followed the house of al-Husayn did not admit the claims of Muhammad b. al-Hanafiya or his descendants, but they supported Muhammad b. 'Ali's efforts under the impression that he was a Shi'ite champion.

The propaganda in favour of Muhammad b. 'Ali is sometimes referred to as 'Abbasid because he was descended from al-'Abbas, one of the three sons of 'Abdu l-Muttalib, and so brother of Abu Talib the father of the Imam 'Ali and of 'Abdullah who was grandfather of the Prophet Muhammad. At the time, however, the missionaries claimed rather to be the supporters of the Hashimites, a term which was ambiguous, perhaps intentionally so. It was afterwards explained as referring to the house of Hashim which was the rival clan of the Quraysh opposed to the 'Umayyads and that to which the Prophet, and 'Ali,

and al-'Abbas belonged : but in the minds of many of
the Shi'ites it was taken to mean the followers of Abu
Hashim, the grandson of Al-Hanafiya.

Muhammad b. 'Ali died in 126 A.H. leaving three
sons, Ibrahim, Abu l-Abbas, and Abu Ja'far, the first
of these being recognised as his successor. About the
same time Abu Muslim, who became governor of
Khurasan in 129 comes into prominence. It is
dubious whether he was an Arab or a native of 'Iraq
(cf. Masudi. vi. 59), indeed, the claim was made that he
was a descendant of Gandarz, one of the ancient kings
of Persia (id.) Now Khurasan was the area most
disaffected towards the 'Umayyads, and there the
Hashimite missionaries had been most active and
successful. Abu Muslim threw himself into this work
heartily and began gathering together an armed body
of men who before long numbered 200,000. Information and warning was sent to the Khalif Marwan
II. but was ignored : indeed the court at Damascus
took no notice until 130. Abu Muslim at length
openly raised the black standard as the signal of revolt
against the 'Umayyads whose official colour was white.
Then all the Khalif did was to seize Muhammad b.
'Ali's son Ibrahim and put him to death. The other
two sons escaped and fled to Kufa where they were
sheltered and concealed by some Shi'ites, the second
son Abu l-'abbas, known to history as *as-Saffah* " the
butcher " being recognised as the Hashimite leader.

Abu Muslim's success was rapid and complete, and
in 132 the 'Umayyad dynasty was overthrown and

partly exterminated, and so "the butcher" became the first of the 'Abbasid Khalifs, so called as being of the family of al-'Abbas the son of 'Abdu l-Muttalib.

As soon as the Khalif Abu l-'Abbas was seated on the throne his chief aim was to secure the establishment of his dynasty by getting rid of all possible rivals, and it was the vigour he showed in doing this which earned for him the title of " the Butcher." First of all he hunted down and slew all the representatives he could find of the 'Umayyad family. One of these escaped, 'Abdu r-Rahman, and went to Africa where he endeavoured to form a body of supporters without success, and then crossed over to Spain where in 138 he established himself at Cordova, and there he and his descendants ruled until 422 A.H. These Spanish 'Umayyads claimed to be legitimist rulers, but never assumed the divine claims of the 'Alid section.

Abu Muslim, who had done most to establish the 'Umayyad dynasty, next provoked the Khalif's jealousy, probably with good cause for he was indignant to find that " the Butcher " was no sooner on the throne than he entirely discarded the Shi'ites who had helped to place him there, and so within the first year of the 'Abbasid rule Abu Muslim was put to death.

The fall of the 'Umayyads brought an end to the tyranny of the Arab minority, as it now was, and placed the preponderance for a clear century (A.H. 132-232) in Persian hands. The government was remodelled on Persian lines, and to Persian influence was due the institution of the *wazir* or responsible minister at the head of the executive. The title is probably identical with the Old Persian *vi-chir* or " overseer " (thus Darmesteter : *Etudes Iraniennes* i. p. 58. note 3.) ; before this the chief minister was simply clerk (*kàtib*) or adviser (*mushir*) and was simply one of the Khalif's attendants who was employed to conduct correspondence, or to give advice when occasion required. In 135 the noble Persian family of Barmecides began to supply *wazirs*, and these controlled the policy of the Khalifate until 189. From the time of al-Mansur (A.H. 136-158) onwards the Persians began to assert their pre-eminence and a party was formed known as the *Shu'ubiyya* or " anti-Arab party " of those who held, not only that the alien converts were equal to the Arabs, but that the Arabs were a half savage and inferior race in all respects, contrasting unfavourably with the Persians, Syrians, and Copts. This party produced considerable mass of controversial literature in which free course was given to the general dislike felt towards the Arabs and which reveals the intensity of the contempt and hatred felt towards these parvenus. The Arabs had boasted of their racial descent and had devoted much attention to the keeping of their genealogies, at least in the century immediately preceding the rise of Islam ; as they had then only just commenced to count descent in the father's line these genealogies were purely fictitious in so far as they dealt with pre-

Islamic ancestors. The Arabs were in fact a parvenu people only just emerging out of barbarism (cf. Lammens : *Le berceau de l'islam*. p. 117). But the Persians, no less careful about genealogical records, to which their caste system had caused them to pay considerable attention, boasted authentic genealogies of much greater antiquity. In literature, in science, in Muslim canon law, in theology, and even in the scientific treatment of Arabic grammar, the Persians very rapidly surpassed the Arabs, so that we must be careful always to refer to Arabic philosophy, Arabic science, etc., in the history of Muslim culture, rather than to Arab philosophy, etc., remembering that, though expressed in the Arabic language, the common medium of all the Muslim world, only in a very few cases was it the work of Arabs : for the most part the Arabic philosophers and scientists, historians, grammarians, theologians, and jurists were Persians, Turks, or Berbers by birth, though using the Arabic language. The fall of the 'Umayyads and the replacing of the Arabs by the Persians commences the golden age of Arabic literature and scholarship. The older Arabic literature, that namely which was written by Arabs as yet untouched by external influences, consists entirely of poetry, the work of professional bards who sing of desert life and warfare, lament over the deserted camping grounds, boast of their tribe, and abuse their enemies. It forms a distinct class of poetic composition, which has developed its own literary standards, and attained a high standard of

excellence in its way. In many respects this older
Arab poetry makes a special appeal to us, it shows an
observation of nature which is very striking, it has an
undercurrent of melancholy which seems an echo of
the desert, and an emotional side which seems con-
vincing in its reality. At the same time it has very
distinct limitations in its range of interest and subject
matter. Undoubtedly a careful study of this early
Arab poetry is a necessary preparation for a proper
appreciation of the literary forms of Arabic and of its
oldest vocabulary and syntax, and of recent years
much attention has been given to it. But this older
Arabic poetry, apparently a native production, but
possibly influenced in pre-Islamic times by some
external contacts as yet undefined, comes to an end
soon after the fall of the 'Umayyads, save in Spain,
where, under the exiled and fugitive remnant of the
'Umayyad dynasty, the production of such poetry
survived. But this type of poetry is really outside
our present enquiry, save to note that it was a Persian
scholar, Hammad b. Sabur ar-Rawiya (d. circ. 156-159)
who collected and edited the seven ancient Arabic
poems known as the *Mu'allaqat* or " suspended,"
i.e., the catena or series, and thus set what may be
called the classical standard of the ancient poetry and
vocabulary. At the accession of the Abbasids the old
Arab type passes away and the intellectual guidance
of the Muslim community passes into the hands of
the Persians.

CHAPTER IV

THE TRANSLATORS

One of the first and most significant indications of the new orientation of Muslim thought was the extensive production of Arabic tranlations of works dealing with philosophical and scientific subjects, with the result that eighty years after the fall of the 'Umayyads the Arabic speaking world possessed Arabic translations of the greater part of the works of Aristotle, of the leading neo-Platonic commentators, of some of the works of Plato, of the greater part of the works of Galen, and portions of other medical writers and their commentators, as well as of other Greek scientific works and of various Indian and Persian writings. This period of activity in translating falls into two stages, the first from the accession of the Abbasids to the accession of al-Ma'mum (A.H. 132-198), when a large amount of work was done by various independent translators, largely Christians, Jews, and recent converts from non-Islamic religions ; the second under al-Ma'mun and his immediate successors, when the work of translation mainly centered in the academy newly founded at Baghdad, and a consistent effort was made to render the material necessary for philosophical and scientific research available for the Arabic speaking student.

The earlier translation work is especially associated with '*Abdullah b. al-Muqaffa'*, a native of Fars and originally a Zoroastrian, who made his profession of faith before a brother of Muhammad b. 'Ali, the father of as-Saffah, and became his secretary. Presuming on his employer's protection he ventured to make derisive and impertinent remarks to Arab dignitaries and especially to Sufyan, the governor of Basra, whom he used to salute with a lewd jest against his mother's chastity. It seems that men of Arab birth who held political office under the early 'Abbasids often had to put up with such insults from the ex-serfs. After an unsuccessful attempt at revolt by another of the Khalif's uncles Ibn al-Muqaffa' was directed to prepare a draft letter of pardon to be presented to the Khalif al-Mansur, who succeeded his brother as-Saffah, for his official seal, but he drew up the letter in such terms as to arouse the Khalif's indignation ; amongst other things the letter said, " if at any time the Commander of the Faithful act perfidiously towards his uncle 'Abdullah b. 'Ali, his wives shall be divorced from him, his horses shall be confiscated for the service of God (in war), his slaves shall become free, and the Muslims loosed from their allegiance to him." The Khalif enquired who had prepared this letter and on being informed directed Sufyan to put him to death. Pleased thus to gratify his personal rancour the governor of Basra executed Ibn al-Muqaffa' with great cruelty, though the details differ in different accounts, in A.H. 142 or 143.

Although conforming to Islam, Ibn al-Muqaffa' was generally regarded as a *Zindiq*, a term properly signifying a Manichæan but used loosely by the Arabic writers to denote a member of one of the Persian religions who professed outward conformity to Islam, but secretly adhered to his own creed, or as a term of abuse to denote a heretic of any sort. The word itself is a Persian rendering of *siddiq* or " initiate," a title assumed by full members of the Manichæan sect. It implies the possession of esoteric knowledge and from this idea rose the practice common amongst the Shi'ite sects of concealing their real beliefs from general profession and assuming the external appearance of orthodoxy. Masudi (viii. 293) states that " many heresies arose after the publication of the works of Mani, Ibn Daysan, and Marcion translated from Persian and Pahlawi into Arabic by 'Abdullah b. al-Muqaffa' and others." Under al-Mansur and by his orders, translations were made from Greek, Syriac, and Persian, the Syriac and Persian books being themselves translations from Greek or Sanskrit. The best known work of Ibn Muqaffa, was the translation of the *Kalila wa-Dimna* or " Fables of Bidpai " from the Old Persian which was itself a translation from the Sanskrit. Ibn al-Muqaffa's translation into Arabic is generally regarded as a standard model of Arabic prose. The Persian original is lost, but a version in Syriac made from it by the Nestorian missionary Budh, about A.D. 570, is extant and has been published (ed. Bickell and Benfey,

1876) ; the Sanskrit original also is lost in what was
presumably its earlier form, but we find its material
in a much expanded form in two Sanskrit books, (i)
in the *Panchatantra*, which contains the stories which
appear as 5, 7, 8, 9, 10, 17, of de Sacy's Arabic text,
and (ii) the *Mahabharata*, which contains chapters
11, 12, 13.   Evidently the old Syriac of Budh, a
translation of the Persian translation of the original, is
the best representative of the older form of the text.
The Arabic version of Ibn al-Muqaffa' shows a number
of interpolations and additions which all, of course,
appear in the derived versions, in the later Syriac, the
several mediæval Persian translations which are made
from the Arabic and not from the old Persian, and in
the numerous Latin, Hebrew, Spanish, Persian, and
Greek versions.   It was this Arabic translation which
gave to the book a wider circulation than possessed
before or than it could ever have had, and introduced
it to the western world.   The case was exactly
parallel with Aristotle and similar material : Arabic
became a medium of extremely wide transmission
and the additions made as material passed through
Arabic received a wide circulation also.

   Ibn Muqaffa' lived in the reign of al-Mansur and
during that same period we are told (Masudi. viii.
291-2) that Arabic versions were made of several
treatises of Aristotle, of the *almajasta* of Ptolemy, of
the book of Euclid, and other material from the Greek.
About 156 A.H. an Indian traveller brought to
Baghdad a treatise on arithmetic and another on

astronomy : the astronomical treatise was the *Siddhanta* which came to be known to the Arabic writers as the *Sindhind*, it was translated by Ibrahim al-Fazari and opened up a new interest in astronomical studies : some little time afterwards Muhammad b. Musa al-Kharizmi combined the Greek and Indian systems of astronomy, and from this time forth the subject takes a prominent place in Arabic studies. The great Arabic astronomers belong to a later generation, such as Abu Ma'shar of Baghdad, the pupil of al-Kindi, who died in A.H. 272 (= A.D. 885), known to the Latin mediæval writers as " Abumazar," and Muhammad b. Jabir b. Sinan al-Battani (d. 317 A.H. = A.D. 929) who was known as " Albategnius." The Indian work on arithmetic was even more important as by its means the Indian numerals were introduced, to be passed on in due course as " Arabic " numerals, and this decimal system of numbering has made possible an extension of arithmetical processes and indeed of mathematics generally which would have been difficult with any of the older and more cumbersome systems.

Al-Mansur, after founding Baghdad in A.H. 148 (= A.D. 765), summoned a Nestorian physician, George Boktishu', from the school at Junde-Shapur and established him a court physician, and from this time there was a series of Nestorian physicians connected with the court and forming a medical school at Baghdad. George fell ill in Baghdad and was allowed to retire to Junde-Shapur, his place being taken by his pupil Issa b. Thakerbokht, who was the author of a book on therapeutics. Later came Bokhtishu' son of George who was physician to Harunu r-Rashid in 171 (=A.D. 787), and then Gabriel, another son of George, who was sent to attend Ja'far the Barmecide in 175 and stood high in Harun's favour : he wrote an introduction to logic, a letter to al-Ma'mun on foods and drinks, a manual of medicine based on Dioscorus, Galen, and Paul of Aegina, medical pandects, a treatise on perfumes, and other works. In medicine, as will be remembered, the Indian system had been introduced at Junde-Shapur and combined with the Greek, but the latter clearly predominated. Another important settler in Baghdad was the Jewish Syrian physician John bar Maserjoye, who translated the *Syntagma* of Aaron into Syriac and presided over the medical school gathered in the Muslim capital. For a long time the Arabic work in medicine was limited to translation of the great Greek authorities and practice on the lines learned in Alexandria. We have already referred to the unfortunate influence derived from the Egyptian school which diverted both medicine and chemistry into semi-magical lines, an evil tendency from which the Arabic school never quite freed itself. A considerable time elapsed before the Arabic speaking community produced any original writers on medicine. About the end of the third century we find Abu l-Abbas Ahmad b. Thayib as-Sarakhsi, a pupil of al-Kindi, who is stated to have written a treatise on the soul, an abridgment of Porphyry's *Isagoge*, and an introductory manual of medicine (Masudi. ii. 72). At that time medical studies were still very largely in Christian and Jewish hands, and we find the Syriac physician John ben Serapion (end of 9th cent. A.D.) writing in Syriac medical pandects which were circulated in two editions, the latter of which was translated into Arabic by several writers independently and long afterwards into Latin by Gerard of Cremona.

The father of Arabic medicine proper was Abu Bakr Muhammad b. Zakariyya ar-Razi (d. A.H. 311-320 = A.D. 923-932) who was known to Latin mediæval writers as " Razes," a student of music, philosophy, literature, and finally medicine. In his medical pandects he uses both Greek and Indian authorities, and the introduction of these latter in subordination to the classic authorities used at Alexandria was the really important contribution made by the Arabic students to the progress of science. Unfortunately ar-Razi's work suffered from the defect that it greatly lacks order and arrangement, it is a collection of more or less separate treatises, and so not at all convenient to use. For this reason more perhaps than any other he was replaced by Ibn Sina (Avicenna) whose work, if anything, errs in the opposite direction and suffers from an extremely elaborate arrangement and systematization. It will be noticed that with the Arabic writers, as with their Syriac predecessors, the leading medical writers were usually also exponents of logic and commentators on Aristotle as well as Galen.

The Khalif al-Mansur was the patron who did most to attract the Nestorian physicians to the city of Baghdad which he had founded, and he was also a prince who did much to encourage those who set themselves to prepare Arabic translations of Greek, Syriac, and Persian works. Still more important was the patronage given by the Khalif al-Ma'mun who in A.H. 217 (=A.D. 832) founded a school at Baghdad, suggested no doubt by the Nestorians and Zoroastrian schools already existing, and this he called the *Bayt al-Hikma* or " House of Wisdom," and this he placed under the guidance of Yahya b. Masawaih (d. A.H. 243 =A.D. 857), who was an author both in Syriac and Arabic, and learned also in the use of Greek. His medical treatise on " Fevers " was long in repute and was afterwards translated into Latin and into Hebrew.

The most important work of the academy however was done by Yahya's pupils and successors, especially *Abu Zayd Hunayn b. Ishaq al-Ibadi* (d. 263 A.H. = A.D. 876), the Nestorian physician to whom we have already referred as translating into Syriac the chief medical authorities as well as parts of Aristotle's Organon. After studying at Baghdad under Yahya he visited Alexandria and returned, not only with the training given at what was then the first medical school, but with a good knowledge of Greek which he employed in making translations in Syriac and Arabic.

With him were associated his son Ishaq and his nephew Hubaysh. Hunayn prepared Arabic translations of Euclid; of various portions of Galen, Hippocrates, Archimedes, Apollonius, and others, as well as of the Republic Laws, and Timæus of Plato, the Categories, Physics, and Magna Moralia of Aristotle, and the commentary of Themistius on book 30 of the Metaphysics, as well as an Arabic translation of the Bible. He also translated the spurious Mineralogy of Aristotle, which long served as one of the leading authorities on chemistry, and the medical pandects of Paul of Aegina. His son, besides original works on medicine, produced Arabic versions of the Sophist of Plato, the Metaphysics, *de anima, de generatione et de corruptione*, and the Hermeneutica of Aristotle which Hunayn had translated into Syriac, as well as some of the commentaries of Porphyry, Alexander of Aphrodisias, and Ammonius. A little later we find the Syrian Christian Questa b. Luqa, a native of Ba'albek, who had studied in Greece, prominent as a translator.

The fourth century A.H. was the golden period of the Arabic translators, and it is worth noting that, although the work was done chiefly by Syriac speaking Christians, and inspired by Syriac tradition a very large number of the translations were made directly from the Greek, by men who had studied the language in Alexandria or Greece; very often the same scholar made Syriac and Arabic translations from the Greek text. There were also translators from the Syriac, but these usually come after the translators from the Greek. Amongst the Nestorian translators from Syriac was *Abu Bishr Matta b. Yunus* (d. 328 A.H. =A.D. 939), who rendered into Arabic the Analytica Posteriora and the poetics of Aristotle, Alexander of Aphrodisias' commentary on the *de generatione et de corruptione*, and Themistius' commentary on book 30 of the Metaphysics, all from the existing Syriac versions. He was also the author of original commentaries on Aristotle's Categories and the Isagoge of Porphyry.

The Jacobite translators come on the scene after the Nestorians. Amongst the Jacobites translating from Syriac to Arabic we find *Yahya b. Adi* of Takrit (d. 364), a pupil of Hunayn, who revised many of the existing versions and prepared translations of Aristotle's Categories, Sophist. Elench., Poetics, and Metaphysics, Plato's Laws and Timæus, as well as Alexander of Aphrodisias' commentary on the Categories and Theophrastus on the Moralia. The Jacobite *Abu 'Ali Isa b. Zaraah* (d. 398) translated the Categories, the Natural History, and the *de partibus animalium*, with the commentary of John Philoponus.

This is a convenient place to summarize briefly the range of Aristotelian material available to Arabic students of philosophy. The whole of the logical Organon was accessible in Arabic, and in this were included the Rhetoric and Poetics, as well as Porphyry's *Isagoge*. Of the works on natural science they had the *Physica, de coelo, de generatione et corruptione, de sensu,* the *Historia animalium,* the spurious *Meteorologia,* and the *de anima.* On mental and moral science they had the *Metaphysics,* the *Nicomachœan Ethics* and the *Magna Moralia.* Strangely enough the *Politics* was not included in the Aristotelian canon, its place being taken by Plato's *Laws* or *Republic.* Besides these the Arabic students accepted as Aristotelian a *Mineralogy,* of which we have no knowledge, and a *Mechanics.*

Of these the logical Organon always remained the basis of a humane education, side by side with the indigenous study of grammar, and this essentially logical basis of education seems to have been influenced by the example of the existing system developed amongst the Syrians, although it must be remembered a similar system was developed quite independently in Latin scholasticism prior to the earliest contact with the Arabic writers. The Aristotelian logic has always remained an orthodox and generally accepted science. The philosophical and theological controversies and the developments produced by the Arabic philosophers centred mainly in questions of metaphysics and psychology, and so were particularly concerned with the 12th book of *Metaphysics* and the treatise *de anima,* more especially the 3rd book. As we have already noted the psychology of Aristotle was interpreted in the light of Alexander of Aphrodisias' commentary, and thus received a theistic and supernatural colouring which receives its fuller development in neo-Platonic teaching.

Most important in the fuller development of this neo-Platonic doctrine was the so-called *Theology of Aristotle* which appeared in Arabic about 226 A.H. It was in fact an abridged paraphrase of the last three books (iv-vi) of the *Enneads* of Plotinus made by Naymah of Emessa, boldly circulated and generally received as a genuine work of Aristotle. It might be regarded as a literary fraud, but it is quite possible that Plotinus was confused with Plato whose name appears in Arabic as *'Aflatun*, it seems indeed that this particular confusion was made by some other writers, and the translators accepted the current belief, maintained by all the neo-Platonic commentators, that the teaching of Aristotle and that of Plato were substantially the same, the superficial appearances of difference being such as could be easily explained away. By means of this *Theology* the fully developed doctrine of the neo-Platonists was put into general circulation and combined with the teaching of Alexander of Aphrodisias and thus exercised an enormous influence on the philosophy of Islam in several directions. In the hands of the philosophers properly so called it developed an Islamic neo-Platonism which received its final form at the hands of Ibn Sina (Avicenna) and Ibn Rushd (Averroes), and in this form exercised a powerful influence over Latin scholasticism. Transmitted in another atmosphere it affected Sufism or Muslim mysticism, and was mainly responsible for the speculative theology which that mysticism developed.

In a modified form some of the resultant principles gathered from these two sources finally entered into orthodox Muslim scholastic theology.

The main points of this neo-Platonic doctrine as it figures in Muslim theology present the teaching of the active intellect or *'aql fa''al*, the Agent Intellect of Alexander Aph. as an emanation from God, and the *'aql hayyulani* or passive intellect in man only aroused to activity by the operation of this Agent Intellect, which is substantially the doctrine of Alexander Aph. : the aim of man is to attain a union or *ittisal* in which his intellect becomes one with the Agent Intellect, although the means of attaining this union and the nature of the union differ in the doctrines of the philosophers and the mystics, as we shall see in due course.

Next to philosophy proper medical science is the most important heritage received by the Arabic world from Hellenism. But this science derived through an Alexandrian medium had a serious defect in the accretions which the later Egyptian school had added to the pure teaching of Galen and Hippocrates. As we have already noted this accretion is of a quasi magical character and shows itself in talismans, etc., and theories which are based on ideas which are now classed as " sympathetic magic."

The real impetus came ultimately from transmitted Hellenism, but this influence was derived immediately from the Nestorians in philosophy proper, and from the Nestorians and the Zoroastrian school at Junde-

Shapur in medicine. A good deal later comes the influence of the pagan school at Harran, which also had a neo-Platonic tendency. When the second Abbasid Khalif al-Mansur passed by Harran on his way to fight against the Byzantine Emperor he was astonished to observe the strange appearance of some of the citizens who came out to meet him, wearing their hair long and having close fitting tunics. When the Khalif asked whether they were Christians, Jews, or Zoroastrians, they replied that they were neither. He then enquired if they were " people of a book," for it was only those who possessed written scriptures who could be tolerated in Muslim dominions ; but to this they returned such hesitating and ambiguous replies that the Khalif at length felt convinced that he had discovered a colony of pagans, as was the case, and he ordered them to adopt some one or other of the " religions of the book " before his return from the war, or to suffer the penalty of death. At this they were greatly alarmed : some of them became Muslims, others Christians or Zoroastrians, but some declined to desert their traditional beliefs. These latter naturally had the most anxious time, wondering how they could contrive to evade the Khalif's demands. At length a Muslim lawyer offered to show them a way out of the difficulty if they paid him a substantial fee for doing so. The fee was paid and he advised them to claim to be Sabians, because Sabians are mentioned in the Qur'an as belonging to a religion " of the book," but no one knew who the Sabians were. There is a

sect known as *Sabiyun* or *Sabaean*, whose religion is a
strange mixture of ancient Babylonian state worship
Christian Gnosticism, and Zoroastrianism, living in
the mashe lands near Basra, but they had always
been careful to keep their religious beliefs secret
from all outsiders, and although they were no doubt
the sect mentioned in the Qur'an under the name of
Sabiyun or *Sabians*, none could prove that the pagans
of Harran were not also comprised under this term.
The Khalif never did pass back by Harran, the pagans
who had assumed the name of Sabian continued to use
it, those who had become Christians or Zoroastrians
reverted to their old faith and submitted to its new
name ; those who had become Muslims were obliged
to remain so as the penalty of death lay upon any who
became renegades from that religion.

The most distinguished of the *alumni* of Harran
was Thabit b. Qurra (d. 289 A.H.), a scholar familiar
with Greek, Syriac, and Arabic, who produced many
works on logic, mathematics, astrology, and medicine,
as well as on the ritual and beliefs of the paganism to
which he remained faithful. Following in his foot-
steps were his son Abu Sa'id Sinan, his grandsons
Ibrahim and Abu l-Hasan Thabit, and his great
grandsons Ishaq and Abu l-Faraj. All these special-
ized in mathematics and astronomy.

It seems that we ought to associate with Harran
Jabir b. Hayyan a perfectly historical character but
of somewhat uncertain date, but believed to have been
a pupil of the 'Umayyad prince Khalid, who dis-

tinguished himself by his researches in chemistry.
Many chemical treatises bear the name of Jabir and a
great proportion of these are probably quite authentic.
M. Berthelot in the 3rd volume of his *La chimie au
moyen age* (Paris, 1893) has made a careful analysis of
the Arabic chemists and regards the whole material
capable of division into two classes, the one a reproduction of the investigations of the Greek chemists
of Alexandria, the other as representing original
investigations, though based upon the Alexandrian
studies in the first place, and all this original material
he regards as due to the initiative of Jabir who thus
becomes in chemistry very much what Aristotle was in
logic.   Berthelot publishes in this book six treatises
claiming to be by Jabir, and these he regards as
representative of all Arabic chemical material, the
later investigators continuing in the lines laid down by
this first investigator.   For a long time the main
object in view was the transmutation of metals, but at
a later period chemistry enters into closer connection
with medical work though never losing the metallurgi-
cal character which we imply when we speak of
" alchemy."   The object in view of the Arabic
students of alchemy does not appeal to the modern
scientist, although the possibility of transmuting
elements is no longer regarded as the impossible
dream which it appeared to the chemists of the
nineteenth century : and, at the same time, it is
perfectly clear that with admitted limitations, the
Arabic chemists were bona fide investigators, though

not understanding correctly the results of the experiments they made.

All the texts published by M. Berthelot begin with the warning that the contents are to be kept strictly secret, and often contain a statement that some essential process is omitted in order that the unenlightened student may not be able to perform the experiments successfully, lest the wholesale production of gold should be a means of corrupting the whole human race. Undoubtedly the Arabic chemists did claim to have attained a knowledge of the means of transmuting the baser metals into gold but the histories contain various references which show that these claims were adversely criticised by many contemporary thinkers, and that a great many of the Arabic writers regarded chemistry, as it was then understood, as a mere imposture. More than once it was noted that the philosopher al-Farabi, who fully believed that it was possible to change other metals into gold and wrote a treatise on how it might be done, himself lived and died in great poverty, whilst Ibn Sina, who did not believe in alchemy, enjoyed modest comfort and could have commanded wealth had he been willing to accept it.

In the course of the middle ages various treatises by Jabir were translated into Latin, where his name appears as Geber, and exercised a considerable influence in producing a western school of alchemy. Before long many original alchemical works were produced in Western Europe and a considerable proportion of these were published under the name of Geber but are pure forgeries. As a result the personality of Geber took a semi mythical character and attempts have been made to account for the diverse and contradictory statements about his life and death, and about the country and century in which he lived by supposing that there were several persons who bore the name ; but the fact seems to be that he early attained a position of great prominence as a chemical writer, and that later ages fathered on him a number of apocryphal productions. Berthelot considers that the best evidence associates him with Harran in the early part of the second century of the Hijra.

Arabic chemistry largely reproduces the work of the Greek chemists of Alexandria, but probably had an underlying native Egyptian stratum. J. Ruska (*Tabula smaragdina*, 1926) regards the material as transmitted through Coptic to Arabic, but this certainly was not the case as the Coptic texts show that they have been translated from Arabic originals.

CHAPTER V

THE MU'TAZILITES

When the Aristotelian philosophy was first made known to the Muslim world it was received almost as a revelation supplementing the Qur'an. At that time it was very imperfectly understood and the discrepancies between it and orthodox theology were not perceived. Thus the Qur'an and Aristotle were read together and regarded as supplementing one another in perfect good faith, but inevitably the conclusions, and still more perhaps the methods, of Greek philosophy began to act as a powerful solvent on the traditional beliefs.

Maqrizi refers to the Mu'tazilites as seizing with avidity on the books of the philosophers, and certainly now new difficulties begin to appear as well as the two great problems which had been prominent at the beginning of the second century—the eternity of the Qur'an and the question of free will. The new difficulties were especially concerned with the qualities of God and, later, with the Qur'anic promise of the beatific vision. The problem of the qualities of God is very closely parallel to the earlier difficulty as to the eternity of the Qur'an, indeed it appears as an enlargement of it. Christian theologians educated in the methods of Greek philosophy had already debated this matter, and in their hands it had taken the form of the question, " how many, and what, attributes are compatible with the unity of God ? " If God's wisdom, whether expressed in the Qur'an or not expressed, were eternal there was something which God possessed, and consequently something other than God which was equal to him in eternity and was not created by him, so that it could not be said that God was alone and that all other things proceeded from him as their cause as the eternal quality always was side by side with God, and so Wasil b. 'Ata declared " he who affirms an eternal quality beside God, affirms two gods." But this applies equally to all qualities, justice, mercy, etc., and, as was suggested by the study of Aristotle, all the categories, all that could be predicated of God as subject, were either created by God and so were not essential and eternal attributes, or else were external things equal with God.

The second generation of Mu'tazilites, of those who begin to show direct acquaintance with Greek philosophy, begins with *Abu l-Hudayl al- Allaf* of Basra (d. 226 A.H.), who lived at the time when Greek philosophy was beginning to be studied with great ardour and was received without question. He admits the attributes of God and regards them as eternal, but treats them on lines very similar to those employed by the Christians in dealing with the divine hypostases, that is to say, they are not external things possessed by God but modes or phases of the divine essence. The will of God for example, he treats as a mode of knowledge, that is to say that God wills what is good is equivalent to saying that God knows it to be good. But in dealing with the will we must distinguish between (a) that which exists in place, as the moral rules in God's commandments to men, for there could be no will against theft until the creation of things which could be stolen ; in such case the will exists in time and is created, for it depends upon a created thing : and (b) that which exists not in place and without an object to which the will refers, as when God willed to create before the thing to be created existed. In man the inner volition is free, but the outer acts are not free ; sometimes they are controlled by external forces in the body, or even outside the body, and sometimes they are controlled by the inner volition. Aristotle speaks of the universe as existing from eternity, but the Qur'an refers to its creation, yet these are not inconsistent : we must suppose that it existed eternally, but in perfect quiescence and stillness, as it were latent and potential rather than actual, and without those qualities which appear in the categories of logic and are to us the only known terms of existence. Creation meant that God brought in movement so that things began to exist in time and space, and the universe comes to an end when it returns again to the state of absolute rest in which it was at the beginning. Men can distinguish between good and evil by the light of reason, for good and evil have objective characters which can be recognised so that our knowledge of this difference does not depend only on God's revelation : but no man can know anything about God but by the medium of revelation which is given principally for this purpose.

Ibrahim b. Sayar an-Nazzam (d. 231), the next great Mu'tazilite leader was a devoted student of the Greek philosophers and an encyclopædic writer. In this he was typical of the earlier Arabic philosophers whose endeavour was to apply Greek science to the interpretation of life and nature generally, an aim which necessarily tended to produce encyclopædic compilations rather than original studies in any one field of knowledge. Already the Mu'tazilites had reached the position that good and evil represent objective realities and that God, knowing the good, does not will that which is contrary to it ; but an-Nazzam presses this further and asserts that God can do nothing in the creature save what is for its good and is in itself just. To this the objection was raised that in such case God's own acts are determined and are not free. An-Nazzam replied that he admitted this determination, not in action but in potentiality as God is restricted by his own nature. He attempted to reproduce the ancient doctrine that the soul is the form of the body, as had already been asserted by Aristotle, but he misunderstood the terminology employed and represents the soul as of the same shape as the body. This implies that the soul is a very

subtile kind of substance permeating the whole body
in the same way as butter permeates milk, or as oil
permeates the sesame : both soul and body are equal
in size and alike in shape. Freedom of the will is
peculiar to God and man, all other created things are
subject to necessity. God created all things at once
in remote eternity, but reserved them in a state of
quiescence so that they may be described as " concealed," and then projected them into active existence
at successive intervals.

The next great Mu'tazilite leader was *Bishr b.
Mu'tamir* (d. 226 circ.) in whose work we find a more
definite attempt to apply philosophical speculation
to the practical needs of Islam. In the case of free
will he enters directly into the question of how far
external influences limit freedom of the will and so
diminish responsibility. Infants cannot be condemned
to eternal punishment because they have no responsibility, having never exercised free will. Unbelievers,
however, are condemned to punishment because,
although they have not the help of revelation, it is
possible for them to know that there must be a God,
and only one God, by the light of reason. In dealing
with actions and their moral values we have to
consider not only one agent and one object, but often
a series, the act being transmitted from one to the
other so that each of the intervening objects becomes
the agent to the next object. This serial connection
he termed " begetting " (*tawullud*).

Ma'mar b. Abbad as-Sulami (d. 220) describes God

as creating substances but not accidents, so that he
produced a kind of universal matter common to all
existing things and to this matter or essence the
accidents are added, some produced by a force inherent in the essence created, others by free will on
the part of the creature.   Following the neo-Platonic
commentators on Aristotle he treats the attributes of
God as purely negative, so that God is unknowable by
man.   In the case of wisdom or knowledge, that which
is known must either be identical with God, or external
to him : if God is the agent who knows and that
which is known as object is also himself, there is a
distinction between God the agent and God the object
which implies two persons, and this is subversive of
the divine unity : but if God is the agent and knows
something external to himself, that knowledge depends
on the external object, and God therefore is not
absolute but in some sense dependent on something
other than himself.   Hence the attributes of God
cannot be such as the positive qualities which exist in
man, but only the negation of those which are dis-
tinctively human and dependent : we can only say
that he is infinite, meaning unlimited in space, or
eternal as unlimited in time, or other like terms
negative of the known things which can be predicated
of man.   The general tendency of Ma'mar's teaching
is distinctly pantheistic : partly this is due to the
logical development of a tendency already inherent
in the neo-Platonic doctrine with which all Arabic
thought was now becoming saturated, and partly it

was due to oriental influences which were now beginning to appear in Islam.

Ma'mar's pantheism was more fully developed by *Tumameh b. al-Ashras* (d. 213) who treats the world as indeed created by God, but created according to a law of nature so that it is the expression of a force latent in God and not due to an act of volition. Tumameh entirely deserts al-Allaf's attempt to reconcile the Aristotelian doctrine of the eternity of matter with the teaching of the Qur'an, and quite frankly states that the universe is eternal like God. This is by no means the last word in Islamic pantheism, but its subsequent development rather belongs to the doctrines of the extremer Shi'ite sects and to Sufism.

Reverting to an-Nazzam, the great leader of the middle age of the Mu'tazilites, we find his teaching continued by his pupils *Ahmad b. Habit, Fadl al-Hudabi.* and *'Amr b. Bakr al-Jahiz.* On the theological side all the Mu'tazilites admitted the eternal salvation of good Muslims, and most agreed that unbelievers would receive eternal punishment : but there were differences of view as to those who were believers but died unrepentant in sin. For the most part the Mu'tazilites took the lax view that these would be favourably treated as against the rigorist opinion which reserved eternal salvation to good Muslims, an opinion which appeared amongst the stricter believers during the 'Umayyad period. The two first named of an-Nazzam's pupils, however, introduced a new theory entirely repugnant to ortho-

dox Islam, though familiar to the extremer Shi'ite
sects, that those neither decisively good nor absolutely
bad. pass by transmigration into other bodies until
they finally deserve either salvation or damnation.
With these two thinkers also we are brought into
contact with another problem which now began to
present itself to Islam, the doctrine of the " beatific
vision." Islam generally had expected the vision of
God to be the chief of the rewards enjoyed in paradise,
but the treatment of the attributes of God had been
so definitely against the anthropomorphic ideas
expressed in the Qur'an that it became difficult to
explain what could be meant by " seeing God."
Ahmad and Fadl dealing with this subject deny that
men ever will or can see God ; the beatific vision can
at most mean that they are brought face to face with
the " Agent Intellect " which is an emanation from
the First Cause, and " seeing " in such a connection
must of course mean something quite different from
what we understand as vision.

'Amr b. Bakr al-Jahir (d. 255), the third of an-
Nazzam's pupils mentioned above, may be regarded
as the last of the middle period of the Mu'tazilites.
He was an encyclopædic writer according to the
fashion of the time and wrote on literature, theology,
logic, philosophy, geography, natural history, and
other subjects (cf. Masudi viii. 33, etc.) To free will
he gives rather a new bearing. The will he regards as
simply a manner of knowing and so as an accident
of knowledge ; a voluntary act he defines as one known

to its agent. Those who are condemned to the fire of
hell do not suffer eternally by it, but are changed by
its purification. The term " Muslim " must be taken
to include all who believe that God has neither form
or body, since the attribution of a human form to
God is the essential mark of the idolater, that he is
just and wills no evil, and that Muhammad is his
prophet. Substance he treats as eternal, accidents
are created and variable.

We have now reached the third stage of the history
of the Mu'tazilites, that which marks their decline.
During this latter period they divide into two schools,
that of Basra giving its attention mainly to the
attributes of God, that of Baghdad being chiefly
occupied with the more purely philosophical discussion of what is meant by an existing thing.

The Basrite discussions received their final form
in the dispute between *al-Jubbay* (d. 303) and his son
Abu Hashim (d. 321). The latter held that the attributes of God are distinct *modes* of being, we know the
essence under such varying modes or conditions, but
they are not *states*, nor are they thinkable apart from
the essence, though they are distinct from it but do
not exist apart from it. Against this his father
objected that these subjective attributes are only
names and convey no concept. The attributes are
thus asserted to be neither qualities nor states so as
to imply subject or agent, but they are inseparably
united with the essence.

Against all views of this sort the orthodox adhered,

and still adhere to the opinion that God has real
qualities. Those who laid emphasis on this in
opposition to the Mu'tazilite speculations are commonly known as *Sifatites* (*sifat*, qualities), but they
admit that, as God is not like a man, the qualities
attributed to him in the Qur'an are not the same as
those qualities bearing the same names which are
referred to men, and it is not possible for us to know
the real import of the qualities attributed to God.

A more pronounced recoil against the Mu'tazilite
speculations appears in Abu 'Abdullah b. Karram
(d. 256) and his followers who were known as Karram-
ites. These returned to a crude anthropomorphism
and held that God not only has qualities of precisely
the same kind as a man may have, but that he actually
sits on a throne, etc., taking in plain literal sense all
the statements made in the Qur'an.

The Mu'tazilite school of Baghdad concerned itself
mainly with the metaphysical question—" what is a
thing ? " It was admitted that " thing " denotes a
concept which could be known and could serve as
subject to a predicate. It does not necessarily exist,
for existence is a quality added to the essence : with
this addition the essence becomes an entity (*mawjud*),
without this addition it is a non-entity (*ma'dum*)
but still has substance and accident, so that God
creates by adding the single attribute of existence.

The whole course of Mu'tazilite speculation shows
the influence of Greek philosophy as applied to
Muslim theology, but the influence is for the most

part indirect. The ideas of Aristotle, as the course of speculation projected to the fore-front the problems with which he had dealt in times past, were received through a Syriac Christian medium, for the most part imperfectly understood and somewhat modified by the emphasis which Christian controversy had given to certain particular aspects. More or less directly prompted by the Mu'tazilite controversy we have three other lines of development : in the first place we have the " philosophers " as the name is used by the Arabic writers, meaning those students and commentators who based their work directly on the Greek text or at least on the later and better versions. In their hands philosophical enquiry took a somewhat changed direction as they began to understand better the real meaning of what Aristotle had taught. In the second place we have the orthodox theology of al-Ash'ari, al-Ghazali, and others, which represents Muslim theological science as modified and partly directed by Aristotelian philosophy, consciously endeavouring to make a working compromise between that philosophy and Muslim theology. The older Mu'tazilite tradition came to an end in the time of al-Ash'ari : men who felt the force of philosophical questions either adopted the orthodox scholasticism of al-Ash'ari and those who came after him, or followed the course of the philosophers and drift away from the traditional beliefs of Islam altogether. In the third place we have the Sufi movement, in which we find neo-Platonic elements mingled with others from the east, from India and Persia. The M'utazilites proper come to an end with the fourth century A.H.

CHAPTER VI

THE EASTERN PHILOSOPHERS

The Aristotelian philosophy was first made known to the Muslim world through the medium of Syriac translations and commentaries, and the particular commentaries used amongst the Syrians never ceased to control the direction of Arabic thought. From the time of al-Ma'mun the text of Aristotle began to be better known, as translations were made directly from the Greek, and this resulted in a more accurate appreciation of his teaching, although still largely controlled by the suggestions of the commentaries circulated amongst the Syrians. The Arabic writers give the name of *failasuf* (plur. *falasifa*), a transliteration of the Greek φιλόσοφος, to those who based their study directly on the Greek text, either as translators or as students of philosophy, or as the pupils of those who used the Greek text. The word is used to denote a particular series of Arabic scholars who arose in the third century A.H. and came to an end in the seventh century, and who had their origin in the more accurate study of Aristotle based on an examination of the Greek text and the Greek commentators whose work was circulated in Syria, and is employed as though these *falasifa* formed a par-

ticular sect or school of thought.   Other philosophical
students were termed *hakim* or *nazir*.

The line of these *falasifa* forms the most important
group in the history of Islamic culture.   It was they
who were largely responsible for awakening Aristotelian studies in Latin Christendom, and it was they
who developed the Aristotelian tradition which Islam
had received from the Syriac community, correcting
and revising its contents by a direct study of the
Greek text and working out their conclusions on lines
indicated by the neo-Platonic commentators.

The first of the series is *Yaqub b. Ishaq al-Kindi*
(d. circ. 260 A.H. = 873 A.D.), who began very much
as a Mu'tazilite interested in the theological problems
discussed by the members of that school of thought,
but desirous of testing and examining these more
accurately, made use of the translations taken
directly from the Greek and then only recently
published.   By this means he brought a much stricter
method to bear, and thus opened the way to an
Aristotelian scholarship much in advance of anything
which had been contemplated so far.   As a result
his pupils and those who came after them raised new
questions and ceased to confine themselves to
Mu'tazilite problems, and al-Kindi was their intellectual ancestor in those new enquiries which his
methods and his use of the Greek text alone made
possible.   It is a strange fact that al-Kindi, the
parent of Arabic philosophy, was himself one of the
very few leaders of Arabic thought who was a true

Arab by race. For the most part the scientists and
philosophers of the Muslim world were of Persian,
Turkish, or Berber blood, but al-Kindi was descended
from the Yemenite kings of Kinda (cf. genealogy
quoted from the *Tarikh al-Hakama* cited in note
(22) of De Slane's trans. of Ibn Kkallikan, vol. i. p.
355). Very little is known about his life, save that
his father was governor of Kufa, that he himself
studied at Baghdad, under what teachers is not
known, and stood high in favour with the Khalif
Mu'tasim (A.H. 218-227). His real training and
equipment lay in a knowledge of Greek, which he
used in preparing translations of Aristotle's *Metaphysics*, Ptolemy's *Geography*, and a revised edition
of the Arabic version of Euclid. Besides this he
made Arabic abridgments of Aristotle's *Poetica*
and *Hermeneutica*, and Porphyry's *Isagoge*, and wrote
commentaries on Aristotle's *Analytica Posteriora*,
Sophistica Elenchi, the *Categories*, the apocryphal
Apology ; on Ptolemy's *Almagesta* and Euclid's
Elements, and original treatises, of which the essay
" On the Intellect " and another " On the five
essences " are the most noteworthy (Latin tr. by
A. Nagy in Baeumker and Hertling's *Beitrage zur
Geschichte der philosophie des MA*. II. 5. Munster,
1897).

He accepted as genuine the *Theology of Aristotle*
which had been put into circulation by Naymah of
Emessa, and, we are told, revised the Arabic translation. The *Theology* was an abridgment of the

last three books of Plotinus' *Enneads*, and presumably al-Kindi compared this with the text of the *Enneads*, corrected the terminology and general sense in accordance with the original, and evidently did so without any suspicion that it was not a genuine work of Aristotle. The *Theology* had not been long introduced to the Muslim world, and it is certain that the use of it made by al-Kindi was a main cause of its subsequent importance. Endorsed by him it not only took an assured place in the Aristotelian canon, but became the very kernel of the teaching developed by the whole series of *falasifa*, emphasizing the tendencies already marked in the commentary of Alexander of Aphrodisias. The influence of the *Theology* and of Alexander appear most clearly in the treatise " On the Intellect " which is based on the doctrine of the faculties of the soul as described in Aristotle's *de anima* II. ii. Al-Kindi, developing the doctrine as presented by the neo-Platonic commentators, describes the faculties or degrees of intelligence in the soul as four, of which three are actually and necessarily in the human soul, but one enters from outside and is independent of the soul. Of the three former one is latent or potential, as the knowledge of the art of writing is latent in the mind of one who has learned to write ; the second is active, as when the scribe evokes from the latent state this knowledge of writing which he desires to put into practice ; the third is the degree of intelligence actually involved in the operation of writing, where the knowledge now quickened into activity guides and directs the act. The external faculty is the " Agent Intellect " (*'aql fa"al*) which proceeds from, God by way of emanation and which, though acting on the faculties in the body, is independent of the body, as its knowledge is not based upon perceptions obtained through the senses.

It is futile to maintain that the history of Arabic philosophy shows a lack of originality in the Semitic mind ; for one thing not one of the philosophers of first rank after al-Kindi was of Arab birth, very few could be described as Semitic. It would be more correct to say that the Greek philosophers stood alone, until quite modern times, in attempting anything which could be described as a scientific psychology. Until the methods and material of modern natural science came to be applied to psychological research there was little, if any, advance on the psychological theories of the ancient Greek investigators, and the only point of difference in later schools was as to which particular aspect af ancient research would be selected as the starting-place. Here lies the great importance of al-Kindi, for it was he who selected and indicated the starting-point which all the later Arabic philosophers began from, and selected the material which they developed. The particular basis thus selected by al-Kindi was the psychology of Aristotle's *de Anima* as expounded by Alexander of Aphrodisias. This was suggested but not in all respects clearly indicated by the Syriac philosophers,

and it seems certain that al-Kindi's development
was very largely influenced by the *Theology of
Aristotle,* a work which he evidently esteemed very
greatly. The relation between Alexander Aphr. and
Plotinus, whose teaching appeared in the *Theology,*
may be described as being that Alexander's teaching
contained all the germs of neo-Platonism, whilst
Plotinus shows the neo-Platonic system fully worked
out. As first presented this system must have
seemed fully consistent with the teaching of the
Qur'an, indeed it would appear as complementary
to it. In man was an animal soul which he shared
with the lower creation, but added to it was a rational
soul or spirit which proceeded directly from God and
was immortal because it was not dependent on the
body. The possible conclusions which proved to
be inconsistent with the teachings of revelation were
not as yet fully worked out.

We need not linger over al-Kindi's logical teaching
which carried on and corrected Arabic study of the
Aristotelian logic. This was not a mere side issue,
it is true, although logic did not play so important
a part in Arabic education as it did in Syriac. In
Syriac it was the basis of all that we should regard
as the humanities, but in Arabic this position was
taken by the study of grammar, which was developed
on rather fresh and independent lines, though slightly
modified by the study of logic in later times. Still,
so long as the Muslim world had any claim to be
regarded as fostering philosophical studies, and to

a less degree even in later times, the Aristotelian logic has been only second to grammar as the basis of a humane education. Al-Kindi's real influence is shown in the introduction of the problems of psychology and of metaphysics, and the work of the *falasifa* centres in these two studies on the lines indicated by al-Kindi.

In psychology, as we have seen, al-Kindi introduced a system already fully developed by Alexander and the neo-Platonic commentators on Aristotle, kept alive amongst the Syriac students of philosophy, and then further developed from this point by his successors. In metaphysics the circumstances were different. Al-Kindi apparently was the one who introduced the problems of metaphysics to the Muslim world, but it is obvious that he did not clearly understand Aristotle's treatment of these problems. The problems involved in the ideas of movement, time, and place are treated by Aristotle in books iv., v. and vii. of the *Physics*, which had been translated by al-Kindi's contemporary, Hunayn b. Ishaq, and in the *Metaphysics*, of which at the time no Arabic translation existed, so that, so far as it was used, al-Kindi must have consulted the Greek text.

The essay " On the Five Essences " treats the ideas of the five conditions of matter, form, movement, time, and place. Of these he defines (a) matter as that which receives the other essences but cannot itself be received as an attribute, and so if the matter is taken away the other four essences are necessarily removed also. (b) Form is of two kinds, that which is the essential of the genius, being inseparable from the matter, and that which serves to describe the thing itself, i.e., the ten Aristotelian, categories—substance, quantity, quality, relation, place, time, situation, condition, action, and passion; and this form is the faculty whereby a thing (*shay'*) is produced from formless matter, as fire is produced from the coincidence of dryness and heat, the matter being the dryness and heat, the form being the fire; without form the matter is abstract but real, becoming a thing when it takes form. As De Vaux points out (*Avicenne*, p. 85) this illustration shows that al-Kindi does not grasp Aristotle's meaning correctly. (c) Movement is of six kinds: two are variations in substance, as either generation or corruption, i.e., production or destruction; two are variations in quantity by increase or decrease; one is variation in quality, and one is change of position. (d) Time is itself akin to movement, but proceeds always and only in one direction; it is not movement, though akin, for movement shows diversities of direction. Time is known only in relation to a " before " or " after," like movement in a straight line and at a uniform rate, and so can only be expressed as a series of continuous numbers. (e) Place is by some supposed to be a body, but this is refuted by Aristotle: it is rather the surface which surrounds the body. When the body is taken away the place does not cease to exist, for the vacant space is instantly filled by some other body, air, water, etc., which has the same surrounding surface. Admittedly al-Kindi shows a crude treatment of these ideas, but he was the first to direct Arabic thought in this direction, and from these arose a new attitude towards the revealed doctrine of creation on the part of those who came after him.

Al-Kindi, the " Philosopher of the Arabs," as he was called (circ. 365), contains our best account of the various sects existing in Islam towards the end of the 3rd century A.H. as he met them in the course of his travels. It has been published as the second volume of De Goeje's *Bibliotheca Geographorum Arab.* (Leiden., 1873).

The next great philosopher was *Muhammad b. Muhammmad b. Tarkhan Abu Nasr al-Farabi* (d. 339), of Turkish descent. He was " a celebrated philosopher, the greatest indeed that the Muslims ever had; he composed a number of works on logic, music, and other sciences. No Musulman ever reached in the philosophical sciences the same rank as he, and it was by the study of his writings and the imitation of his style that Avicenna attained proficiency and rendered his own works so useful." (Ibn Khallikan, iii. 307). He was born at Farab or Otrar near Balasaghum, but travelled widely. In the course of his wanderings he came to Baghdad but, as at the time he knew no Arabic, he was unable to enter into the intellectual life of the city. He set himself first to acquire a knowledge of the Arabic language, and then became

a pupil of the Christian physician Matta b. Yunus,
who was at that time a very old man, and under him
he studied logic. To increase his studies he removed
to Harran, where he met the Christian philosopher
Yuhanna b. Khailan, and continued to work at logic
under his direction. He then returned to Baghdad,
where he set to work at the Aristotelian philosophy,
in the course of his studies reading the *de anima*
200 times, the *Physics* 40 times. His chief interest,
however, was in logic, and it is on his logical work
that his fame chiefly rests. From Baghdad he went
to Damascus, and thence to Egypt, but returned to
Damascus, where he settled for the rest of his life.
At that time the empire of the Khalifa of Baghdad
was beginning to split up into many states, just like
the Roman Empire under the later Karlings, and the
officials of the Khalifate were forming semi-
independent principalities under the nominal
suzerainty of the Khalif and establishing hereditary
dynasties. The Hamdanids Shi'ites, who began to
rule in Mosul in 293, established themselves at Aleppo
in 333 and achieved great fame and power as successful leaders against the Byzantine emperors. In 334
(=946 A.D.) the Hamdanid Prince Sayf ad-Dawla
took Damascus, and al-Farabi lived under his protection. At that period the orthodox were distinctly
reactionary, and it was the various Shi'ite rulers
who showed themselves the patrons of science and
philosophy.

At Damascus al-Farabi led a secluded life. Most of his time he spent by the borders of one of the many streams which are so characteristic a feature of Damascus, or in a shady garden, and here he met and talked with his friends and pupils. He was accustomed to write his compositions on loose leaves, " for which reason nearly all his productions assume the form of detached chapters and notes ; some of them exist only in fragments and unfinished. He was the most indifferent of men for the things of this world ; he never gave himself the least trouble to acquire a livelihood or possess a habitation. Sayf ad-Dawla settled on him a daily pension of four dirhams out of the public treasury, this moderate sum being the amount to which al-Farabi had limited his demand." (Ibn Khallikan, iii. 309-310.)

Al-Farabi was the author of a series of commentaries on the logical Organon, which contained nine books according to the Arabic reckoning, namely :

(i.)   The Isagoge of Porphyry.
(ii.)   The Categories or al-Maqulat.
(iii.)   The Hermeneutica or al-'Ibara or al-Tafsir.
(iv.)   The Analytica Priora or al-Qiyas I.
(v.)   The Analytica Posteriora or al-Burhan.
(vi.)   The Topica or al-Jadl.
(vii.)   The Sophistica Elenchi or al-Maghalit.
(viii.) The Rhetoric or al-Khataba.
(ix.)   The Poetics or ash-Shi'r.

He also wrote an " Introduction to Logic " and an "Abridgment of Logic "; indeed, as we have already noted, his main work lay in the exposition of logic. He took some interest in political science and edited a summary of the laws of Plato, which very often replaces the Politics in the Arabic Aristotelian canon. In Ethics he wrote a commentary on the Nicomachæan Ethics of Aristotle, but ethical theory did not, as a rule, appeal greatly to Arabic students. In natural science he was the author of commentaries on the *Physics, Meteorology, de coelo* et *de mundo* of Aristotle, as well as of an essay " On the movement of the heavenly spheres." His work in psychology is represented by a commentary on Alexander of Aphrodisias' commentary on the *De Anima,* and by treatises " On the soul," " On the power of the soul," " On the unity and the one," and " On the intelligence and the intelligible," some of which afterwards circulated in mediæval Latin translations, which continued to be reprinted well into the 17th century (e.g., De intelligentia et de intelligibili. Paris, 1638). In metaphysics he wrote essays on " Substance," " Time," " Space and Measure," and " Vacuum." In mathematics he wrote a commentary on the *Almajesta* of Ptolemy, and a treatise on various problems in Euclid. He was a staunch upholder of the neo-Platonic theory that the teaching of Aristotle and that of Plato are essentially in accord and differ only in superficial details and modes of expression ; he wrote treatises " On the agreement between Plato

and Aristotle " and on " The object before Plato and
Aristotle." In essays " Against Galen " and
" Against John Philoponus " he criticised the views
of those commentators, and endeavoured to defend
the orthodoxy of Aristotle by making them responsible
for apparent discrepancies with the teaching of
revelation. He was interested also in the occult
sciences, as appears from his treatises " On geomancy,"
" On the Jinn," and " On dreams." His chemical
treatise called *kimiya t-Tabish*, " the chemistry of
things heated," has been classed as a work on natural
science and also as a treatise on magic ; this was the
unfortunate direction which Arabic chemistry was
taking. He also wrote several works on music.
(Cf. Schmölders : *Documenta Philos. Arab.* Bonn.,
1836, for Latin versions of select treatises).

As we have already noted, his primary importance
was as a teacher of logic. A great deal of what he
has written is simply a reproduction of the outlines
of the Aristotelian logic and an exposition of its
principles, but De Vaux (*Avicenne*, pp. 94-97) has
drawn attention to evidences of original thought in
his " Letter in reply to certain questions."

Like al-Kindi he accepted the *Theology* as a genuine
work of Aristotle, and shows very clear traces of its
influences. In his treatise " On the intelligence " he
makes a careful analysis of the way in which the term
'*aql* (reason, intelligence, spirit) is employed in general
speech and in philosophical enquiry. In common
language " a man of intelligence " denotes a man of

reliable judgment, who uses his judgment in an upright
way to discern between good and evil, and thus is distinguished from a crafty man who employs his mind
in devising evil expedients. Theologians use the
term *'aql* to denote the faculty which tests the validity
of statements, either approving them as true or
rejecting them as false. In the *Analytica* Aristotle
uses " intelligence " for the faculty by which man
attains directly to the certain knowledge of axioms
and general abstract truths without the need of proof ;
this faculty al-Farabi explains as being the part of
the soul in which intuition exists, and which is thereby
able to lay hold of the premises of speculative science,
i.e., the reason of intelligence proper as the term is
employed in the *de anima*, the rational soul which
Alexander of Aphrodisias takes as an emanation
from God. Following al-Kindi, al-Farabi speaks of
four faculties or parts of the soul : the potential or
latent intelligence, intelligence in action, acquired
intelligence, and the agent intelligence. The first
is the *'aql hayyulani*, the passive intelligence, the
capacity which man has for understanding the
essence of material things by abstracting mentally
that essence from the various accidents with which it
is associated in perception, more or less equivalent
to the " common sense " of Aristotle. The intelligence in action or *'aql bi-l-fi'l* is the potential faculty
aroused to activity and making this abstraction. The
agent intelligence or *'aql fa''al* is the external power,
the emanation from God which is able to awaken

the latent power in man and arouse it to activity, and the acquired intelligence or *'aql mustafad* is the intelligence aroused to activity and developed under the inspiration of the agent intelligence. Thus the intelligence in action is related to the potential intellect as form is to matter, but the agent intelligence enters from outside, and by its operation the intelligence receives new powers, so that its highest activity is " acquired."

Al-Farabi appears throughout as a devout Muslim, and evidently does not appreciate the bearing of the Aristotelian psychology on the doctrine of the Qur'an. The earlier belief of Islam, as of most religions, was a heritage from primitive animism, which regarded life as due to the presence of a perfectly substantial, though invisible, thing called the soul : a thing is alive so long as the soul is present, it dies when the soul goes away. In the earlier forms of animism this is the explanation of all movement : the flying arrow has a " soul " in it so long as it moves, it ceases to move when this soul goes away or desires to rest. This involves no belief in the immortality of the soul, nor is the soul invested with any distinct personality, all that comes later ; it is simply that life is regarded as a kind of substance, very light and impalpable but perfectly self-existent. What may be described as the " ghost" theory marks a later stage of evolution, when the departed soul is believed to retain a distinct

personality and still to possess the form and some at
least of the sensations associated with the being
in which it formerly dwelt. Such was the stage
reached by Arab psychology at the time of the
preaching of Islam. The Aristotelian doctrine represented the soul as containing different energies
or parts, such as it had in common with the vegetable
world and such others as it possessed in common
with the lower kinds of animals: that is to say the
faculties of nutrition, reproduction, and all the perceptions obtained from the use of the organs of sense,
as well as the intellectual generalisations derived
from the use of those senses, are simply laid on one
side as forms of energy derived from the potentiali-
ties latent in the material body, very nearly the
position indeed of modern materialism, as the term
is used in psychology. This does not oppose a
belief in God, who is the prime source of the powers
which exist, although that is brought out more by
the commentators than by Aristotle himself; nor
does it infringe the doctrine of an immortal and
separable soul or spirit which exists in man in addition
to what we may describe as the vegetative and
animal soul. It is this spirit, the rational soul which
has entered from outside and exists in man alone,
which is immortal. Such a doctrine sets an impas-
sible gulf between man and the rest of creation, and
explains why it is impossible for those whose thought
is formed on Aristotelian lines, whether in orthodox

Islam or in the Catholic Church, to admit the
" rights " of animals, although ready to regard
benevolent action towards them as a duty. But
more, the highly abstract rational soul or spirit of
the Aristotelian doctrine, void of all that could be
shared with the lower creatures, and even of all that
could be developed from anything that an animal is
capable of possessing, is the only part of man which
is capable of immortality, and such a spirit separated
from its body and the lower functions of the animal
soul can hardly fit in with the picture of the future
life as portrayed in the Qur'an. Further, the Qur'an
regards that future life as incomplete until the
spirit is re-united with the body, a possibility which
the Aristotelians could hardly contemplate. The
Aristotelian doctrine showed the animal soul not as
an invisible being but merely as a form of energy in
the body : so far as it was concerned, death did not
mean the going away of this soul, but the cessation
of the functions of the bodily faculties, just as com-
bustion ceases when a candle is blown out, the flame
not going away and continuing to exist apart ; or
as the impression of a seal on wax which disappears
when the wax is melted and does not continue a
ghostly existence on its own account. The only
immortal part of man, therefore, was the part which
came to him as an emanation from the Agent Intellect,
and when this emanation was set free from its association with the human body and lower soul it became
inevitable to suggest its re-absorption in the omni-

present source from which it had been derived. The logical conclusion was thus a denial, not of a future life, nor of its eternity, but of the separate existence of an individual soul, and this, as we shall see, was actually worked out as a result of Arabic Aristotelianism. Thus the scholastic theologians, both of Islam and of Latin Christianity, attack the philosophers as undermining belief in individual personality and in opposing the doctrine of the resurrection, and in this latter, it must be remembered, Muslim doctrine is committed to cruder details than prevail in Christianity. But al-Farabi did not see where the Aristotelian teaching would lead him : to him Aristotle seemed orthodox because his doctrines seemed to prove the immortality of the soul.

Al-Farabi expresses his theory of causality in the treatise called " the gems of wisdom." Everything which exists after having not existed, he says, must be brought into being by a cause which itself may be the result of some preceding cause, and so on, until we reach a First Cause, which is and always has been, its eternity being necessary because there is no other cause to precede it, and Aristotle has shown that the chain of causes cannot be infinite. The First Cause is one and eternal, and is God (cf. Aristot. *Metaph.* 12. 7, and similarly Plato, *Timaeus* 28). Being unchanged this First Cause is perfect, and to know it is the aim of all philosophy, for obviously everything would be intelligible if the cause of all were known. This First Cause is the " necessary being " whose

existence is necessary to account for all other existence;
it has neither genus, species, nor differentia; it is
both external and internal, at once apparent and
concealed; it cannot be perceived by any faculty
but is knowable by its attributes, and the best
approach to knowledge is to know that it is inaccessible. In this treatment al-Farabi is mingling the
teaching of philosophy proper with mysticism, in
his days rapidly developing in Asiatic Islam, and
especially in the Shi'ite community with which he
was in contact. From the philosophical point of
view God is unknowable but necessary, just as eternity
and infinity are unknowable but necessary, because
God is above all knowledge: but in another sense God
is beneath all knowledge, as the ultimate reality must
underlie all existing things, and every result is a
manifesting of the cause.

The proof of the existence of God is founded upon
the argument in Plato, *Timaeus* 28, and Aristotle,
Metaphysics 12. 7, and was later on used by Albertus
Magnus and others. In the first place a distinction
is made between the possible, which may be only
potential, and the real. For the possible to become
real it is necessary that there should be an effective
cause. The world is evidently composite, and so cannot
itself be the first cause, for the first cause must be single
and not multiple: therefore the world evidently proceeds from a cause other than itself. The immediate
cause may itself be the result of another preceding
cause, but the series of causes cannot be infinite, nor

can they return as a circle upon themselves, therefore if we trace back we must ultimately reach an *ens primum*, itself uncaused, which is the cause of all, and this first cause exists of necessity, but not by a necessity caused by anything other than itself. It must be single and unchangeable, free from all accidents, absolute, perfect, and good, and the absolute *intelligentia*, *intelligibile*, and *intelligens*. In itself it possesses wisdom, life, insight, will, power, beauty and goodness, not as acquired or external qualities, but as aspects of its own essence. It is the first will and the first willing, and also the first object of will. It is the end of all philosophy to know this first Cause, which is God, because as He is the cause of all, all can be understood and explained by understanding and knowing Him. That the first Cause is single and one and the cause of all agrees with the teaching of the Qur'an, and al-Farabi freely uses Qur'anic phraseology in perfect good faith, supposing that the Aristotelian doctrine corroborates the doctrine of the Qur'an. The most curious part of al-Farabi's work is the way in which he employs the terminology of the Qur'an as corresponding to that of the neo-Platonists, so that the Qur'anic pen, tablet, etc., represent the neo-Platonic, etc. It may be questioned whether, even in al-Farabi, philosophy really does fit in with Qur'anic doctrine, but the divergence was not yet sufficiently marked to compel attention.

Assured of the conformity of the teaching of Aristotle with the teaching of revelation al-Farabi denies that Aristotle teaches the eternity of matter, and so is inconsistent with the dogma of creation. The whole question depends on what is meant by "creation." God, he supposes, created all things in an instant in unmeasured eternity, not directly, but by the intermediary operation of the 'aql or Agent Intelligence. In this sense Aristotle held that the universe existed in eternity, but it so existed as a created thing. Creation was therefore complete before God, acting through the 'aql, introduced movement, at which time commenced ; as movement and time came into existence simultaneously, forthwith creation already existing in the timeless came out of its concealment and entered into reality. The term "creation" is sometimes used as applying to this emergence from timeless quiesence, but more properly may be taken as denoting the causation, which, as it preceded time, came into unmeasured eternity, which is what Aristotle means when he speaks of the world as eternal. Thus both Qur'an and Aristotle are right, but each uses "creation" to denote a different thing.

It is difficult to over-estimate the importance of al-Farabi. Practically all we afterwards meet in Ibn Sina and Ibn Rushd is already to be found in substance in his teaching, only that these later philosophers have realized that the Aristotelian system cannot be reconciled with the traditional theology, and so, having given up all attempt at formal reconciliation, are able to express themselves more clearly and to press home their tenets to their logical conclusions. When considering the reconciliation between philosophy and Qur'an attempted by al-Farabi it is important to compare and contrast the reconciliation attempted on quite other lines by al-Ash'ari and other founders of orthodox scholasticism. It must be noted that the beginning of scholasticism was contemporary with al-Farabi.

As has been noted, al-Farabi was mixed up with the Shi'ite group; the supporters of 'Alid claims who held aloof from the official Khalifate at Baghdad. About the time of al-Kindi's death (circ. 260), the twelfth Iman of the *Ithna 'ashariya* or orthodox Shi'ite sect, Muhammad al-Muntazar, " disappeared." In the year 320, within the period of al-Farabi's activity, the Buwayhid princes became the leading power in 'Iraq, and in 334, five years before his death, they obtained possession of Baghdad, so that for the next 133 years the Khalifs were in very much the same position as the Frankish kings when they, surrounded with great ceremony and treated with the utmost reverence, were no more than puppets in the hands of the Mayors of the Palace. In exactly the same way the Khalifs, half popes and half emperors, whose sign manual was sought as giving a show of legitimacy to sovereigns even in far-off India, possessed in Baghdad only ceremonial functions, and were treated as honoured prisoners by the Buwayhid Emirs, who themselves were Shi'ites of the *Ithna 'ashariya* sect, and who, consequently, regarded the Khalifs as mere usurpers. At this period the Shi'ites were the patrons of philosophy, and the orthodox Sunnis generally took a reactionary attitude.

Besides the *Ithna 'ashariya*, the comparatively orthodox Shi'ites, there was another branch of extremer type known as the *Sab'iya* or " seveners." The sixth Imam Ja'far as-Sadiq had nominated his son Isma'il as his successor, but as Isma'il was one day found drunk, Ja'far disinherited him and appointed his second son Musa al-Qazam (d. 183). But some did not admit that the Imamate, whose divine right passed by hereditary descent, could be transferred at will, but remained loyal to Isma'il, and these preferred, when Isma'il died in Ja'far's lifetime, to transfer their allegiance to his son Muhammed, reckoning him as the seventh Imam. These " seveners " continued to exist as an obscure sect until, it would appear, somewhere about the year 220, when 'Abdullah, the son of a Persian oculist named Maymun, either was made their head or led a secession from them, and organised his followers with a kind of freemasonry in seven (afterwards nine) grades of initiation and a very admirably organised system of propaganda on the lines already laid down by the Hashimites (cf. supra). In the earlier grades the doctrine of *batn* or allegorical interpretation of the Qur'an was laid down as essential to a right understanding of its meaning, for the literal sense is often obscure, and sometimes refers to things incomprehensible, a doctrine commonly attri-

buted to Ja'far as-Sadiq. The initiate was then
taught that the true meaning could not be discovered
by private interpretation but needed an authoritative teacher, the Imam, or, as he had disappeared,
his accredited representative, the Mahdi 'Abdullah,
son of Maymun. In the higher grades the disciple
had this inner meaning of the Qur'an disclosed to
him, and this proved to be substantially the Aristotelian and neo-Platonic doctrine in general outline,
together with certain oriental elements derived from
Zoroastrianism and Masdekism. These oriental
elements figured chiefly in the doctrines taught to
the intermediate grades, the higher ones attaining a
pure agnosticism with an Aristotelian background.
The sect thus formed spread, developed, and finally
divided. It had a successful career in the Bahrayn
or district near the junction of the two rivers, the
Tigris and Euphrates, and there its followers were
known as Qarmatians, after the name of a leading
missionary. It met with success also in and around
Aden, but we have no account of its subsequent history
there. From Aden missionaries passed over to North
Africa, where it had its chief success, and when Ubayd
Allah, a descendant of 'Abdullah, passed over there
an independent state was founded, with its capital
at Kairawan (297 A.H.). From Kairawan a missionary propaganda was conducted in Egypt, then
suffering from almost perennial misgovernment, and
in the days of the deputy Kafur a definite invitation
was sent by the Egyptian officials asking for the Khalif

of Kairawan to enter Egypt. At length Ubayd
Allah's great-grandson al-Mo'izz did invade Egypt
in 356, and established there the Fatimite Khalifate,
which lasted until the country was conquered by
Saladin in 567.

The Sab'iya sect was thus geographically divided
into two branches, one in Asia represented by the
Qarmatians, the other in Africa under the Fatimite
Khalifs. In the Asiatic branch the members were
chiefly drawn from the Nabatæan peasantry, and
the sect took the form of a revolutionary group with
communist teaching, and violently opposed to the
Muslim religion. In their contemptuous hostility
they finally attacked Mecca, slew many of the dignitaries of the city and a number of pilgrims who were
there, and carried off the sacred black stone, which
they retained for several years. In the hands of the
Qarmatians the sect ceased to be a propaganda of
philosophical doctrine, it became simply anti-religious
and revolutionary. The history of the African
branch took a different turn. Possession of an
important state brought with it a position of re-
spectability, and political ambition replaced religious
enthusiasm. As the majority of the subject population was strictly orthodox, the peculiar tenets of
the sect were, to a large extent, allowed to drop into
the background; candidates were still admitted to
initiation and instructed, but, although the Fatimite
rulers in Egypt were liberal patrons of scholarship,
and generally showed a more tolerant attitude than

other contemporary Muslim rulers, they certainly did not carry out a wholesale Aristotelian propaganda; indeed, the line of " philosophers " proper simply misses over Fatimite Egypt, although there were several distinguished medical workers there. From the Isma'ilians or Sab'iya of Egypt there came two interesting off-shoots. Towards the end of the reign of the sixth Fatimite Khalif, al-Hakim, who may have been a religious fanatic, perhaps insane, or possibly an enlightened religious reformer of views far ahead of his age—his real character is one of the problems of history—there arrived in Egypt certain Persian teachers holding doctrines of transmigration and of theophanies, which seem to be endemic in Persia, and these persuaded al-Hakim that he was an incarnation of the Deity. A riot followed the open preaching of this claim, and the preachers fled to Syria, then a part of the Fatimite dominions, and there founded a sect which still exists in the Lebanon under the name of the Druzes. Soon after this al-Hakim himself disappeared; some said he was murdered, others said he had retired to a Christian monastry, and was recognised there afterwards as a monk; others believed he had gone up to heaven, and more than one claimant appeared asserting that he was al-Hakim returned from concealment. The other off-shoot shows a more definitely philosophical bearing. In the days of al-Mustansir, al-Hakim's grandson, one of the Isma'ilian missionaries, a Persian named Nasir-i-Khusraw, came from Khurasan to Egypt, and after a stay of seven years returned home. This seems to have coincided with a kind of revival in the Isma'ilian sect, which now regarded Cairo as its headquarters. The Qarmatians had quite passed away ; al-Hakim, whatever his later eccentricities, had been a patron of scholarship, the founder of an academy, the *Daru l-Hikma,* or " House of Wisdom," at Cairo, and had enriched it with a large library, and was himself distinguished as a student of astronomy. The reign of his grandson was the golden age of Fatimid science, and apparently Shi'ites from all parts of Asia found their way to Egypt. In 471 another da'i or missionary, Hasan-i-Sabbah, a pupil of Nasir-i-Khusraw, visited Cairo and was received by the Chief Da'i, but not allowed to see the Khalif, and eighteen months later was compelled to leave the country and return to Asia. There were two factions in Cairo, the adherents respectively of the Khalif's two sons, Nizar and Musta'li ; Nasir-i-Khusraw and Hasan-i-Sabbah had already made themselves known as supporters of the elder son Nizar, but the court officials in Egypt adhered to the younger son Musta'li. When the Khalif al-Mustansir died in 487 the Isma'ilian sect divided into two new branches, the Egyptians and Africans generally recognising Musta'li, the Asiatics adhering to Nizar This latter group had already been well organised by Nasir-i-Khusraw and Hasan-i-Sabbah, who for several years previously had been preaching the rights of Nizar. On his return home, about 473, Hasan-

i-Sabbah had secured possession of a stronghold
known as Alamut, " the eagle's teaching " (cf. Browne :
Lit. History of Persia, ii. 203, espec. note 13), and
this became the headquarters of the sect of Nizaris
or Assassins, who figure so prominently in the history
of the Crusades.   They had many mountain strong-
holds, but all were under the control of the Sheikh
or " Old Man of the Mountain," as the Crusaders
and Marco Polo called him, at Alamut.   These
Sheikhs or Grand Masters of the order continued for
eight generations, until Alamut was captured by the
Mongols in 618 A.H. (=1221 A.D.), and the last was
put to death. As the order grew it spread into Syria,
and it was the Syrian branch with which the Crusaders
from Europe came most into contact.   In this order
we find the old system of successive grades of initiation.   The *Lasiqs*, or " adherents," had but little
knowledge of the real doctrines of the sect, and
attached to them were the *Fida'is* or " self-devoted,"
bound to blind obedience and ready to execute
vengeance at the bidding of their superiors ; these
were the men to whom the Crusaders especially
applied the term *Assassins*, that is *Hashishin* or
" users of hashish," referring to the hashish or Indian
hemp which they commonly used as a means of
exaltation.   Above these were the *Rafiqs* or
" companions," and above these was an ordered
hierarchy of *da'is* or missionaries, Chief Missionaries
(*da'i i-Kabir*), and Supreme Missionary (*da'i d-Du'at*).
In the eyes of outsiders the whole sect had a sinister

appearance ; the crimes of the Fida'is, usually committed under striking and dramatic circumstances,
and the reputed heresies of the superior grades were
sufficient to secure this, and the general dread with
which they were regarded was increased by incidents
which showed that they had spies and sympathizers
in all directions. The superior grades, however,
were true heirs of the old Isma'ilian principles and
ardent students of philosophy and science. When
the Mongols under Hulagu seized Alamut in 654
= A.D. 1256) they found an extensive library and
an observatory with a collection of valuable astronomical instruments. The Mongol capture meant the
downfall of the Assassins, although the Syrian branch
still continued in humbler fashion, and the sect has
adherents even at the present day. Scattered relics
survive also in central Asia, in Persia, and in India ;
the Agha Khan is a lineal descendant af Ruknu
d-Din Khurshah, the last Sheikh at Alamut.

Thus the movememt started by Abdullah, the son
of Maymun, whose original purpose seems to have
been to maintain a highly philosophical religion
as revealed by Aristotle and the neo-Platonists, but
to safeguard this as an esoteric faith disclosed only
to initiates, the rank and file being apparently Shi'ite
sectaries, produced a group of very curious sects. In
the Qarmatians the esoteric tenets were compelled
to take a debased form because those who professed
them, and into whose hands this branch fell altogether, were illiterate peasants. In the Fatimid

state of Egypt they were minimised because political considerations rendered it expedient to conciliate orthodox Muslim opinion. And in the Assassins, confined, it seems, to the higher grades of the initiates, they produced a rich intellectual development, though allied to a system which shows fanaticism unscrupulously used by the leaders that they might live out their lives in a philosophical seclusion, protected from the dangers which surrounded them.

Before leaving this particular subject, which shows the promulgation of philosophy as an esoteric creed, we must refer to a society known as the *Ikhwanu s-Safa* or " the brotherhood of purity." We do not know what its connection with 'Abdullah b. Maymun's sect may have been beyond the fact that they were contemporary and of kindred aims, but it certainly seems that there was some connection : it has been suggested that this brotherhood represents the original teaching of Abdullah's sect. It was divided into four grades, but its doctrines were promulgated freely at an early date, though we do not know whether this general divulging of its teaching was part of the original plan or forced upon it by circumstances. It appears openly about 360, some hundred years after Abdullah founded his sect, shortly after the Fatimites had conquered Egypt and some time after the Qarmatians had returned the sacred black stone which they had stolen from the " House of God " at Mecca. It seems tempting to suggest that it may have been a reformation of

the Ishma'ilians on the part of those who wished
to return to the original aims of the movement.

The published work of the brotherhood appears in
a series of 51 epistles, the *Rasa'il ikhwani s-Safa*,
which form an encyclopædia of philosophy and
science as known to the Arabic-speaking world in the
4th cent. A.H. They do not propose any new
theories but simply furnish a manual of current
material. The whole text of these epistles has been
printed at Calcutta, whilst portions of the voluminous
whole have been edited by Prof. Dieterici between
1858 and 1872, and these were followed in 1876 and
1879 by two volumes called *Makrokosmos* and
Mikrokosmos, in which an epitome is presented of
the whole work. It appears that the leading spirit
in the preparation of this encyclopædia was Zayd
b. Rifa'a, and with him were associated Abu Sulayman
Muhammad al-Busti, Abu l-Hasan 'Ali az-Zanjani,
Abu Ahmad al-Mahrajani, and al-Awfi, but it does
not follow that these were the founders of the brotherhood, as some have suppposed.

A great part of the *Epistles of the Brotherhood* deals
with logic and the natural sciences, but when the
writers turn to metaphysics, psychology, or theology,
we find very clear traces of the neo-Platonic doctrines
as contained in Alexander of Aphrodisias and matured
by Plotinus. God, we read, is above all knowledge
and above all the categories of human thought. From
God proceeds the *'aql* or intelligence, a complete
spiritual emanation which contains in itself the forms

of all things, and from the '*aql* proceeds the Universal
Soul, and from that Soul comes primal matter : when
this primal matter becomes capable of receiving
dimensions it becomes secondary matter, and from
that the universe proceeds. The Universal Soul
permeates all matter and is itself sustained by the
perpetual emanation of itself from the '*aql*. This
Universal Soul permeating all things yet remains one ;
but each individual thing has a part-soul, which is
the source of its force and energy, this part-soul
having a varying degree of intellectual capacity.
The union of soul and matter is temporary ; by wisdom
and faith the soul tends to be set free from its material
fetters, and so to approach nearer to the present
spirit or '*aql*. The right aim of life is the emancipation of the soul from matter, so that it may be
absorbed in the parent spirit and thus approach
nearer to the Deity. All this is but a repetition of
the teaching of al-Farabi and the neo-Platonists,
slightly coloured, perhaps, by Sufism, and expressed
less logically and lucidly than in the teaching of the
philosophers. In general character it shows a
tendency towards pantheism, akin to the tendency
we have already observed in certain of the Mu'tazilites.
God, properly so called, is outside, or rather on such
a plane that man does not know, and never can know,
anything about Him. Even the '*aql* is on a plane
other than that on which the human soul lives. But
the Universal Soul which permeates all things is an
emanation from this Spirit, and the Spirit emanates

from the unknowable God. Comparing this with the teaching of al-Kindi and al-Farabi it is clear that it is based upon the same material, but it is in the hands of those who have made it a religion, and this religion has entirely broken away from the orthodox doctrine of the Qur'an. In al-Farabi this breach is not conscious, although really quite complete; in his successors we see a full realization of the cleavage. Comparing it with Sufism the superficial resemblances are very close, the more so as Sufism borrows a great deal of philosophical, i.e., neo-Platonic terminology, but in fact there is an essential divergence: the Epistles of the brethren represent the emancipation of the soul from matter as the aim of life, and the final result is re-absorption in the Universal Soul, but they represent this emancipation as due to an intellectual force, so that the soul's salvation lies in wisdom and knowledge; it is a cult of intellect. But Sufism is spiritual in another sense: it has the same aim in view, but it regards the means as wisdom in the sense of religious truth as found by the devout soul in piety, not as the wisdom obtained by intellectual learning.

We seem, however, justified in saying that Sufism is the heir of the philosophical teaching of al-Farabi and the Brethren of Purity, at least in Asia. After the first quarter of the fifth century philosophical teaching seems to have disappeared altogether in Asia, but this is only apparent. In substance it remains in Sufism, and we may say that the essential change lies in the new meaning given to " wisdom," which ceases to signify scientific facts and specu- lations acquired intellectually, and is taken to mean a supra-intellectual knowledge of God. This, perhaps, represents the Indian contribution working upon elements of Hellenistic origin.

The doctrines of the *Brethren of Purity* were in- troduced to the West by a Spanish doctor, Muslim b. Muhammad Abu l-Qasim al-Majriti al-Andalusi (d. 395-6), and were largely influential in producing the *falasifa* of Spain, who ultimately exercised so great an influence on mediæval Latin scholasticism.

Before leaving this particular section of our subject it will be well to note that all these sects and groups we have mentioned after al-Farabi, from the sect founded by Abdullah b. Maymun to the Brethren of Purity, agreed in treating philosophy, at least in so far as it had any bearing on theological topics, as esoteric, and not to be disclosed to any save the elect. This general attitude will appear again, in a slightly different form, in the works of the Spanish philosophers, and to some extent recurs in all Islamic thought.

The greatest product in Asia of the ferment of thought produced by the general study of the Aristot- elian and neo-Platonic philosophies appears in *Abu 'Ali al-Husayn b. 'Abdullah b. Sina* (d. 428 = A.D. 1027), commonly known as Ibn Sina, which is Latin- ized as Avicenna. His life is known to us from an autobiography completed by his pupil, Abu Ubayd

al-Juzjanl, from his master's recollections. We learn
that his father was governor of Kharmayta, but, after
his son's birth, he returned to Bukhara, which had
been the original home of his family, and it was there
that Ibn Sina received his education. During his
youth some Isma'ilian missionaries arrived from
Egypt, and his father became one of their converts.
From them the son learned Greek, philosophy,
geometry, and arithmetic. This helps to remind us
how the whole Isma'ilian propaganda was associated
with Hellenistic learning. It is sometimes stated
that the Egypt of the Fatimite age was isolated from
the intellectual life of Islam at large: but this is
hardly accurate; from first to last the whole of the
Isma'ilian movement was connected with the intellectual revival due to the reproduction of Greek philosophy in Arabic form, less so, of course, when the
Isma'ilian converts were drawn from the illiterate
classes, as was the case with the Qarmations, and when
the attention of the members was engrossed with political ambitions, as was the case with the Fatimids whilst
they were building up their power in Africa before the
invasion of Egypt. But even under the most un-
favourable conditions it seems that the *da 'is* or
missionaries regarded the spread of science and
philosophy as a leading part of their duties, quite as
much so as the preaching of the 'Alid claims of the
Fatimite Khalif. Learning Greek and Greek philosophy from these missionaries Ibn Sina made rapid
progress, and then turned to the study of juris-

prudence and mystic theology. Jurisprudence, that is to say, the canon law based on one of the orthodox systems laid down by Ab-u Hanifa and the other recognised jurists, or by their Shi'ite rivals, has always been the backbone of Islamic scholarship, and was thus parallel with the study of canon law in mediæval Europe : in each case it turned men's attention to the development of the social structure towards an ideal, and this had an educative influence of the highest value. We, holding very different principles, may be tempted to under-estimate this influence, but it is worth noting that, whilst our aims are opportunist in character, the canonist of Islam or of Christendom had a more definitely constructed ideal, with a more complete and scientific finality, which, in so far as it was an ideal, was an uplifting power. In Muslim lands the canonists were the one power which had the courage and ability to resist the caprices of an autocratic government, and to compel even the most arbitrary princes to submit to principles which, however narrow and defective they may seem to us, yet made the ruler admit that he was subordinate to a system, and defined the limits allowed by that system in conformity with ideals of equity and justice. It is interesting to note that in Ibn Sina's time mystic theology had already taken its place as a subject of serious study.

A short time afterwards a philosopher named an-Natali arrived at Bukhara and became a guest of Ibn Sina's father. Bearing in mind the technical

meaning of *failasuf*, we recognise this guest as a professed Aristotelian, and presumably one able to obtain
his living as a teacher of the Aristotelian doctrine.
From him Ibn Sina learned logic and had his mind
directed towards the Aristotelian teaching, which was
then preached like a religion. After this he studied
Euclid, the *Almajesta*, and the "Aphorisms of the
Philosophers." His next study was medicine, in
which he made so great progress that he adopted the
practice of medicine as his profession. He attempted
to study Aristotle's *Metaphysics*, but found himself
entirely incapable of understanding its meaning,
until one day he casually purchased one of al-
Farabi's books, and by its help he was able to grasp
the meaning and purport of what had so far eluded
him. It is on this ground that we are entitled to
describe Ibn Sina as a pupil of al-Farabi : it was al-
Farabi's work which really formed his mind and
guided him to the interpretation of Aristotle ; al-
Farabi was, in the truest sense, the parent of all
subsequent Arabic philosophers ; great as was Ibn
Sina, he does not enter into the tradition in the same
way as al-Farabi, and does not exercise the same
influence on his successors, although al-Ghazali
classes him with al-Farabi, and calls them the leading
interpreters of Aristotle. Emphasis is sometimes
laid upon the fact that Ibn Sina treats philosophy as
quite apart from revelation as given in the Qur'an ;
but in this he was not original : it was the general
tendency of all who came after al-Farabi ; we can

only say that Ibn Sina was the first important writer who illustrates this tendency.

Called to exercise his medical skill at the court of Nuh b. Mansur, the Samanid governor of Khurasan, he enjoyed that prince's favour, and in his library studied many works of Aristotle hitherto unknown to his contemporaries, and when that library was burned he was regarded as the sole transmitter of the doctrines contained in those books. This represents contemporary Arabic opinion about him : there is no evidence in his existing writings that he had access to Aristotelian material other than that generally known to the Syriac and Arabic writers. When the affairs of the Samanid dynasty fell into disorder Ibn Sina removed to Khwarazan, where he, with several other scholars, enjoyed the enlightened patronage of the Ma'muni Emir. But this Emir was living a somewhat precarious existence in the neighbourhood of the Turkish Sultan Mahmud of Ghazna, the stern champion of orthodoxy and the conqueror of India. It was obvious that the Sultan coveted the Emir's dominions, and that when he chose to seize them it would be impossible to resist ; he actually did take them in 408. Meanwhile the Sultan was treated with the utmost deference by the Emir and such of his neighbours as were allowed to live on sufferance. Mahmud wished to be distinguished as a patron of learning, and " invited " scholars to his court—in plain words, he kidnapped scholars and took care that they never afterwards transgressed the strictest limits of orthodoxy. Amongst others the Emir received a letter inviting such men of learning as were to be found in Khwarazan to his court. The Emir read out the letter to the five most distinguished scholars who were his guests, leaving them to act as they thought fit. Three of the guests were attracted by the Sultan's reputation for generosity and accepted the invitation, but two, Ibn Sina and Masihi, were afraid to venture, so they escaped privately and fled ; overtaken by a sandstorm in the desert Masihi perished, but Ibn Sina, after long wanderings, finally found a refuge in Isfahan, where the Buwayhid 'Ala'u d-Dawla Muhammad held his court. His experiences show plainly that it was the Shi'ites who were the supporters of philosophy, and that the growing Turkish power of Mahmud of Ghazna and of the Seljuks who succeeded him was reactionary and unfavourably disposed towards philosophical research. It was the Turkish power which finally checked the progress of Arabic philosophy in the East.

Ibn Sina wrote many works in Arabic and Persian, and a number of these are still extant. Amongst his productions were *as-Shafa*, an encyclopædia of physics, metaphysics, and mathematics in eighteen volumes (ed. Forget, Leiden, 1892), a treatise on logic and philosophy, and the medical works on which his fame so largely rests. The best known of these are the *Najat* abridged from the *as-Shafa*, and the medical *Canon*, in which he reproduced the teaching of Galen and Hippocrates with illustrative material from the later medical writers. The *Canon* is more methodical in its arrangement than the *al-Hawi* of Razes, hitherto the popular manual of medicine in Arabic ; indeed, its chief defect is an excessively elaborate classification. It became the leading medical authority, and, after translation into Latin by Gerard of Cremona, served for many centuries as the chief representative of the Arabic school of medicine in western Europe, holding its place in the universities of Montpelier and Louvain down to A.D. 1650.

Ibn Sina treats logic as of use rather in a negative than in a positive way : " the end of logic is to give a man a standard rule, by observing which he is preserved from error in reasoning " (*Isharat* ed. Forget, p. 2). His treatise on this subject in *Tis' Rasa'il fi-l-Hikma wa-l-Tabi'yat* (p. 79, pub. Stamboul, 1298), is divided into nine parts corresponding to the Arabic canon of Aristotle, which includes the *Isagoge* as well as the Rhetoric and Poetics. He makes special note to the logical bearing of particular grammatical constructions which in Arabic differ from the forms used in Greek, as, for example, where the Greek expresses the universal negative by " all A is not B," but Arabic renders this " nothing of A (is) B." He lays great emphasis upon accurate definition, which he describes as the essential basis of all sound reasoning, and to this he devotes much attention. Definition proper must state the *quiddity* of a thing, its genus, differentia, and all its essential characteristics, and is thus distinct from mere description, which need only give the propria and accidents in such a way that the thing may be recognised correctly.

In dealing with the universal and the particular he considers that the universal exists only in the human mind : the abstract idea of the genus is formed in the mind of the observer when he compares individuals and makes note of their points of similarity, but this abstract idea exists only as a mental concept and has no objective reality. The universal precedes the individual (genus ante res) only in the way that the general idea existed in the mind of the Creator before the individual was formed, just as the idea of an object to be made exists in the mind of the artificer before the work is executed. The general idea is realised in matter (genus in rebus), but only when accompanied by accidents: apart from these accidents it exists only as a mental abstraction. After the general idea is realised in matter (genus post res) it is possible for the intellect to make a mental abstraction and to use this as a standard of comparison with other individuals. The generic belongs only to the realm of thought, and such abstract ideas have no objective existence, although they may be used as real in logic.

The soul is treated as a collection of faculties (*kowa*) or forces acting on the body : all activity of any sort, in bodies animal or vegetable, as well as human, proceeds either from such forces added to

the body or from the mixture of elements from which
the body is formed. The simplest soul condition is
that of the vegetable whose activity is limited to
nutrition and generation and accretion by growth
(*Najat*, p. 43). The animal soul possesses the vegetable faculties but adds to them others, and the
human soul adds yet others to these, and the addition
made to the human soul enables it to be described
as a rational soul. The faculties present in the soul
may be divided into two classes, the faculties of perception and the faculties of action. The faculties
of perception are partly external and partly internal :
of these the external faculties exist in the body
wherein the soul dwells and are the eight senses,
sight, hearing, taste, smell, perception of heat and
cold, perception of dry and moist, perception of
resistance as by hard and soft, and perception of
rough and smooth. By means of these senses the
form of the external object is reproduced in the soul
of the percipient. There are four internal faculties
of perception : (i.) *al-musawira*, " the formative,"
whereby the soul perceives the object without the
aid of the senses as by an act of imagination ; (ii.)
al-mufakkira, " the cogitative," by which the soul
perceiving a number of qualities associated together
abstracts one or more of them from the others with
which they are associated, or groups together those
which are not seen as connected ; this is the faculty
of abstraction which is employed in forming general
ideas ; (iii.) *al wahm*, or " opinion," by means of which

a general conclusion is drawn from a number of ideas grouped together; and (iv.) *al-hafiza* or *az-zakira*, "memory," which preserves and records the judgments formed. Men and animals perceive pariculars by means of sense; man attains the knowledge of universals by means of reason. The '*aql* or rational soul of man is conscious of its own faculties, not by means of an external, i.e., bodily sense, but immediately by the exercise of its own reasoning power. This proves to be an independent entity, even though accidentally connected with a body and dependent on that body for sense perception: the possibility of direct knowledge without sense perception shows that it is not essentially dependent on the body, and the possibility of its existence without the body, which follows logically from its independence, is the proof of its immortality. Every living creature perceives that it has only one *ego* or soul in itself, and this soul, says Ibn Sina, did not exist prior to the body but was created, that is to say, proceeded by emanation from the Agent Intellect at the time when the body was generated. (*Najat*, p. 51).

Under the head of Physics Ibn Sina considers the forces observed in nature, including all that are in the soul, save only that which is peculiar to the rational soul of man. These forces are of three kinds: some, such as weight, are an essential part of the body in which they occur; others are external to the body on which they act, and are such as cause movement

or rest; and others, again, are such as the faculties
possessed by the non-rational souls of the spheres,
which produce movement directly without external
impulse. No force is infinite; it may be increased or
diminished, and always produces a finite result.

Time is regarded as essentially dependent on movement; although it is not itself a form of movement,
so far as the idea of time is concerned, it is measured
and made known by the movements of the heavenly
bodies. Following al-Kindi place is defined as " the
limit of the container which touches the contained."
Vacuum is " only a name", in fact it is impossible,
for all space can be increased, diminished, or divided
into parts, and so must contain something capable
of increase, etc.

God alone is " necessary being," and so the supreme
reality. Space, time, etc., belong to " actual being,"
and whatever necessity they possess is derived from
God. The objects studied in physical science are
only " possible being," which may or may not become
" actual being." God alone is necessarily existent
through all eternity : He is the truth in the sense
that He alone is true absolutely, all other reality is
so only in so far as it is derived from God. From God
by emanation comes the *'aql* or " Agent Intellect,"
and from this proceeds the intellect or reason which
differentiates the rational soul in man from the soul
in other creatures. To every man this intellect is
given, and in due course it returns to the " Agent
Intellect " which was its source. The soul's possible

activity, independent of the body with which it is associated, proves its immortality, but this immortality does not imply separate existence, but rather re-absorption in the source. From the *'aql* also proceeds the universe, but not like the reason of man by direct emanation, but by the medium of successive emanations.

Ibn Sina was the last of the great philosophers of the East. Two causes combined to terminate philosophy proper in Asiatic Islam. In the first place it had become closely identified with the Shi'ite heresies, and was thus in bad repute in the eyes of the orthodox; whilst the Shi'ite sects themselves, all of the extremer kind (*ghulat*), which had devoted themselves most to philosophical studies, had also taken up a number of pre-Islamic religious theories, such as transmigration of souls, etc., which were detrimental to scientific research. Neo-Platonism had shown itself at an earlier period prone to similar tendencies. As a result the Shi'ites tended towards mystic and often fantastic theories, which were discouraging to the study of Aristotelian doctrines. The second cause lay in the rise of dominant Turkish elements, Mahmud of Ghazna, then the Saljuk Turks, which were of uncompromising orthodoxy, and abhorred everything which was associated with the Shi'ites or tended to rationalism. For all that it left permanent marks in Asiatic Islam in two directions: in orthodox scholasticism and in mysticism.

We have already noted that Muslim b. Muhammad Abu l-Qasim al-Majriti al-Andalusi (d. 395-6), as his name denotes, a native of Madrid, brought the teachings of the *Brethren of Purity* to Spain, and so incidentally aroused an interest there in the philosophy which had been studied in the East. For some time no important results appeared, then followed a series of brilliant philosophical writers and teachers, deriving their inspiration partly from the *Brethren*, and partly from the Jewish students.

CHAPTER VII

SUFISM

Sufism or Islamic mysticism, which becomes prominent in the course of the 3rd cent. A.H., was partly a product of Hellenistic influences, and exercised a considerable influence on the philosophers of the time of Ibn Sina and afterwards. The name *Sufi* is derived from *suf* " wool," and so means " wool-clad," thus denoting a person who from choice used clothing of the simplest kind and avoided every form of luxury or ostentation. That this is the true meaning is proved by the fact that Persian employs as its equivalent the term *pashmina-push*, which also means " wool-clad." By a popular error the Arabic writers on Sufism often treat the word as derived from *safa*, " purity," and so make it something akin to " puritan " ; and still more incorrectly certain Western writers have supposed that it is a transliteration of the Greek σοφός. The emphasis is laid upon the ascetic avoidance of luxury and the voluntary adoption of simplicity in clothing on the part of those to whom the term is applied. If we regard this as a form of asceticism it will be at once objected that asceticism has no place in the teaching of the Qur'an and is alien to the character of early

Islam.   In a sense this is true, and in a sense untrue
according to the meaning we attach to the term
" asceticism."   As it is used in the history of
Christian monasticism, or of the devotees of several
Indian religions, or even of the latter Sufis, it implies
a deliberate avoidance of the normal pleasures and
indulgences of human life, and especially of marriage,
as things which entangle the soul and prevent its
spiritual progress.   In this sense asceticism is alien
to the spirit of Islam, and appears amongst Muslims
only as an exotic.   But the term may be used, not
very accurately perhaps, of the puritanical restraint
and simplicity which avoids all luxury and display,
and deliberately tries to retain a primitively simple
and self-denying manner of life.   In this latter sense
asceticism or puritanism was a distinguishing mark
of the " old believer " as contrasted with the secularised Arab of the Umayyad type, and this attitude
always had its admirers.   The historians constantly
refer with commendation to the abstemious lives of
the early Khalifs and the " Companions " of the
Prophet, and describe how they were abstinent not
from poverty but in order to put themselves on an
equality with their subjects, and to preserve the
traditional mode of life of the Prophet and his first
followers, and very often in the recognised Traditions
we find mention of the bare and simple mode of life
of the first Muslims.   Quite early this simplicity
appears as the distinctive mark of the strict Muslim,
and emphasizes the difference between him and the

worldly followers of the Umayyads, and similar
instances appear amongst the devout Muslims of the
present day. Such were not Sufis, but they may be
regarded as the precursors of the Sufis. The historian al-Fakhri, describing the abstemious life of
the first Khalifs, says that they endeavoured by this
self-restraint to wean themselves from the lusts of
the flesh. This is reading a later idea into a much
earlier practice, which was originally designed simply
as a more accurate following of the Prophet, who was
unable to enjoy any luxury or splendour ; but it
shows that later generations were inclined to ascribe
a more definitely ascetic motive to the affectedly
simple life of the earlier Muslims, and no doubt that
early puritanism, misunderstood by later ages, contributed to spread asceticism.

Al-Qushayri (cited Browne : *Lit. Hist. of Persia*,
i. pp. 297-8), after referring to the " Companions "
and " Followers " of the first age of Islam, then
mentions the " ascetes " or " devotees " as the elect
of a later age, those who were most deeply concerned
with matters of religion, and finally the Sufis as those
elect of still later times, " whose souls were set on God,
and who guarded their hearts from the disasters of
heedlessness." Historically this is an error, for the
saints of early Islam were inspired by a spirit of strict
adherence to the traditional life of their desert
ancestors and rejected luxury as an " innovation,"
very much the same spirit as that observed in the
ancient Hebrew prophets ; whilst the Sufis were no

enthusiasts for tradition, but eschewed bodily in-
dulgence as an entanglement of the flesh which
hindered the progress of the spirit, so that they were
in no sense the successors of the "Companions,"
but were influenced by new ideas unknown to early
Islam. Yet superficially the results were very much
alike, and this caused the two to be connected, and
helped the later custom of connecting the early
puritans with the ascetics of a subsequent age. In
its earliest form, also, Islam made a strong appeal to
the motive of fear, an appeal not based on divine
severity so much as on divine justice and on man's
consciousness of his own sinfulness and unworthi-
ness, and on the fleeting passage of the life lived in
this present world. There was an intense concentra-
tion on the Day of Judgment and on the perils of the
sinner, a teaching which is perceived in the Qur'an
even by the most casual reader : but all this was not
altogether congenial to the Arab, although he in
poetry certainly inclined towards a tone of sadness.
The inevitable result of this teaching was asceticism
in the puritanical sense, or, perhaps we should say,
a tone of severity in religion.

Jami, one of the greatest Persian authorities on
Sufism, tells us that the name "Sufi" was first
applied to Abu Hashim (d. 162), an Arab of Kufa who
spent the greater part of his life in Syria, and is typical
of the early Islamic devotee who followed the
simplicity of the Prophet's life and was deeply
influenced by the Qur'anic teaching about sin,

judgment, and the brief passage of earthly life. Similar devotees, claimed as Sufis by later Sufi writers, but more properly devotees who were their precursors, appear in the course of the 2nd century, such as Ibrahim b. Adham (d. 162), Da'ud of Tayy (d. 165), Fadayl of 'Iyad (d. 188), Ma'ruf of Karkh (d. 200), and others, both men and women. Amongst these there was gradually evolved the beginnings of an ascetic theology in traditional sayings and narratives of their lives and conduct, a hagiology which lays great emphasis upon their penances and self mortification. Of this material the most important is the recorded teaching of Ma'ruf of Karkh, from which we may quote the definition of Sufism as " the apprehension of divine realities," which, in a slightly altered sense perhaps, becomes the keynote of later Sufism.

Can we trace the origin of these early recluses ? Von Kremer (*Herrsch*, p. 67) considers this type as a native Arab growth developed from pre-Islamic Christian influences. Christian monasticism we know was familiar to the Arabs in the country fringing the Syrian desert and in the desert of Sinai : of this we have evidence both in Christian writers like Nilus and in the pre-Islamic poets, as in the words of Imru l-Qays :—

Friend, see the lightning—it flashed and is gone,
  like the flashing of two hands on a crowned pillar :
Did its blaze flash forth ? or was it the lamp of a
  monk who poured oil on the twisted wick ? "

The hermit's life was known even in Arabia itself, and tradition relates that Muhammad received his first call when he had retired to the cave of Hira and was living as a recluse there, returning periodically to his home and taking back food with him to the cave (cf. Bukhari : *Sahih*, i.). It seems likely, indeed, that the early recluses of Islam were inspired by the example of Christian monasticism, either directly or through the medium of Muhammad's traditional retirement. But these recluses were not numerous, and admittedly neglect the Qur'anic command to marry (Qur. 24, 32).

Thus the earlier asceticism shows the character of devout quietism, of a puritanical abstinence from display of wealth and from self-indulgence, of a strict simplicity of life rather than of a voluntary poverty and mortification, of occasional retirement from the world, and only in rare instances of the permanent adoption of the hermit life. An instance of this type occurs in Abu l-'Abbas as-Sabti (d. 184), son of the Khalif Harunu r-Rashid, who renounced rank and fortune for a life of meditation and retirement.

In the latter part of the 3rd cent. we begin to find evidences of a " new Sufism," which was inspired by religious ideals other than those which had been dominant in early Islam, and which developed from those ideals a theology of its own, which for a long time was not admitted as orthodox. Asceticism still occurs, but whilst, on the one hand, it begins to

take a more definite character in the deliberate seeking
of poverty and mortification, it is, on the other hand,
relegated to a subordinate place as a merely preparatory stage in the Sufi life, which is technically
described as a " journey." Poverty, which amongst
the early Muslims was esteemed simply in so far as it
reproduced the modest life of the Prophet and his
companions, and was a standing protest against the
secularisation of the Umayyads, now assumed greater
prominence as a devotional exercise, a change which
appears definitely in Da'ud at-Ta'i (d. 165), who
limited his possessions to a rush mat, a brick which
he used as a pillow, and a leather water bottle. In
later Sufism poverty takes a position of great prominence : the terms *faqir*, "poor man," and *darwish*,
" mendicant," become synonyms for " Sufi." But
in Sufi teaching religious poverty does not mean
absence of possessions only : it implies the absence of
all interest in earthly things, the giving up of all
participation in earthly possessions, and desiring God
as the only aim of desire. So mortification is the
subjugation of the evil part of the animal soul, the
nafs which is the seat of the lust and passions, and
so the weaning of the soul from material interests,
a " dying to self and to the world " as a beginning
of a living to God.

What was the source of the theology developed in
the newer Sufism ? Undoubtedly this was neo-
Platonic, as has been proved by Dr. Nicholson
(*Selected Poems from the Diwan of Shams-i-Tabriz*,

Camb., 1898, and *The Mystics of Islam*, Lond. 1914),
and by Prof. Browne (*Literary Hist. of Persia*, Lond.,
1902, chap. xiii.), and forms part of the influence
which came into Islam at the introduction of Greek
philosophy under the 'Abbasids. But as in philosophy and other cultural transmissions direct Greek
influence was preceded by an indirect influence
brought to bear through Syriac and Persian, so it
was also in neo-platonic theology, for neo-Platonic
influences had already been brought to bear upon
the Syrians and Persians in the pre-Islamic period.
In the forefront of the later direct influence must
be placed the so-called *Theology of Aristotle*, which it
is no exaggeration to describe as the most prominent
and the widest circulated manual of neo-Platonism
which has ever appeared. It is, as we have already
stated, an abridged translation of the last three books
of Plotinus' *Enneads*. Now the mysticism of
Plotinus is philosophical and not religious, but it
lends itself to a theological interpretation very
easily, just as neo-Platonism as a whole very readily
became a theological system in the hands of
Jamblichus, of the pagans of Harran, and such like ;
and the Sufis were inclined to make this application,
whilst the *falasifa* confined themselves to its philosophical side. It seems probable that the influence
of the Pseudo-Dionysius was brought to bear upon
Islam about the same time. The Pseudo-Dionysian
writings consist of four treatises, of which two, a
treatise " On Mystical Theology " in five chapters,

and a treatise " On the Names of God " in thirteen
chapters, have been the chief source of Christian
mystical theology. The first reference to these
writings occurs in A.D. 532, when the claim was made
that they were the work of Dionysius, the
Areopagite, a pupil of St. Paul, or at least represent
his teaching. In several places the writer cites
Hierotheus as his teacher, and this enables us to
identify the source as a Syrian monk named Stephen
Bar Sudaili, who wrote under the name of Hierotheus
(cf. Asseman, *Bibl. Orient.* ii. 290-291). This Bar
Sudaili was abbot of a convent at Edessa, and was
involved in controversy with James of Sarugh, so
that we may refer the writings to the latter part of
the 5th century A.D. They were translated into
Syraic very soon after their first appearance in Greek,
and, as familiar to Syriac Christians, must have
become indirectly known to the Muslims. We have
no direct evidence as to their translation into Arabic,
but Mai gives fragments of other works of Bar Sudaili
which appear in Arabic MSS. in his *Spicilegium
Romanum* (iii. 707). The traditional view of the
relations between Sufism and philosophy is described
in the anecdote cited by Prof. Browne (*Lit. Hist. of
Persia,* ii. 261, from *Akhlag-i-Jalali*) of the Sufi Abu
Sa'id b. Abi l-Khayr (d. 441 A.H.=1049 A.D.), who
is said to have met and conversed with Ibn Sina ;
when they parted Abu Sa'id said of Ibn Sina, " What
I see, he knows," whilst Ibn Sina said, " What I
know, he sees."

But there were other influences of a secondary character at work in Iraq and Persia which become important when we remember that it was the subject population of those parts which had, to a large extent, replaced the Arabs as the leaders of Islam during the 'Abbasid period. In connection with the Sufis probably we cannot refer any influence to the Zoroastrian religion proper, which had a non-ascetic and national character; but the Manichæan and Masdekite religions, the two "free churches" of Persia, show a definitely ascetic tone, and when we find, as is the case, that many of the early Sufis were converts from Zoroastrianism, or the sons of such converts, we are inclined to suspect that, though professing that recognised religion, they were in all probability actually *Zindiqs*, that is to say secretly heretics and initiates of the Manichæan or Masdekite sect making external profession of the more recognised cult, as was the common practice of these *Zindiqs*. Note must also be made of the Gnostic influences transmitted through the Saniya of the fen country between Wasit and Basra, the Mandæans, as they are called to distinguish them from the so-called Sabians of Harran. The Sufi Ma'ruf of Karkh was himself the son of Sabian parents. And again we must not ignore the probability of Buddhist influences, for Buddhist propaganda had been active in pre-Islamic times in Eastern Persia and Transoxiana. Buddhist monasteries existed in Balkh, and it is noteworthy that the ascete Ibrahim b. Adham (d. 162—cf. supra) is

traditionally described as a prince of Balkh who left
his throne to become a darwish. On closer examination, however, it does not appear that Buddhist
influence can have been very strong, as there are
essential differences between Sufi and Buddhist
theories. A superficial resemblance exists between
the Buddhist *nirvana* and the *fana* or re-absorption
of the soul in the Divine Spirit of Sufism. But the
Buddhist doctrine represents the soul as losing its
individuality in the passionless placidity of absolute
quiescence, whilst the Sufi doctrine, though also
teaching a loss of individuality, regards everlasting
life as consisting in the ecstatic contemplation of the
Divine Beauty. There is an Indian parallel to *fana*,
but it is not in Buddhism, but in the Vedantic
pantheism.

It is generally accepted that the first exponent of
Sufi doctrine was the Egyptian, or Nubian, *Dhu
n-Nun* (d. 245-246), a pupil of the jurist Malik b.
'Anas, who lived at the time when there was much
percolation of Hellenistic influence into the Islamic
world. He was indeed nearly contemporary with
'Abdullah, the son of Maymum, whose work we have
already noticed. Dhu n-Nun's teaching was recorded
and systematized by al-Junayd of Baghdad (d. 297),
and in it appears essential doctrine of Sufism, as of
all mysticism, in the teaching of *tawhid*, the final
union of the soul with God, a doctrine which is
expressed in a way closely resembling the neo-
Platonic teaching, save that in Sufism the means

whereby this union is to be attained is not by the exercise of the intuitive faculty of reason but by piety and devotion. Still the two come very close when we find in the teachings of the later philosophers that the highest exercise of reason consists in the intuitive apprehension of the eternal verities rather than in any other activity of the intellect. Al-Junayd is stated by Jami to have been a Persian, and it is chiefly in Persian hands that the doctrines of Sufism develop and turn towards pantheism. Both agnosticism and pantheism are present practically in the later neo-Platonism ; agnosticism as regards the unknowable First Cause, the God from the Agent Intellect is an emanation, a doctrine which develops in the teaching of the philosophers and of the Isma'ilians and kindred sects ; but Sufi teaching centres its attention upon the knowable God, which the philosopher would describe as the Agent Intellect or Logos, and this develops more usually in a pantheistic direction. The doctrines thus developed and expressed by al-Junayd were boldly preached by his pupil, *ash-Shibli* of Kurasan (d. 335).

Al-Husayn b. Mansur al-Hallaj (d. 309) was a fellow-student of ash-Shibli, and shows Sufism as allied with extremely unorthodox elements. He was of Zoroastrian descent and closely in touch with the Qarmatians, and seems to have held those doctrines which are usually associated with the *ghulat* or extreme Shi'ites, such as transmigration, incarnation, etc. He was put to death as a heretic for declaring " I am the truth", thus identifying himself with God. The accounts given of him show great differences of opinion : for the most part the earlier historians, approaching the subject from an orthodox stand-point, represent him as a wily conjurer who by pretended miracles gained a number of adherents, but later Sufi writers regard him as a saint and martyr who suffered because he disclosed the great secret of the union between the soul and God. The doctrine of *hulul,* or the incarnation of God in the human body, was one of the cardinal tenets of the *ghulat.* According to al-Hallaj, man is essentially divine because he was created by God in his own image, and that is why, in Qur. 2, 32, God bids the angels worship Adam. In *hulul,* which is treated as *tawhid* taking place in this present life, the deity of God enters the human soul in the same way that the soul at birth enters the body. This teaching is a fusion of the old pre-Islamic Persian beliefs as to incarnation and the philosophical theories of neo-Platonism, of the Intellect or rational soul or spirit, as it is more commonly called by English writers, the part added to the animal soul as an emanation from the Agent Intellect, to which it will ultimately return and with which it will be united (cf. Massignon : *Kitab al-Tawasin,* Paris, 1913). This is an extremely interesting illustration of the fusion of oriental and Hellenistic elements in Sufism, and shows that the theoretical doctrines of Sufism, whatever they may have borrowed from Persia and India, receive their interpretative hypotheses from neo-Platonism. It is interesting also as shewing in the person of al-Hallaj a meeting-point between the Sufi and the philosopher of the Isma'ilian school.

Very similar was the teaching of Abu Yazid or Bayazid of Bistam (d. 260), who was also of Zoroastrian descent. The pantheistic element is very clearly defined: "God," he said, "is an unfathomable ocean"; he himself was the throne of God, the preserved Tablet, the Pen, the Word—all images taken from the Qur'an—Abraham, Moses, Jesus, and Gabriel, for all who obtain true being are absorbed into God and become one with God.

Pantheistic views and the doctrine of *hulul* occur frequently in Sufi teaching, but they are by no means universal. Indeed, we cannot make any accurate statement of Sufi doctrine in detail, but only of general principles and tendencies. The Sufis do not form a sect, but are simply devotees of mystical tendencies spread through all the branches of the Muslim community. In the 3rd cent. they are most prominent amongst the Shi'ites, and so Shi'ite views seem to be incorporated in Sufism, but they form no integral part of it. Precisely similar conditions occur in Christianity where mysticism has flourished in the extremer Protestant sects as well as in the contemplative orders of the Catholic Church, and, in spite of theological differences, has a very considerable amount of common material. Only it must be noted that no basis of mysticism exists unless some such relations between the human soul and God are pre-supposed, as are suggested by neo-Platonism. Christian mysticism, in the true sense, does not begin in the West until the works of the Pseudo-Dionysius were translated into Latin in the 9th cent. A.D., and Muslim mysticism dates from the translation of the *Theology of Aristotle.* On the other hand, it must also be noted that mysticism exercises a strong modifying influence on theology generally. The tendency of mysticism is towards a latitudinarian type : it is consequently opposed, consciously or unconsciously, to definite dogmatic teaching and so to speculative theology and philosophy.

Superficially Muslim mysticism seems to be organised like a sect. Reference is often made to the various " grades " of Sufis. But these are not official grades like those of the Isma'ilians and similar bodies, but denote successive stages on the path of personal holiness : it is no more than a fanciful terminology, perhaps borrowed from some of the sects because it seems that Sufism flourished earliest and most freely in some of the extremer Shi'ite groups. It was, and is, most usual for the beginner in the path of holiness to put himself under the direction of some experienced spiritual guide, who acts as his teacher, and is known as *sheikh, murshid,* or *pir.* In many cases this pupilage involves absolute and blind obedience to the teacher, because the renunciation of personal wishes and inclinations and all that can be described as self-will is one of the forms of abnegation required of those who seek to be weaned from earthly interests. From the grouping of devotees around some prominent teacher has arisen the foundation of darwish confraternities, sometimes as sodalities of laymen, who pursue their secular occupations and meet from time to time for religious exercises and instruction, and sometimes as permanent communities living in strict obedience under a sheikh. Traces of such monastic institutions appear in Damascus about 150 A.H., and in Khurasan some fifty years later. None of the existing orders of Islam, however, seem to be of so early a date. We hear of a sheikh Alwan (circ. 149), whose shrine is at Jedda, and who is the reputed founder of the Alwaniya community, a body now existing only as a sub-division of the Rifa'ite order. There are also orders known as the *Adhamiya, Bastamiya,* and *Saqatiya,* which trace their origin to Ibrahim b. Adham (cf. above), to Bayazid Bastami, and to Sari as-Saqati respectively, but whose real origin is uncertain.

In the 6th century we are on surer ground. There is no reason to question the claim of the Rifa'ite order to trace its foundation to *Abu l-'Abbas Ahmad b. 'Ali l-Hasan 'Ali ibn Abi l-'Abbas Ahmad Rifa'i* (d. 578), a native of the village of Umm Abida, near the junction of the Tigris and Euphrates. In his lifetime he gathered a large body of disciples, whom he incorporated in an order in 576, the members living in community under a sheikh, to whom they owed unquestioning obedience, but having also, like other orders, a number of lay adherents. Dying without issue the headship of his order passed to his brother's family. It exists to-day in two main branches (i.) the Alwaniya, already mentioned, and (ii.) the Gibawi, who are best known from their association with the ceremony of the *dawsa*, at which the sheikh used to ride over the prostrate bodies of his followers. Of all the orders now flourishing in Egypt it is the one most inclined to fanatical observances at its *zikr* or prayer-meeting, the members cutting themselves, driving sharp skewers and knives into their bodies, swallowing snakes, etc., and in prayer allowing the name of God oft-repeated to become at last no more than a half articulate groan. They are usually distinguished by black turbans. The Qadariya claim 'Abdu l-Qadir Jilani (d. 561) as their founder. At their *zikr* there is none of the fire-eating, serpent-swallowing, or self-mutilation of the Rifa'ites, but only the name of God is repeated, always clearly enunciated and followed by a pause. The Badawiya were founded by Abu l-Fita Ahmad (d. 675), whose shrine is at Tanta, in Lower Egypt. The *zikr* is of a sober kind, the Divine name being repeated in a loud voice without cutting, fire-eating, etc. The Mawlawiya or dancing darwishes were founded by the Persian mystical poet Jalalu d-Din Rumi, the author of the poem known as the *Masnawi*. The *Suhrwardiya* trace their origin to Shihabu d-Din, a pantheistic Sufi of Baghdad, who was put to death by Saladin in 587.

In each of these orders a special course of instruction has taken a more or less conventional form, and there have been certain great teachers whose writings have come into use as manuals, and so have impressed their views upon Sufism generally. Yet the fact remains that Sufi teaching is essentially eclectic, and can be formulated only in broad principles and tendencies. Of these the following seem to be of most general application :—

(i.) God alone exists ; God is the only reality, all else is illusive. This is the Sufi rendering of the doctrine of the unity of God. Strictly speaking " God " here signifies the Agent Intellect, that is to say, the revelation of God who in Himself is unknowable, but the Sufi does not make this philosophical distinction clear, or else deliberately regards the revelation of God as God. But in man there is a rational soul, which is to God as a mirrored image is to the object which it reflects, and is capable of approaching the Divine reality. As other than God is merely illusive it is obvious that a knowledge of God the Reality cannot be attained by the medium of created things, and thus the Sufis were led, like the neo-Platonists, to attach greater value to immediate intuition by the rational soul than to the use of arguments, and so to place direct revelation above what is ordinarily described as reason. This is a line of development common to all forms of mysticism, and results in a preference for ecstasy or similar spiritual experience above the record of past revelation as given in the Qur'an. The doctrine of ecstasy (*hal* or *maqama*) was first formulated by Dhu n-Nun, and implies *fana* or " passing away," i.e., insensibility to the things of this world, and finally *baqa* or " continuance " in God. Usually this experience is accompanied by loss of sensation, though this is not always the case, and there are many legends of Sufi saints which represent them as totally unconscious of violence of wounds ; and this is not confined to legend, for most extraordinary sufferings are endured, apparently with perfect placidity, by darwishes at the present day, perhaps in accordance with psychological laws which are imperfectly understood, and this is the underlying idea in the exercises undergone by the Rifa'i darwishes and others. The exercise known as *zikr* (*dhikr*) or " remembering," in accordance with the command in Qur. 33, 41, " remember God often," is an attempt to make an advance towards the ecstatic state. It was perhaps under Sufi influence that we find philosophy inclining to prefer knowledge obtained by immediate intuition ; it was certainly under such influence that ecstasy is treated as a means of obtaining such direct apprehension of truth in the later philosophers.

(ii.) The Sufi doctrine of God as the only reality has a direct bearing not only on creation but also on the problem of good and evil. As a thing can only be known by its opposite, light by darkness, health by sickness, being by non-being, so God could only be made known to man as reality contrasted with non-reality, and the mingling of these two opposites produces the world of phenoma in which light is made

known by a background of darkness, which darkness
is itself only the absence of light : or, as being proceeds by successive emanations from the First Cause,
and becomes weaker or less real in each emanation as
it recedes further from the great Reality, it
incidentally becomes more perceptible as it becomes
less real. Thus evil, which is merely the negation
of the moral beauty of the Reality, appears in the
latest emanation as the unreal background which
is the inevitable result of a projection of the emanation
from the First Cause, who is entirely good, into a
world of phenomena. Evil is therefore not real, it
is merely the result, the inevitable result, of the
mingling of reality with unreality. In fact, this is
implied in the doctrine that all other than God is
unreal.

(iii.) The aim of the soul is union with God. This
doctrine of *tawhid*, as we have seen, received early expression in Muslim mystic theology. Dr. Nicholson is of
opinion that " the Sufi conception of the passing away
(*fana*) of individual self in universal being is certainly
. . . of Indian origin. Its first great exponent
was the Persian mystic Bāyazīd of Bistām, who may
have received it of his teacher, Abū 'Alī of Sind
(Scinde.") (Nicholson : *Mystics of Islam*, p. 17.)
But this is only one particular way of presenting a
doctrine which has a much wider range and is present
in all mystical teaching, including that of the neo-
Platonists. In the highest sense it is the basis of
Sufi ethics, for the *summum bonum* is defined as the

union of the individual soul with God, and all is good which helps towards this, all is evil which retards it, and this is true of Christian and all other forms of mysticism equally. We cannot say definitely that the doctrine of the unitive state is borrowed from neo-Platonism, from Buddhism, or from Gnosticism; it is the common property of all, and is the natural conclusion from the mystics premises as to the nature of God and of the human soul. It may well be that certain presentations of this doctrine show Indian details, but in this as in all other parts of Sufi specu- lation it seems that the constructive theory employed in forming a theological system was neo-Platonic: even in mysticism the Greek mind exercised its influence in analysing and constructing hypotheses.

At quite an early age the soul's desire for union with its Divine source began to be clothed in terms borrowed from the expression of human love. With some hesitation we may say, perhaps, that this is distinctly oriental, although it was so only as a means of expressing a desire which is characteristic of all mysticism. We find the same, at a later period, though in a much more restrained fashion, in Christian mysticism, and it is not easy to see the actual line of contact, if any. Perhaps we must be content to regard it as independently developed as a means of expressing the soul's longing.

The rise of Sufi teaching was not without opposition, and this was mainly on three grounds (i.) the Sufis advocated constant prayer in the form of unceasing silent intercourse with God, and by this tended to discard the fixed *salawat* or five obligatory prayers at appointed hours, one of the compulsory duties of Islam and one of its distinctive marks. Ultimately the Sufi position was that these fixed ritual observances were for the people at large who had not made any advance in the deeper spiritual knowledge, but might be disregarded by those who were more mature in grace, a position which is closely parallel to that attained by the philosophers. (ii.) They introduced *zikirs* or religious exercises, consisting in a continuous repetition of the name of God, a form of devotion unknown to older Islam, and consequently an innovation. And (iii.) many of them adopted the practice of *tawakkul*, or complete dependence on God, neglecting all kinds of labour or trade, refusing medical aid in sickness, and living on alms begged from the faithful. All these were "innovations," and as such met with very definite opposition, mostly, no doubt, because they were repugnant to the sober tone of traditional Islam, which has always been suspicious of oriental fanaticism. The more serious objection, that it really dispensed with the religion of the Qur'an is implied if not expressed ; it introduced an entirely new concept of God and a new standard of religious values ; if Sufi ideas prevailed the practices of the Muslim religion would be at best the tolerable and harmless usages of those who were not initiated into vital religion. In fact, however, the philosophical principles brought forward by the neo-Platonic Aristotelian works in general circulation were so far influential and regarded as reconcileable with the Qur'an that Sufism, in so far as it was neo-Platonic, did not appear to be destructive of Islam, but only at variance with customary usage.

Nevertheless, Sufism was generally looked upon as heretical, not only from the " innovations " we have mentioned, but because of the close alliance between the doctrines of its extremer advocates and those of the more advanced Shi'ites. It is indeed most significant that it developed chiefly amongst the same elements which gave the readiest hearing to philosophy and still adhered to Zoroastrian and Masdekite ideas. No doubt the ill repute of Sufism was largely due to the bad company it kept. It was not until the time of al-Ghazali (d. 505) that Sufism began to take its place in orthodox Islam. Al-Ghazali, left an orphan at an early age, had been educated by a Sufi friend, and, after becoming an Ash'arite and as such acting as president of the Nazimite academy at Baghdad, found himself in spiritual difficulties, and spent eleven years in retirement and in the practices of devotion, with the result that when he returned to work as a teacher in 449 his instruction was strongly leavened by mysticism, practically a return to the principles he had been taught in his early years. As al-Ghazali became in course of time the dominant influence in Muslim scholasticism, a modified and orthodox Sufism was

introduced into Sunni theology and has since held
its own.   At the same time he reduced Sufism to a
scientific form, and gave, or rather supported, a
terminology derived from Plotinus.   Such a Sufism
may be described as Muslim mystic theology purged of
its Shi'ite accretions.   This admission of a modified
Sufism into the orthodox church of Islam took place
in the sixth century A.H.

In the following century Sufism appeared in Spain,
but there it arrived as transmitted through an orthodox
medium, and hence differs from Asiatic mysticism.
The first Spanish Sufi seems to have been *Muhyi
d-Din ibn 'Arabi* (d. 638), who travelled in Asia and
died at Damascus.   He was a follower of Ibn Hazm,
who, as we shall see later, represents a system of
jurisprudence of a type more reactionary even than
that of Ibn Hanbal.   In Spain itself the leading
Sufi was *'Abdu l-Haqq ibn Sab'in* (d. 667), who shows
the more characteristic Spanish attitude of a Sufi
who was also a philosopher, for Spanish Sufism was
essentially speculative.   Like many other philosophers of the Muwahhid period he adhered out-
wardly to the Zahirites, the most reactionary party
of the narrowest orthodoxy.

In the 7th century, also, we have *Jalalu d-Din
Rumi* (d. 672), who practically completes the golden
age of Sufism.   Although a Persian he was an
orthodox Sunni.   He was a native of Balkh, but his
father was compelled to leave that city and migrate
westward, and finally settled at Qonya (Iconium),

where he died. Jalalu d-Din had been educated by
his father, and after his death he sought further
instruction at Aleppo and Damascus, where he came
under the influence of Burhanu d-Din of Tirmidh,
who had been one of his father's pupils, and continued
his training in Sufi doctrines. After this teacher's
death he came in touch with the eccentric but saintly
Shams-i-Tabriz, a man of great spiritual power but
illiterate, who left a great impress on his age by his
tremendous spiritual enthusiasm and the strange
crudity of his conduct and character. It was after
the death of Shams-i-Tabriz that Jalalu d-Din
commenced his great mystical poem, the *Masnawi*,
a work which has attained an extraordinary eminence
and reverence throughout the whole of Turkish Islam.
As already mentioned, Jalalu d-Din founded an
order of Darwishes known as the Mawlawi order, or
" dancing darwishes," as they are called by Europeans.

The whole course of doctrinal Sufism begins with
Dhu n-Nun and ends with Jalalu d-Din ; later writers
do little more than repeat their teaching in new
literary form, and it will be sufficient to select a few
typical examples. In the 8th cent. we have *'Abdu
r-Razzaq* (d. 730), a pantheistic Sufi who wrote a
commentary on and defended the teaching of Muhiyyu
d-Din ibnu l-'Arabi. He advocated the doctrine
of free will on the ground that the human soul is
an emanation from God, and so shares the Divine
character. This world, he holds, is the best possible
world : differences in condition exist and justice

consists in accepting these and adapting things to their situation ; ultimately all things will cease to exist as they are re-absorbed in God, the only reality. Men are divided into three classes : the first contains the men of the world, whose life centres in self and who are indifferent towards religion ; a second class contains the men of the reason, who discern God intellectually by his external attributes and manifestations ; and as a third class are the men of the spirit, who perceive God intuitively.

Although Sufism has now taken a recognised place in the life of Islam, it was not allowed to pass without occasional challenge. The leading opponent was the Hanbalite reformer, Ibn Taymiya (d. 728), who represented the reactionary but popular theology. He rejected formal adherence to any school, dismissed all importance attached to *Ijma* or "consensus" save that based on the agreement of the Prophet's Companions ; he denounced the scholastic theology of al-Ash'ari and al-Ghazali, and defined the Divine attributes on the lines laid down by Ibn Hazm. At that time the Sufi an-Nasr al-Manbiji was prominent in Cairo, and to him Ibn Taymiya wrote a letter denouncing the Sufi doctrine of *ittihad* as heresy. From this arose a quarrel between the two rival forces of Islam, traditional orthodoxy and mysticism, in the course of which Ibn Taymiya suffered persecution and imprisonment. Towards the end of his life, in 726, he issued a *fatwa* or declaration of opinion against the lawfulness of the reverence paid to the tombs of saints and of the invocation of saints, the Prophet himself included. In this he was the precursor of the Wahibi reformation of the 18th cent. A.D. MSS. exist in which the works of Ibn Taymiya are copied out by the hand of 'Abdu l-Wahhab, who was evidently a close student of that reformer, all of whose theories he reproduces.

Ash-Sha'rani of Cairo (d. 973) is typical of the later orthodox Sufi. He was a follower of Ibn 'Arabi on general lines but without his pantheism. His writings are a strange mixture of lofty speculation and lowly superstition, his life was full of intercourse with jinns and other supernatural beings. The truth, he states, is not to be reached by the aid of reason, but only by ecstatic vision. The *wali* is the man who possesses the gift of illumination (*ilham*), or direct apprehension of the spiritual, but that grace differs from the inspiration (*wahy*) bestowed upon the prophets, and the wali must submit to the guidance of prophetic revelations. All walis are essentially under the *qutb*, but the qutb is inferior to the companions of Muhammad. Whatever rule (*tariqa*) a darwish follows he is guided by God, but ash-Sha'rani himself preferred the rule of al-Junayd. The varying opinions of the canonists are adapted to the different needs of men. Ash-Sha'rani was the founder of a darwish order which forms a sub-division of the Badawiya (cf. above). His writings have considerable influence in modern Islam, and form the programme of those who advocate a neo-Sufi reformation.

CHAPTER VIII

ORTHODOX SCHOLASTICISM

The formation of an orthodox scholasticism within the Muslim church appears as a development spread over the 4th-5th centuries of the Hijra (10-11 cent. A.D.), and is in three strata associated with the three leaders, al-Ash'ari, al-Baqilani, and al-Ghazali. Such a development, of course, is principally of interest for the internal history of Islam and the evolution of Muslim theology, but it had its influence also on the transmission of Arabic thought to Latin Christendom in two ways: (i.) directly, in that al-Ghazali was established as one of the great Arabic authorities when the Latins began to study the interpreters of Aristotle, and his teaching is quoted by St. Thomas Aquinas and other scholastic writers ; and (ii.) indirectly, because a considerable part of the work of Ibn Rushd (Averroes) takes the form of controversy against the followers of al-Ghazali; his *Destruction of the Destruction*, for example, is a refutation of al-Ghazali's *Destruction of the Philosophers*. It thus becomes imperative to know something about the position and teaching of al-Ghazali and the influences which prepared the way for his work.

Such a movement as orthodox scholasticism was inevitable. The position at the end of the third century was quite impossible. The orthodox Muslim adhered strictly to tradition, and entirely refused to admit " innovation " (*bid'a*) : he had been forced into this position as a reaction against his earlier ready acceptance of Plato and Aristotle as inspired teachers, for the later errors of the Mu'tazilites showed what extremely dangerous conclusions could be drawn by those who came under Hellenistic influence, and the more accurately the Greek philosophers were studied the worse the heresies gathered from them. Orthodox thought held itself carefully aloof from the Mu'tazilites and philosophers on the one side, and from the Shi'ites and Sufis on the other, confining itself to the safe studies of Qur'an exegesis, tradition, and the canon law in which at Baghdad the reactionary influence of Ibn Hanbal was predominant. The whole of the third century had been a time of reaction on the part of the orthodox, very largely due to the unfortunate attempt of al-Ma'mun to force rationalism on his subjects. Al-Ghazali tells us in his " Confessions " that some sincere Muslims felt themselves bound to reject all the exact sciences as of dangerous tendency, and so repudiated scientific theories as to eclipses of the sun and moon. All speculation lay under a ban, because it led to " innovation " in belief or in practice ; it was contrary to orthodoxy to use the methods of Greek philosophy to prove revealed doctrine as much as it was to impugn it, for both alike were innovations

on the traditional usage ; nothing was known of
spiritual matters save what is actually stated in the
Qur'an and tradition, and from this nothing could be
deduced by the use of argument, for logic itself was
a Greek innovation, at least as applied to theology :
only that was known which was actually stated, and
no explanation of the statement was lawful. Thus,
when Ahmad ibn Hanbal was examined by the
inquisitors of al-Ma'mun he replied only by quoting
the words of the Qur'an or tradition, refusing to draw
any conclusions from these statements and admitting
no conclusions drawn, keeping silence when arguments
were proposed to him, and protesting that such examination as to religious belief was itself an innovation.

This position was hardly satisfactory to those who
had inherited any part of the Hellenic tradition,
and it ultimately became impossible. An organic
body which cannot adapt itself to its surroundings
is doomed to decay. The Islamic state had sufficient
vitality to meet the new conditions introduced by
its expansion to Syria and Persia, and now the time
had come for Islamic theology to adapt itself to the
new thought that was invading it. As we have seen,
the philosophers al-Kindi and al-Farabi were loyal
Muslims, and had no suspicion that their investigations
were leading to heretical conclusions, and such was undoubtedly the case with the earlier Mu'tazilites also,
but results had justified the orthodox in a suspicious
attitude towards " argument " (*kalam*). Now, towards
the close of the third century the attempt to find an

orthodox *kalam* appears as a movement which originates with the Mu'tazilites, of whom a section of the more conservative sought to return to an orthodox stand-point, and to use *kalam* in theology in defence of the traditional beliefs as against the heretical conclusions which were in circulation. Following a somewhat later usage we may employ this term *kalam* to denote an orthodox philosophical theology, that is to say, one in which the methods of philosophy were used, but the primary material was obtained from revelation, and thus one which was closely parallel with the scholastic theology of Latin Christendom.

We have cited the name of al-Ash'ari as representative of the first stage of this movement, but it is equally represented by the contemporary al-Mataradi in Samarqand and by at-Tahawi in Egypt. Of these, however, at-Tahawi has quite passed into oblivion. For long the Ash'arites and the Matar-idites formed rival orthodox schools of *kalam*, and al-Mataridi's system still has a certain vogue amongst Turkish Muslims, but the Ash'arite system is that which commands the widest assent. Theologians reckon thirteen points of difference between the two schools, all of purely theoretical importance.

Al-Ash'ari was born at Basra in 260 or 270, and died at Baghdad about 330 or 340. At first he was an adherent of the Mu'tazilites, but one Friday in A.H. 300 he made a public renunciation of the views of that party, and took up a definitely orthodox position ; in the pulpit of the great mosque at Basra

he said, " They who know me know who I am ; as
for those who do not know me, I am 'Ali b. Isma'il
al-Ash'ari, and I used to hold that the Qur'an was
created, that the eyes of men shall not see God, and
that we ourselves are the authors of our evil deeds ;
now I have returned to the truth ; I renounce these
opinions, and I take the engagement to refute the
Mu'tazilites and expose their infamy and turpitude "
(Ibn Khallikan, ii. 228). From this it will be perceived that the doctrines then regarded as characteristic of the Mu'tazilites were (i.) that the Qur'an
was created, (ii.) the denial of the possibility of the
beatific vision, and (iii.) the freedom of the will.

In the period after this change al-Ash'ari wrote a controversial work against the Mu'tazilites, which bears
the name *Kitab ash-Sharh wa-t-Tafsil,* " the book
of explanation and exposition " ; he was the author
also of religious treatises called *Luma* " flashes,"
Mujaz " abridgment," *Idah al-Burhan* " elucidation
of the Burhan," and *Tabiyin* " illustrations." His
real importance, however, lay in founding a school
of orthodox scholasticism, afterwards more fully
developed by al-Baqilani, and gradually spreading
through the Muslim world, although strongly opposed
on the one side by the *falasifah,* who saw in its teaching
the introduction of traditional beliefs limiting and
restricting the Aristotelian doctrine, and on the
other side by the more reactionary orthodox, who
disapproved the use of philosophical methods as
applied to theological subjects. This use of philoso-

phy in the explanation and defence of religion came to be known as *kalam*, and those who employed it were called *mutakallamin*.

In dealing with the old problems of Muslim theology, such as the eternity of the Qur'an, the freedom of the will, etc., the Ash'arites do seem to have produced a reasonable statement of doctrine, which yet safeguarded the main demands of orthodoxy.

(a) As to the Qur'an, they held that it was eternal in God, but its expression in words and syllables was created in time. This does not of course mean that the expression was due to the Prophet to whom it was revealed, but to God, so that the doctrine of literal inspiration was asserted in the strictest form. Nor was it thus created when it was revealed, but long before in remote ages when it was first uttered to the angels and " august beings," and was afterwards disclosed by the angel Gabriel to the Prophet Muhammad. This, which is now the orthodox belief, has furnished an opportunity for controversy to Christians and modern rationalists, who have fixed upon the use of particular words, introduced into Arabic as loan words from Syriac, Persian, and Greek, and appear in the Qur'an : how, they ask, can it be explained that words revealed at a remote period of past eternity, long before the creation of the world, as it is commonly asserted, show the influence of foreign languages which were brought to bear upon Arabic in the 7th cent. A.D. ? and Muslim apologists, who have always maintained the absolute

purity of Qur'anic Arabic as one of the evidences
of Divine origin, seem to regard this as a serious
difficulty. The view that the Qur'an is eternal in
substance, and thus in substance revealed to the
Prophet, who was left to express it in his own words,
which would thereby show the limitations of his time,
is not admitted by the orthodox. It will be noted
also that the Ash'arite teaching evades and does not
answer an old difficulty : if the substance of the
Qur'an is the wisdom of God and is co-eternal with
Him, even though emanating from Him, we have
something other than God, namely, His wisdom,
eternally existing with Him, and this can be represented as parallel with the persons of the Christian
Trinity, so as to be inconsistent with the absolute
unity of God.

(*b*) This brings us to the attributes of God generally.
The Ash'arites in this controversy side with the
traditional school against the philosophers. Of the
ten Aristotelian categories they regard only two—
existence, i.e., *ens*, and quality as objectively real ;
the other eight are merely relative characteristics
(*i'tibar*) subjective in the mind of the knower, and
having no objective reality. God has qualities—
indeed, no less than twenty are enumerated, but
amongst these is *mukhalafa*, which is the quality
of uniqueness in qualification, so that the qualities
and attributes ascribed to God must either be such
as cannot be applied to men, or else, if the terms can
be used of created beings, they must have quite

different meanings when applied to God, and these qualities thus signified must be such as could not be predicated of men or of any other created being. Thus, that God has power and wisdom means that He is almighty and omniscient in a way which could not possibly be stated of any men. In practice this works so that no attribute can be applied to God unless it is expressly so applied in the text of the Qur'an ; if it occurs there it may be used, but must be understood as having a meaning other than such a term would have when used in the normal way of men. It cannot be that God's attributes differ from those of men only in degree, as that He is wiser and more powerful than man, but they differ in their whole nature. It is noted also that God is *qiyam bi-n-nafs,* or " subsisting in Himself, " that is to say, independent of any other than Himself, and so God's knowledge does not depend on the existence or nature of the thing known.

(c) As to freedom of the will. God creates power in the man and creates also the choice, and He then creates the act corresponding to this power and choice. Thus the action is " acquired " by the creature.

Of the categories existence is the first substratum, and to this the other predicables are added : none of these others are separable or *per se,* they can only exist in the essence. It is admitted that such qualities exist in the *ens,* but they are only adjuncts which come into being with the *ens* and go out of existence

with it. Therefore the world consists of *entia* or
substances on which the mind reflects the qualities
which are not in the thing itself but only in the mind.
Against the Aristotelian theory that matter suffers
the impress of form, he argues that all impress is
subjective in the mind : if all qualities fall out substance itself ceases to exist, and so substance is not
permanent but transitory, which opposes the
Aristotelian doctrine of the eternity of matter.

The substances perceived by us are atoms which
come into existence from vacuity and drop out of
existence again. Thus, when a body moves from one
position to another the atoms in the first position
cease to be, and a group of new similar atoms come
into existence in the second position, so that movement involves a series of annihilations and creations.

The cause of these changes is God, the only permanent and absolute reality. There is no secondary
cause, as there are no laws of nature ; in every case
God acts directly upon each atom. Thus, fire does
not cause burning, but God creates a being burned
when fire touches a body, and the burning is directly
His work. So in the freedom of the will, as, for
example, when a man writes, God gives the will
to write and causes the apparent motion of the pen
and of the hand, and also directly creates the writing
which seems to proceed from the pen.

Existence is the very self of the thing. This is
peculiar to al-Ash'ari and his followers : all others
hold existence to be the state (*ḥāl*) necessary to the

essence, but in al-Ash'ari it is the essence. So God exists, and His existence is the self (*'ayn*) of His essence.

Such a system involves ethical difficulties ; it appears that there can be no responsibility if there is no connection between action and the act done. Al-Ash'ari replied that there is a unity in the will of God, so that cause and effect are not isolated as though independent atoms, but all is disposed according to a Divine plan. This answer, however, can hardly be regarded as adequate.

This system is an attempt to deal with the difficulties raised by philosophy, but al-Ash'ari considers it preferable that the difficulties should never be raised, and so strongly urges that the mysteries of philosophy should never be discussed with the multitude. We shall see the same conclusion set forth by the later philosopher of the West, but on a somewhat different ground ; they regarded the mysteries of philosophy as containing the supreme truth, for which the multitude was not ripe, and so they should not be discussed publicly, as the people were not able to understand ; but al-Ash'ari seems rather to regard these mysteries as likely to be not edifying, as introducing questions which are of small importance compared with the great truths of revelation.

The Ash'arite system thus described was completed by al-Baqilani (d. 403), but it did not become general until it was popularised by al-Ghazali in the East and by Ibn Tumart in the West.

Al-Mataridi, of Samarqand was a contemporary of al-Ash'ari, and reached very similar results. Amongst the points peculiar to al-Mataridi we may note (*a*) the attribute of *creating* has been an attribute of God from all eternity, but this attribute is distinct from the thing created ; (*b*) Creatures have certain choice of action, and for the things done by this choice they are rewarded or punished ; good actions are only done by the pleasure (*rida*) of God, but bad actions are not always by His pleasure ; (*c*) Ability to do the action goes with the will and the act, so that the creature cannot have an action imposed on him as a task which is not in his power.

He agrees with al-Ash'ari in holding that the world and all it contains have been created by God from nothing : it consists of substances and attributes. The substances exist in themselves, either as compounds, such as bodies, or as non-compounds, as essences which are indivisible. Attributes have no separate existence, but depend for their existence on bodies or essences. God is not essence, nor attribute, nor body, nor anything formed, bounded, numbered, limited, nor compounded. He cannot be described by *mahiya* (quiddity), nor *kayfiya* (modality) ; He does not exist in time or place, and nothing resembles Him or is outside His knowledge or power. He has qualities from all eternity existing in His essence ; they are not He nor is He other than they.

For some time the Ash'arites had to meet keen opposition and even persecution, and it was not until the middle of the 5th cent. that they came to be admitted generally as orthodox Muslims. Their triumph was assured in 459 A.H., when Nizam al-Mulk, the wazir of Alp Arslan, founded at Baghdad the Nizamite academy as a theological college of Ash'arite teaching. Still the Hanbalites raised occasional riots, and demonstrated against those whom they regarded as free thinkers; but these were put down by authority, and in 516 the Khalif himself attended the Ash'arite lectures. The Mu'tazilites were now merely a survival; as broad church theologians they had fallen into general disrepute in the eyes of the orthodox, and they were equally disliked by the philosophers as defective in their adherence to the Aristotelian system. The educated fell now into three broad groups : on the one hand were the orthodox, who came under the influence of al-Ash'ari or al-Mataridi; on the other were those who accepted the doctrines of the philosophers, and in the third place were those who rejected all philosophy, and confined their attention solely to Qur'an tradition and the canon law, and who should not be excluded from the ranks of the educated, although their studies ran in somewhat narrow lines.

The final triumph of the Ash'arite theology was the work of *al-Ghazali* (d. 505). He was born at Tus in 450 (= 1058 A.D.); early left an orphan he was educated by a Sufi friend, and then attended the school at Naisabur. As his education progressed he cut loose from Sufi influence and became an Ash'arite, and in 484 he was appointed president of the Nazmiite Academy at Baghdad. Gradually, however, he became a prey to spiritual unrest, and in 488 resigned his post and retired to Syria, where he spent some years in study and the practices of devotion. In 499 he returned to active work as a teacher in the Nazimite Academy at Naisabur, where he became the leader of a modified Ash'arite system strongly leavened by mysticism, which we may regard as the final evolution of orthodox Muslim theology.

Al-Ghazali, following al-Ash'ari, taught that philosophical theory cannot form the basis of religious thought, thus opposing the position of the philosophers. By revelation only can the primary essentials of truth be attained. Philosophy itself is no equal or rival of revelation : it is no more than common sense and regulated thinking, which may be employed by men about religion or any other subject ; at best it acts as a preservative against error in deduction and argument, the primary material for which, so far as religion is concerned, can be furnished only by revelation. But against this he appears also as the transmitter of the teaching already given, by al-Qushayri, which introduced the mysticism of the Sufis into orthodox Islam. Revelation indeed is given by means of the Qur'an and tradition, and it is sufficient to accept what is thus revealed, but the ultimate truth of revelation can be tested and proved only by the experience of the individual. So far as men are concerned this is possible by means of ecstasy whereby one becomes a knower (*'arif*), and receives assurance and enlightenment by direct communication from God. The soul of man differs from all other created things ; it is essentially spiritual, and so outside the categories which are applicable only to material things. The soul has been breathed into man by God (Qur. 15, 29 ; 38, 72), and this is comparable to the way in which the sun sends out its rays and gives warmth to those things on which its rays rest. The soul, which has no dimension, shape, or locus, rules the body in the same way as God rules the world, so that the body is a microcosm reproducing the conditions of the world. The essential element of this soul is not the intelligence which is concerned with the bodily frame, but the will : just as God is primarily known not as thought or intelligence, but as the volition which is the cause of creation. Thus God cannot be considered as the spirit animating the world, which is the pantheistic position, but as volition outside the world which has willed it to be.

The aim of scholastic theology is to preserve the purity of orthodox belief from heretical innovation : " God raised up a school of theologians and inspired them with the desire to defend orthodoxy by means of a system of proofs adapted to unveil the devices of the heretics and to foil the attacks which they made on the doctrines established by tradition " (Al-Ghazali : *Confessions*). Aristotle himself was an unbeliever using arguments he should not, but, in

spite of his errors, his teaching as expounded by al-
Farabi and Ibn Sina is the system of thought which
comes nearest to Islam (id.). Because of its
unavoidable difficulties and the grave errors contained in Aristotle and his Arabic commentators
men are not to be encouraged to read philosophy (id.).

There are three different worlds or planes of
existence (i.) the *'alam al-mulk* is that in which
existence is apparent to the senses, the world made
known by perception, and this is in a state of constant
change ; (ii.) the *'alam al-malakut*, the changeless
and eternal world of reality established by God's
decree, of which the world of perception is but the
reflexion ; (iii.) and the *'alam al-jarabut* or intermediate state, which properly belongs to the world
of reality, but seems to be in the plane of perception.
In this intermediate state is the human soul, which
belongs to the plane of reality, though apparently
projected into the perceptible plane to which it does
not belong, and then returns to reality. The pen,
tablet, etc., mentioned in the Qur'an are not mere
allegories ; they belong to the world of reality, and
so are something other than what we see in this world
of perception. These three worlds or planes are not
separate in time or space, they are rather to be considered as modes of existence

The theories of the astronomers as to movements
of the heavenly bodies are to be accepted—al-Ghazali
adhered, of course, to the Ptolemaic system—but these
deal only with the lowest plane, the world of sense.

Behind all nature is God, who is on the plane of reality. This higher plane cannot be reached by reason or intellect, whose operations must rely on the evidence of sense perception. To reach the plane of reality man must be raised by a spiritual faculty, " by which he perceives invisible things, the secrets of the future and other concepts as inaccessible to reason as the concepts of reason are inaccessible to mere discrimination and what is perceived by discrimination of the senses " (op. cit.). Inspiration means the disclosing of realities to the prophets or saints, and these realities can only be known by such revelation or by the personal experience of ecstasy by which the soul is raised to the plane of reality. Not only are the religious truths in the Qur'an revealed, but all ideas of good and evil are similarly revealed, and could not be attained by the unaided use of reason, a view which is obviously intended to refute the Mu'tazilite claim that moral differences can be perceived by reason. The philosophers also have attained truths by revelation, and the main substance of medicine and astronomy is based on such revelation (op. cit.).

Unlike Ibn Rushd, al-Ghazali thus emphasizes supra-rational intuition attained in a state of ecstasy, whereby the soul is raised above the world of shadow and reflection to the plane of reality. This was pure mysticism, and thus al-Ghazali introduces a Sufi element into orthodox Islam. At the same time he reduced Sufism to a scientific form, and endorsed the Plotinian terminloogy. Macdonald summarises his work under four heads : (i.) he established an orthodox mysticism : (ii.) he popularised the use of philosophy ; (iii.) he rendered philosophy subordinate to theology, and (iv.) he restored the fear of God when the element of fear was tending to be thrust into the background, at least by the educated. From this time on the term *kalam* was usually applied to philosophy adapted to the use of theologians.

The chief works left by al-Ghazali are the *Ihya 'Ulum ad-Din*, of which it is understood that a translation by H. Bauer is in preparation, and the *Mi'yar al-'Ilm*, a treatise on logic. To posterity, however, he is best known by his *Confessions*, an autobiographical account of his spiritual life and development, which may not unfitly be placed beside the Confessions of St. Augustine.

Al-Ghazali completes the development of orthodox Muslim theology. From this time forth it ceased to have any originality, and for the most part showed signs of decadence. Here and there we find Sufi revivals ; indeed, Sufism is the only phase of Islam which kept free from the rigid conservatism which has laid its iron hand of repression upon Muslim life and thought generally. In Yemen the system of al-Ghazali was kept alive by generations of Sufis, but for the most part Sufism preferred less orthodox paths. Against these Sufi movements we see from time to time others of a distinctly reactionary character, such as that of the Wahabis, who opposed the theology of al-Ghazali when it was generally recognised as the orthodox teaching at Mecca, and in this they were followed by the Sanusi.

Sayyid Murtada (d. 1205 A.H. = 1788 A.D.), a native of Zabid in Yihama, wrote a commentary on al-Ghazali's *Ihya 'Ulum ad-Din*, and thus revived the study of the great scholastic theologian. From that time the Islamic community has not lacked neo-Ghazalian students, and many consider that that school contains the best promise for modern Islam.

CHAPTER IX

WESTERN PHILOSOPHY

Muslim rule in North Africa west of the Nile valley was commenced under conditions very different from those prevailing in Egypt and Syria. The Arabs found this land occupied by the Berbers or Libyans, the same race which from the time of the earliest Pharaohs had been a perpetual menace to Egypt, and which, on the Mediterranean seaboard, had offered a serious problem to Phœnician, Greek, Roman and Gothic colonists. For some thousands of years these Berbers had remained very much the same as when they had emerged from the neolithic stage, and were hardy desert men like the Arabs in pre-Islamic times. Their language was not Semitic, but shows very marked Semitic affinities, and, although language transmission is often quite distinct from racial descent, it seems probable that in this case there was a parallel, and this is best explained by supposing that both were derived from the neolithic race which at one time spread along the whole of the south coast of the Mediterranean and across into Arabia, but that some cause, perhaps the early development of civilization in the Nile valley, had cut off the eastern wing from the rest, and this segrated portion developed the peculiar characteristics which we describe as Semitic. The series of Greek, Punic, Roman, and Gothic settlements had left no permanent mark on the Berber population, on their language, or on their culture. At the time of the Arab invasion the country was theoretically under the Byzantine Empire, and the invading Arabs had to meet the resistance of a Greek army ; but this was not a very serious obstacle, and the invaders were soon left face to face with the Berber tribes.

The Muslim invasion of North Africa followed immediately after the invasion of Egypt, but the internal disputes of the Muslim community prevented a regular conquest. It was not until a second invasion took place in A.H. 45 (= A.D. 665) that we can regard the Arabs as commencing the regular conquest and settlement of the country. For centuries afterwards the Arab control was precarious in the extreme, revolts were constantly taking place, and many Berber states were founded, some of which had an existence of considerable duration. As a rule there was a pronounced racial feeling between Berbers and Arabs, but there were also tribal feuds, and Arab policy generally aimed at playing off one powerful tribe against another. Gradually the Arabs spread all along North Africa and down to the desert edge, their tribes as a rule occupying the lower ground, whilst the older population had its chief centres in the mountainous districts. During the invasion of 45 the city of Kairawan was founded

some distance south of Tunis. The site was badly
chosen, and is now marked only by ruins and a scanty
village, but for some centuries it served as the
capital city of *Ifrikiya*, which was the name given to
the province lying next to Egypt, embracing the
modern states of Tripoli, Tunis, and the eastern part
of Algeria up to the meridian of Bougie. West of
this lay *Maghrab*, or the " western land," which was
divided into two districts, Central Maghrab extending
from the borders of Ifrikiya across the greater part
of Algeria and the eastern third of Morocco, and
Further Maghrab, which spread beyond to the Atlantic
coast. In these provinces Arabs and Berbers lived
side by side, but in distinct tribes, the intercourse
between the two varying in different localities and
at different times. For the most part each race
preserved its own language, the several Arabic
dialects being distinguished by archaic forms and a
phonology somewhat modified by Berber influences;
but there are instances of Berber tribes which have
adopted Arabic, and some of the Arab and mixed
groups have preferred the Berber language.

The religion of Islam spread rapidly amongst the
Berbers, but it took a particular development, which
shows a survival of many pre-Islamic religious ideas.
The worship of saints and the devotion paid at their
tombs is a corruption which appears elsewhere,
on lines quite distinct from the Asiatic beliefs as
to incarnation or transmigration, and in the west
this saint worship takes an extreme form, although

here and there are tribes which reject it altogether, as is the case with the B. Messara, the Ida of South Morocco, etc. Pilgrimages (*ziara*) are made to saints' tombs, commemorative banquets are held there (*wa'da* or *ta'an*), and acts of worship, often taking a revolting form, are paid to living saints, who are known as *murabits* or *marabouts*, a word which literally means " those who serve in frontier forts (*ribat*)," where the soldiers were accustomed to devote themselves to practices of piety. These saints are also known as *sidi* (lords), or *mulaye* (teachers), and in the Berber language of the Twaregs as *aneslem*, or " Islamic." Very often they are insane persons, and are allowed to indulge every passion and to disregard the ordinary laws of morality. Even those living at the present day are credited with miraculous powers, not only with gifts of healing, but with exemption from the limitations of space and from the laws of gravity (cf. Trumelet : *Les saints de l'islam*, Paris, 1881) ; in many cases the same saint has two or more tombs, and is believed to be buried in each, for it is argued that, as he was able to be in two or more places at once during life, so his body can be in several tombs after death. All this, of course, is no normal development of Islam, to which it is plainly repugnant. How thin a veneer of Muslim usages covers over a mass of primitive animism may be seen from Dr. Westermarck's essay on " Belief in spirits in Morocco," the firstfruits of the newly established Academy at Abo in Finland (*Humaniora*.

I. i. Abo, Finland, 1920), and from Dr. Montet's *Le culte des saints musulmans dans l'Afrique du nord* (Geneva, 1905).

Amongst the Berber tribes in perpetual conflict with the Arab garrisons there was always a refuge and a welcome for the lost causes of Islam, and so almost every heretical sect and every defeated dynasty made its last stand there, so that even now those parts show the strangest survivals of otherwise forgotten movements. No doubt this was mainly due to a perennial tone of disaffection towards the Arab rulers, and anyone in revolt against the Khalif was welcomed for that very fact.

The conquest of Spain towards the end of the 1st cent. A.H. (early 8th cent. A.D.) was jointly an Arab and Berber undertaking, the Berbers being in the great majority in the invading army, and most of the leaders being Berber. Thus in Andalusia the old rivalries between Arab and Berber figure largely in the next few centuries. At first Andalusia was regarded merely as a district attached to the province of North Africa, and was ruled from Ifrikiya.

In A.H. 138, after the fall of the Umayyads in Asia, a fugitive member of the fallen dynasty, 'Abdu r-Rahman, failing in an attempt to restore his family in Africa, crossed over to Spain, and there established a new and independent power, with its seat of goverment at Cordova, and in A.H. 317 one of his descendants formally assumed the title of " Commander of the Faithful." The Umayyads of

Spain very closely reproduced the general characteristics of their rule in Syria. They were tolerant, and
made free use of Christian and Jewish officials; they
encouraged the older literary arts, and especially
poetry, and employed Greek artists and architects;
but though doing much for the more material elements
of culture, there is no evidence under their rule of
any interest in Greek learning or philosophy. Yet,
though in a sense old-fashioned, the country was by
no means isolated, and we find frequent intercourse
between Spain and the east. The religious duty of
the pilgrimage has always been an important factor
in promoting the common life of Islam, and there is
abundant evidence that the Spanish Muslims looked
steadily eastwards for religious guidance, accepting
the *hadith*, the canon law, and the development of
a scientific jurisprudence as it took shape in the east.
Both Muslims and Jews travelled to Mesopotamia
in order to complete their education, and thus kept
in contact with the more cultured life of Asia. But
Spanish Islam had no feeling of sympathy with the
philosophical speculation popular in the east, and
certainly disapproved the latitudinarian developments
which were taking place under the 'Abbasids of the
third century : its tendency was to a rigid orthodoxy
and strict conservatism, its interests were confined
to the canon law, Qur'anic exegesis, and the study
of tradition.

The reactionary character of Spanish Islam is well
illustrated by *Ibn Hazm* (d. 456 A.H.), the first

important theologian which it produced. Rejecting
the four recognised and orthodox schools of canon
law, and discarding even the rigid system of Ibn
Hanbal as not strict enough, he became an adherent
of the school founded by Da'ud az-Zahiri (d. 270),
which has never been admitted as on the same footing
as the other four, and now is totally extinct. In the
teaching of that school Qur'an and tradition were
taken in their strictest and most literal sense; any
sort of deduction by analogy was forbidden; "it is
evident that here we have to do with an impossible
man and school, and so the Muslim world found.
Most said roundly that it was illegal to appoint a
Zahirite to act as judge, on much the same grounds
that objection to circumstantial evidence will throw
out a man now as juror. If they had been using
modern language, they would have said that it was
because he was a hopeless crank." (Macdonald:
Muslim Theology, p. 110). This was the system
which Ibn Hazm now introduced into Spain, and it
was one calculated to appeal to the stern puritan
strain which undoubtedly exists in the Iberian
character. The novel point was that Ibn Hazm
applied the principles and methods of jurisprudence
to theology proper. Like Da'ud he entirely rejected
the principles of analogy and *taqlid*, that is, the following of authority in the sense of accepting the dictum
of a known teacher. As this undermined all existing
systems, and required every man to study Qur'an and
tradition for himself, it did not receive the approval

of the canonists, who, in Spain as elsewhere, were the followers of recognised schools, such as that of Abu Hanifa and the other orthodox systems, and it was not until a full century afterwards that he gained any number of adherents. In theology he admitted the Ash'arite doctrine of *mukhalafa*, the difference of God from all created beings, so that human attributes could not be applied to him in the same sense as they were used of men ; but he carried this a stage further, and opposed the Ash'arites, who, though admitting the difference, had then argued about the attributes of God as though they described God's nature, when the very fact of difference deprives them of any meaning intelligible to us. As in the Qur'an ninety-nine descriptive titles are applied to God we may lawfully employ them, but we neither know what they imply nor can we argue anything from them. The same method is applied to the treatment of the anthropomorphical expressions which are applied to God in the Qur'an ; we may use those expressions, but we have not the slightest idea of what they may indicate, save that we know they do not mean what they would mean as used of men. In ethics the only distinction between good and evil is based on God's will, and our only knowledge of that distinction is obtained from revelation. If God forbids theft it is wrong only because God forbids it ; there is no standard other than the arbitrary approval or disapproval of God.

Although it took a century for these views to

obtain any number of adherents, Ibn Hazm was no
obscure figure during his lifetime. He became
prominent as a violent and abusive controversialist,
an opponent of the Ash'arite party and of the Mu'tazilites, curiously enough treating the latter more
gently as having limited God's qualities.

Ibn Hazm lived at a time when the Umayyads of
Cordova were already in their decay, and in 422 the
dynasty fell. Very soon the whole of Andalusia
was split into a number of independent principalities, and this was followed by a period of anarchy,
during which the country was exposed more and
more to Christian attacks, until at length Mu'tamid,
King of Seville, fearing that the Muslim states would
disappear altogether under the tide of Christian
conquest, advised his co-religionists to appeal for
help to the Murabit power in Morocco, which, with
much misgiving, they did.

The Murabits, the name is that commonly applied
to saints in Morocco, were the product of a religious
revival led by Yahya b. Ibrahim of the clan of the
Jidala, a branch of the great Berber tribe of Latuna,
one of those light-complexioned Berber races such as
can still be seen in Algeria, and are apparently nearest
akin to the Lebu as they are represented in ancient
Egyptian paintings. In 428 (=1036 A.D.) Yahya
performed the pilgrimage to Mecca, and was astonished
and delighted at the evidences of culture and prosperity which he saw in the lands through which he
travelled, so far exceeding anything which had

previously entered his experience. On his return
journey he stopped at Kairawan and became a hearer
at the lectures given there by Abu Amran. The
lecturer was greatly struck by the diligence and
attention of his pupil, and greatly surprised when he
discovered that he was a product of one of the wild
and barbarous tribes of the far west. But when
Yahya asked that one of the alumni of Kairawan
might be sent home with him to teach his fellow-
tribesmen no one was found willing to venture
amongst a people who were generally regarded as
fierce and savage, until at last the task was under-
taken by Abdullah ibn Jahsim. Helped by his
companion Yahya commenced a religious revival
amongst the Berbers of the West, and seems to have
modelled his work on the example of the Prophet, by
force of arms urging his reforms upon the neighbouring
tribes and laying the foundation of a united kingdom,
a work which was continued by his successor, Yusuf
b. Tashfin, and so at length a powerful kingdom was
established, which extended from the Mediterranean
to the Senegal. Many such Berber states were
established at various times, but, as a rule, they fell
into decay after a couple of generations.

Yusuf b. Tashfin was the champion now invited by
the Muslims of Spain, not without misgivings in
many quarters, but the choice seemed to lie only
between Christian or Berber, and the Berbers were
at least of their own religion and of the same race as
the majority of the Spanish Muslims. Yusuf came

as a helper, but a second time invited he stayed on
and established his authority over the country, and
thus Spain became a province under the rule of the
Murabit princes of Morocco. Yusuf was succeeded
by 'Ali, who was successful in restraining the Christians,
and at one time even formed plans to drive them out
of Spain altogether.

Murabit rule, which lasted 35 years, brought many
changes and itself experienced many changes. The
rulers   were   rough   men   of   uncouth   manners
and fanatical outlook. Not many years before, it
will be remembered, the Arabs of Kairawan were
reluctant to venture into their land, such was their
ill repute. They were partially humanised by a
religious movement, and thus naturally show a religious
character which bordered on fanaticism. 'Ali himself
was entirely in the hands of the *faqirs* or mendicant
devotees and qadis, and the government was liable to
interference from these irresponsible fanatics at every
turn. It was a state of affairs which awakened the im-
patience of the cultured Muslims of Spain, who expressed
their feelings in many caustic epigrams and satirical
poems. But very soon a change began to work. The
Murabits and their followers did not become less
attached to the devotees, who swarmed unchecked on
every side and received idolatrous attentions from the
multitude, but they learned the luxuries and refine-
ments of the cultured life then prevailing in Spain and
showed themselves apt pupils. Indeed, their downfall
may be explained either as due to effete luxury or to

faqir-ridden superstition, as we shall see later on.

The intellectual life of Muslim Spain up to the Murabit period was conservative rather than backward. Its literary men were nearer the old traditional Arab type than was the case in the eastern Khalifate, where Persian influences had pushed the Arab so much into the background ; its scholars were still occupied exclusively with the traditional sciences, exegesis, canon law, and traditions. The Murabit invasion offered a stimulus to satirical verse, but otherwise did nothing to promote either literature or science. Yet it is under Murabit rule that we find the first beginnings of western philosophy, and the line of transmission is from the Mu'tazilites of Baghdad through the Jews and thence to the Muslims of Spain. The Jews act as intermediaries who bring the Muslim philosophy of Asia into contact with the Muslims of Spain.

For a long time the Jews had taken no part in the development of Hellenistic philosophy, although in the later Syriac period they had participated in medical studies and in natural science, of which we have seen evidence in the important work of Jewish physicians and scientists at Baghdad under al-Ma'mun and the early 'Abbasids. Outside medicine and natural science Jewish interest seems to have been mainly confined to Biblical exegesis, tradition, and canon law.

One of the few exceptions to this restriction of interests was *Sa'id al-Fayyumi* or Saadya ben Joseph

(d. 331 A.H. =942 A.D.), a native of Upper Egypt, who became one of the Geonim of the academy at Sora on the Euphrates, and is best known as the translator of the Old Testament into Arabic, which had now replaced Aramaic as the speech of the Jews both in Asia and in Spain. As an author his most important work was the *Kitab al-Amanat wa-l-I'tiqadat*, or " Book of the articles of faith and dogmatics," which was finished in 321-2 (=A.D. 933), and was afterwards translated into Hebrew as *Sefer Emunot we-De'ot* by Judah b. Tibbon. He was the author also of a commentary on the Pentateuch, of which only a portion (on Exod. 30, 11-16) survives, as well as other works ; but it is in the first-named and in the commentary that his views appear most clearly. For the first time a Jewish writer shows familiarity with the problems raised by the Mu'tazilites, and gives these a serious attention from the Jewish stand-point. It does not seem, however, that we should class Sa'id as a Mu'tazilite ; he more properly represents the movement which produced his Muslim contemporaries, al-Ash'ari and al-Mataridi, that is to say, he is one of those who use orthodox *kalam* and adapt philosophy to apologetic purposes. His position is shown most clearly in the " Book of the articles of faith and dogmatics " in dealing with the three problems of (*a*) creation, (*b*) the Divine Unity, and (*c*) free will. In the first of these he defends the doctrine of a creation *ex nihilo*, but in giving proofs of the necessity of a creator he shows in three out of

the four arguments employed distinct traces of
Aristotelian influences. In treating the doctrine of
the Divine Unity he is chiefly concerned with opposing
the Christian teaching of the Trinity, but incidentally
is compelled to deal with the idea of God and the
Divine attributes, and in doing so maintains that none
of the Aristotelian categories can be applied to God.
As to the human will he defends its freedom, and his
task is mainly an effort to reconcile this with the
omnipotence and omniscience of God. In the
fragment on Exodus he refers to the commands of
revelation and the commands of reason, these latter,
he asserts, being based on philosophical speculation.

Evidently the *Mutakallamin* movement, pro-
fessedly an orthodox reaction from the Mu'tazilites,
represents a great widening of philosophical
influences. Philosophy was no longer a subject
confined to one group of scholars who were interested
in Greek writings, but had spread out until it reached
the mosques, and could no longer be thrust aside as
an heretical aberration, and in its outspread it had
penetrated the Jewish schools as well. But Sa'id
produced no immediate disciples, and those who
followed him in the Jewish academies of Mesopotamia
showed no interest in his methods. Yet his work,
apparently barren, was destined to have results of
the widest importance after a century's interval. In
spite of distance and the difficulties of travel there
was a very close and frequent intercourse maintained
between all the Jews of the Sefardi group, those,

namely, who had adopted Arabic as their ordinary
speech and who were living under Muslim rule.   The
Ashkenazi Jews in the north and centre of Europe
who lived in Christian lands and did not use Arabic
were definitely separated from these others by the
barrier of language, and thus in different surroundings
the two groups developed marked differences in their
use of Hebrew, in their liturgical formularies, and
in their popular beliefs and folk-lore.   Thus we must
bear in mind that a synagogue in Spain would
naturally be in close touch with synagogues in
Mesopotamia, but it was not likely to have any
contact with one in the Rhine valley.

Although the earlier Jewish settlers in Spain and
Provence had enjoyed considerable freedom, restrictions had been imposed by the council of Elvira
(A.D. 303-4), and they had to suffer considerable
severity under the later West Goths.   The coming
of the Muslims had greatly eased their position,
chiefly because the Jews had taken a leading part in
assisting and probably in inviting the invaders ; they
often furnished garrisons to occupy towns which
the Muslims had conquered, and were the means of
supplying them with information as to the enemy's
movements.   It seems probable that they had been
in correspondence with the Muslims beforehand, so
that they shared with Witiza's partisans the responsibility of inviting the invasion.   Under
Umayyad rule their prosperity continued and increased.   Very often we find Jews occupying high

positions at court and in the civil service, and these favourable conditions seem to have prevailed until the time of the Muwahhids, for it does not appear that the Murabits, for all their fanaticism, took any measures against Christians or Jews.

Important amongst the Jews of the Umayyad period was *Hasdai ben Shabrut* (d. 360 or 380 A.H.), a physician under 'Abdu r-Rahman, who sent presents to Sora and Pumbaditha, and carried on a correspondence with Dosa, son of the Gaon Sa'id al-Fayyumi. Hitherto it had been the custom for the western Jews to refer all difficult problems of the canon law to the learned of the academies in Mesopotamia, just as their Muslim neighbours referred to the East for guidance in jurisprudence and theology. But Hasdai took advantage of the accidental presence of Moses Ben Enoch in Cordova to found a native Spanish academy for rabbinical studies there, and appointed Moses its president, a step which received the warm approval of the Umayyad prince. This turned out to be more important than its founder had anticipated; it was not merely a provincial school reproducing the work of the eastern academies, but resulted in the transference of Jewish scholarship to Spain. At that time Asiatic Islam was beginning to feel the restricting power of the orthodox reaction, whilst Spain, on the other hand, saw the opening of a golden age. Shortly before this date the Umayyad Hakim II. had been working to encourage Muslim scholarship in the west, and had sent his agents to purchase books

in Cairo, Damascus, Baghdad, and Alexandria.   In
the reactionary age of Mahmud of Ghazna (388-421)
Muslim b. Muhammad al-Andalusi had been instrumental in introducing the teachings of the " Brethren
of Purity " to the Muslims of Spain.   We cannot say
that the Jews anticipated the Muslims of Spain in
their study of philosophy, but it is clear that the Jews
were associated with the first dawn of the new learning in Spain, and thus as the sun was setting in the
East a new day was beginning to break in the West.

The first leader of Spanish philosophy was the Jew
Abu Ayyub Sulayman b. Yahya b. Jabirul (d. 450 A.H. =
1058 A.D.), commonly known as Ibn Gabirol (Jabirul),
and hence " Avencebrol " in the Latin scholastic
writers.   He is chiefly known as the author of *Maqor
Chayim*, "The Fountain of Life," a title based on
the words of Psalm 36, 10, which was one of the works
translated into Latin at the college of Toledo and so
well known to the scholastic writers as the *Fons Vitae*
(ed. Baumer : *Avencebrolis Fons Vitae*, Munster,
1895).   It was this work which really introduced
neo-Platonism to the West.   Ibn Jabirul teaches that
God alone is pure reality, and He is the only actual
substance ; He has no attributes, but in Him are
will and wisdom, not as possessed attributes but as
aspects of His nature.   The world is produced by
the impress of form upon pre-existing universal
matter.   " Separate substances " in the sense of
ideas abstracted from the things in which they exist
(cf. Aristot. *de anima*. iii. 7, 8, " and so the mind when

it thinks of mathematical forms thinks of them as separated, though they are not separated ") do not exist apart in reality ; the abstracting is only a mental process, so the general idea exists only as a concept, not as a reality.   But between the purely spiritual being of God and the crudely material observed in the bodies existing in this world are intermediate forms of existence, such as angels, souls, etc., wherein the form is not impressed upon matter.

Besides this " Fountain of Life " Ibn Gabirol was the author of two ethical treatises, the *Tikkun Midwoth han-Nefesh*, " the correction of the manners of the soul," in which man is treated as a microcosm after the kabbalistic fashion ; and *Mibchar hap-Peninim*, a collection of ethical maxims collected from the Greek and Arabic philosophers.   The former has been published at Luneville in 1804, the latter at Hamburg in 1844.

At the beginning of the sixth century A.H., a younger contemporary of al-Ghazali, we have *Abu Bakr ibn Bajja* (d. 533 A.H. =1138 A.D.), the first of the Muslim philosophers of Spain.   By this time, some three-quarters of a century after the death of Ibn Sina, Arabic philosophy was almost extinct in Asia and was treated as a dangerous heresy.   In Egypt, it is true, there was a greater degree of toleration, though less than in the golden age of the Fatimids, but Egypt was regarded with suspicion as the home of heresy and of forms of superstition which were uncongenial to the philosopher.   Spain thus becomes the place

of refuge for Muslim philosophy as it had already
become the nursery of Jewish speculation. Ibn
Bajja, known to the Latin schoolmen as " Avempace,"
found in Murabit Spain the freedom and toleration
which Asia no longer afforded. He continues the
work of al-Farabi, not, it will be noted, of Ibn Sina,
and develops the neo-Platonic interpretation of
Aristotle on sober and conservative lines. He wrote
commentaries on Aristotle's Physics, *de generatione
et corruptione*, and the *Meteora* ; he produced original
works on mathematics, on " the soul," and a treatise
which he called " The Hermit's Guide," which was
used by Ibn Rushd (Averroes) and by the Jewish
writer Moses of Narbonne in the 14th cent. A.D. In
this last work he makes a distinction between " animal
activity," in which action is due to the prompting of
the emotions, passions, etc., and " human activity,"
which is suggested and directed by abstract reason,
and from this distinction draws a rule of life and
conduct. He is chiefly cited by the Latin schoolmen
with reference to the doctrine of " separate
substances." " Avempace held that, by the study
of the speculative sciences, we are able by means of
the images which we know from these ideas to attain
to the knowledge of separate substances " (St. Thomas
Aq. *c. Gentiles*, 3, 41). This question as to the
possibility of knowing substances separated, i.e.
abstracted, from the concrete bodies in which they
exist in combination—and the " separate substances "
were regarded as spiritual things—was prominent in

mediæval scholasticism, which inherited it from the
Arabic philosophers, and from it came the further
question whether the contemplation of such abstract
ideas gives us a better knowledge of realities than
observation of the concrete bodies. Both Albertus
Magnus and St. Thomas Aquinas associate Avempace
especially with this question and with the doctrine
of the " acquired intellect," to which we have
already referred in our notes on Ibn Sina, and which
completes the theory of " separate substances " by
supposing that intelligible forms stream into our
souls from an outside Agent Intellect by way of
emanation as substantial forms descend on corporeal
matter. St. Thomas Aquinas shows direct knowledge
of Avempace's treatment of these subjects, but this
is not so evident in Albertus. Avempace, like all
other Arabic philosophers, describes *ittisal* or union
of the human intellect with the Agent Intellect, of
which it is an emanation, as the supreme beatitude
and final end of human life. By the operation of the
Agent Intellect on the latent intellect in man this is
awakened to life, but eternal life consists in the complete union of the intellect with the Agent Intellect.
In Avempace the Sufi strain is much weaker than in
al-Farabi ; the means of attaining this union is not
by ecstasy, but by a steady disentangling of the soul
of those material things which hinder its pure intellectual life and consequent union. This leads us to the
teaching of asceticism as the discipline of the soul for
its spiritual progress, and the ascetic and solitary life

is the ideal proposed by Avempace. This ascetic
and contemplative hermit life is not, however, in any
sense a religious life, for in this respect Avempace
has advanced far beyond al-Farabi; he is fully
conscious that pure philosophy cannot be reconciled
with the teachings of revelation, a conviction which
now marks the definite separation of the
" philosophers " from the orthodox scholastics of
Islam, such as al-Ghazali and his school; he regards
the teachings of revelation as an imperfect presentation of the truths which are more completely and
correctly learned from Aristotle, and only admits the
Qur'an and its religion as a discipline for the multitude
whose intelligence neither desires nor is capable of
philosophical reasoning. Strangely enough he lived
in security, protected from the attacks of hostile
theologians, under the protection of the Murabit
princes.

Within a few years after the death of Avempace
the Murabit dynasty came to an end. The succeeding dynasty, the Muwahhids, were of Berber origin
like the Murabits, and, like them, had their origin in
a religious revival.

The foundation of the Muwahhids is associated
with *Ibn Tumart* (d. 524 A.H. = 1129 A.D.). He
was a native of Morocco, and a strange combination
of fanatic and scholastic. He claimed to be a descendant of 'Ali, and posed as the " Mahdi " possessing
the supernatural grace of *isma* or " security from
error," and thus introduced Shi'ite ideas into Morocco;

and at the same time it was he who introduced to the
West the orthodox scholasticism of al-Ghazali, although at the same time he professed to be a follower
of Ibn Hazm. He travelled in Asia, where, no doubt,
he learned of al-Ghazili and his doctrines. Roughly
treated at Mecca he removed to Egypt, where he
rendered himself prominent and objectionable by his
puritanical criticisms on the manners of the people.
Setting out from Alexandria in a ship travelling
westwards he occupied himself with a reformation of
the morals of the crew, compelling them to observe
the correct hours of prayer and the other duties of
religion. In 505 he appeared at Mahdiya, where he
took up his abode in a wayside mosque. There he
used to sit at the window watching the passers-by,
and, whenever he saw any of them carrying a jar of
wine or a musical instrument, he used to sally out
and seize the offensive article and break it. The
common people reverenced him as a saint, but many
of the wealthier citizens resented his activities, and
at length brought a complaint against him before the
Emir Yahya. The Emir heard their complaints and
observed Ibn Tumart and took note of the impression
he had made upon the populace. With characteristic craft the Emir treated the reformer with all
possible respect, but advised, nay rather urged, him
to bestow the favour of his presence upon some other
town as soon as convenient to him, and so he removed
to Bijaiya (Bougie in Algeria). Here his ways were
extremely unpopular, and he was driven away. He

next settled at Mellala, where he met a boy named
'Abdu l-Mumin al-Kumi (d. 558), a potter's son,
whom he made his disciple and declared to be his
successor. At this time the Murabit dynasty had
fallen from its original puritanism and was distinguished for the wealth and luxury which had been
made possible by the conquest of Spain, and the
splendour and ostentation of the royal family at
Morocco laid it open to criticism. One Friday a
faqir entered the public square where a throne was
made ready for the Emir, and, pushing his way through
the guards who stood round, boldly took his seat upon
the throne and refused to leave. It was the Mahdi
Ibn Tumart, and, so great was the superstitious
reverence accorded to all faqirs, and to him above
all, that none of the guards standing round ventured
to remove him by force. At length the Emir himself
appeared and, finding who had occupied his official
seat, declined to interfere with the redoubtable faqir's
will, but it was privately made plain to Ibn Tumart
that it would be wise for him to leave the city for
a while. The Mahdi therefore retired to Fez, but
soon afterwards returned to Morocco. One day he
met in the streets the Emir's sister, who had adopted
the shameless foreign custom of riding in public
without a veil. The Mahdi stopped her and poured
out a stream of abuse at her for this neglect of
established custom, then, overcome by his indignation,
he pulled her off the beast she was riding. He seems,
however, to have felt some alarm at his own temerity

and fled forthwith to Tinamel, where he openly raised
the standard of revolt against a corrupt and un-
faithful dynasty. At first this rebellion did not
meet with much success, but, after the Mahdi's death,
the leadership fell to his pupil, 'Abdu l-Mumin, who
took Oran, Tlemsen, Fez, Sale, Ceuta, and in 542
became master of Morocco, and in due course seized
all the empire of the Murabits. The new dynasty
established by 'Abdu l-Mumin is known by the name
of the Muwahhids or " Unitarians," a title which the
Spanish historians render by " Almohades," and
their rule endured until 667 A.H. (= 1268 A.D.).

Ibn Tumart professed to be a follower of al-Ghazali,
and introduced his system of orthodox scholasticism
to the West. In canon law he followed the reactionary school of Da'ud az-Zahiri and Ibn Hazm, like
the Murabits who preceded him. To the multitude
he was the champion of Berber nationality ; he
translated the Qur'an into the Berber language, and
caused the call to prayer to be made in Berber instead
of Arabic.

Muwahhid rule introduced a period of bigotry and
of religious persecution. It was under the rule of
this dynasty that we find the Jews leaving the country
in large numbers and migrating to Africa or to
Provence, and many Christians also fled to join the
Castilian forces in the north. Modern historians tend
to condemn the later severities of Christian rulers
towards their Muslim subjects, and often seem to
speak of those subjects as the peaceable and cultured

population which had lived under the Umayyads and the Murabits. But Spain's last experience of the Muslims was of the fierce, bigoted, and persecuting Muwahhids, whose tone was very different. Strangely, however, it was under these intolerant rulers that Spanish Islam passed through its golden age of philosophical speculation, and not only so, but the philosophers were protected and favoured by the Muwahhid court. Quite early in this period the position seems to have been tacitly arranged that the philosophers were absolutely free in their work and teaching, provided that teaching was not spread abroad amongst the populace : it was to be regarded as a species of esoteric truth reserved for the enlightened. It seems almost certain that this attitude was deliberately arranged by the philosophers themselves ; it had already been sketched out by some of the Asiatic writers, and definitely laid down by al-Ash'ari and al-Ghazali, and the Muwahhids, it must be remembered, professed to be Ghazalians. But whilst the philosophers enjoyed this exceptional freedom of speculation, so different from the repressive orthodoxy of the Turkish dynasties in Asia, and defended the system in their writings, the rulers officially were enforcing amongst the multitude of their subjects the severest orthodoxy and the most reactionary system of jurisprudence, so reactionary that it was never admitted by the Asiatic sultans.

The first great leader of philosophical thought in Muwahhid Spain was *Ibn Tufayl* (d. 581 = 1185), who was wazir and court physician under the Muwahhid Abu Yaqub (A.H. 558-580). His teaching was in general conformity with that of Ibn Bajja (Avempace), but the mystic element is much more strongly marked. He admits ecstasy as a means of attaining the highest knowledge and of approaching God. But in Ibn Tufayl's teaching this knowledge differs very much from that aimed at by the Sufis : it is mystic philosophy rather than mystic theology. The beatific vision reveals the Agent Intellect and the chain of causation reaching down to man and then back again to itself.

In his views as to the need of removing the doctrines of philosophy from the multitude he shows the same principles as Ibn Bajja, which are those which came to be recognised as the proper official attitude under the Muwahhids, and defends them in a romance called *Hayy b. Yaqzan*, " the Living One son of the Wakeful," the work by which his name is best remembered. In this story we have the picture of two islands, one inhabited by a solitary recluse who spends his time in contemplation and thereby raises his intellect until he finds that he is able to apprehend the eternal verities which are in the One Active Intellect. The other island is inhabited by ordinary people who are occupied in the commonplace incidents of life and follow the practices of religion in the form known to them. In this way they are content and happy, but fall far short of the complete and perfect happiness of the recluse on the other

island. In course of time the recluse, who is perfectly well aware of the neighbouring island and
its inhabitants, begins to feel great pity for them in
that they are excluded from the more perfect felicity
which he enjoys, and in an honest desire for
their welfare, goes over to them and preaches the
truth as he has found it. For the most part he is
quite unintelligible to them, and the only result is
that he produces confusion, doubt, and controversial
strife amongst those whom he desired to benefit, but
who are incapable of the intellectual life which he
has led. In the end he returns to his island convinced that it is a mistake to interfere with the conventional religion of the multitude.

Ibn Rushd (A.H. 520 = 595), known to the West
as Averroes, was the greatest of the Arabic philosophers, and was practically their last. He was a
native of Cordova and the friend and protégé of Ibn
Tufayl, by whom he was introduced to Abu Ya'qub
in 548. He was, however, more outspoken than Ibn
Tufayl, and wrote several controversial works against
al-Ghazali and his followers. The family to which
he belonged was one whose members usually became
jurists, and Ibn Rushd acted as Qadi in various Spanish
towns; like most of the Arabic philosophers he studied
medicine, and in 578 was appointed court physician
to Abu Ya'qub. By this time he had finished his
career as an author. Under the Muwahhid Abu
Yusuf al-Mansur he was censured as a heretic and
banished from Cordova. It must be remembered

that the Muwahhids, like the Murabits, were really Moroccan rulers, to whom Spain was a foreign province. It was whilst the Emir was in Spain and at Cordova, making ready for an attack upon the Christians, that Ibn Rushd was disgraced, and it seems probable that this was mainly a matter of policy, as the Emir, on the eve of a religious war, was desirous of proving his own strict orthodoxy by the public disapproval of one who had been rather too outspoken in his speculative theories. As soon as the Emir returned to Morocco the order of exile was revoked, and later on Ibn Rushd appears at the court of Morocco, where he died in 595.

Amongst the Muslims Ibn Rushd has not exercised great influence ; it was the Jews who supplied the bulk of his admirers, and they, scattered in Provence and Sicily by Muwahhid persecution, seem to have been chiefly instrumental in introducing him to Latin Christendom.

His chief medical work was known as the *Kulliyat*, " the universal," which, under the Latinized name of " colliget," became popular as a manual in the mediæval universities where the Arabic system of medicine was in use. He wrote also on jurisprudence a text-book of the law of inheritance, which is still extant in MS., and also produced works on astronomy and grammer. He maintained that the task of philosophy was one approved and commended by religion, for the Qur'an shows that God commands men to search for the truth. It is only the prejudice of the

unenlightened which fears freedom of thought,
because for those whose knowledge is imperfect the
truths of philosophy seem to be contrary to religion.
On this topic he composed two theological treatises—
" On the Agreement of Religion with Philosophy "
and " On the Demonstration of Religious Dogmas,"
both of which have been edited by M. J. Mueller.
The popular beliefs he does not accept, but he regards
them as wisely designed to teach morality and to
develop piety amongst the people at large; the
true philosopher allows no word to be uttered against
established religion, which is a thing necessary for
the welfare of the people.   Aristotle he regards as
the supreme revelation of God to man : with it
religion is in total agreement, but as religion is known
to the multitude it only partially discloses Divine
truth and adapts it to the practical needs of the many ;
in religion there is a literal meaning, which is all the
uneducated are able to attain, and there is an
" interpretation," which is the disclosing of deeper
truths beneath the surface which it is not expedient
to communicate to the multitude.   He opposes the
position of Ibn Bajja, who inclined to solitary meditation and avoided the discussion of philosophical
problems ; he admits and desires such discussion
provided it is confined to the educated who are able
to understand its bearing, and not brought before the
multitude who are thereby in danger of having their
simple faith undermined.   He agrees with Ibn Bajja,
however, as against Ibn Tufayl in disapproval of

ecstasy ; such a thing may be, but it is too rare to need serious consideration.

There are different classes of men who fall roughly into three groups. The highest of these are those whose religious belief is based on demonstration (*burhan*), the result of reasoning from syllogisms which are *à priori* certain ; these are the men to whom the philosopher makes his appeal. The lowest stratum contains those whose faith is based on the authority of a teacher or on presumptions which cannot be argued out and are not due to the exercise of pure reason ; it is mischievous to put " demonstration " or reason or controversy before people of this type, for it can only cause them doubt and difficulty. Intermediate between these two strata are those who have not attained the use of pure reason—which, with Ibn Rushd, seems to be simply intuition—but are capable of argument and controversy by means of which their faith can be defended and proved ; " demonstration " proper is not to be laid before these, but it is right to enter into argument with them and to assist them to rise above the level of those whose belief is based only upon authority.

Most of all, Ibn Rushd opposed the teaching of the *mutakallimin* or orthodox scholastic theologians, whom he regarded as subverting the pure principles of the Aristotelian philosophy, and of these he considered the worst to be al-Ghazali, " that renegade of philosophy " His leading controversial work is the *Destruction of the Destruction* (Tahafat at-Tahafat),

which he designed as a refutation of al-Ghazali's
Destruction of the Philosophers.

But it was as a commentator on the text of Aristotle
that he became best known to subsequent generations
amongst the Jews and the later Latin scholastics;
he was the great and final commentator. Strangely,
however, Ibn Rushd never perceived the importance
of reading Aristotle in the original; he had no knowledge of Greek, and gives no sign of supposing that a
study of the Greek text would at all assist a student
of the philosopher. The method of his commentaries
is the time-honoured form derived from the Syriac
commentators: a sentence of the text is given and
the explanatory comments follow.

In main substance Ibn Rushd reproduces the psychology of Aristotle as interpreted by al-Farabi and
Ibn Sina, but with some important modifications.
In man is a passive and an active intellect : the active
intellect is roused to action by the operation of the
Agent Intellect, and thus becomes an acquired intellect; the individual intellects are many, but the Agent
Intellect is but one, though present in each, just as
the sun is one, but there are in action as many suns
as there are bodies which it illuminates. This is the
form of the Aristotelian doctrine as it had been
transmitted through Ibn Sina; the Agent Intellect
is one, but it is as by emanation present in each, so
that the quickening power in each one is part of the
universal Agent Intellect. But Ibn Rushd differs
from his predecessors in his treatment of the passive

intellect, the *'aql hayyulani,* which is the seat of latent
and potential faculties upon which the Agent operates.
In all the earlier systems this passive intellect was
regarded as purely individual and as operated on
by the emanation of the universal Agent, but Ibn
Rushd regarded the passive intellect also as but a
portion of a universal soul and as individual only
in so far as temporarily occupying an individual body.
Even the passive powers are part of a universal
force animating the whole of nature. This is the
doctrine of *pampsychism,* which exercised so strong
an attraction for many of the mediæval scholastics,
and has its adherents at the present day; thus
James (*Principles of Psychology,* p. 346) says: " I
confess that the moment I become metaphysical and
try to define the *more,* I find the notion of some sort
of an *anima mundi* thinking in all of us to be a more
promising hypothesis, in spite of all its difficulties, than
that of a lot of absolutely individual souls." Ibn
Rushd regards Alexander of Aphrodisias as mistaken in
supposing that the passive intellect is a mere dis-
position; it is in us, but belongs to something outside;
it is not engendered, it is incorruptible, and so in a
sense resembles the Agent Intellect. This doctrine
is the very opposite to what is commonly described
as materialism, which represents the mind as merely
a form of energy produced by the activity of the
neural functions. The activity of brain and nerves,
according to Ibn Rushd, are due to the presence of
an external force; not only, as Aristotle teaches,

at least according to Alexander Aph.'s interpretation, is the highest faculty of the reason due to the operation of the external one Agent Intellect, but the passive intellect on which this agent acts is itself part of a great universal soul, which is the one source of all life and the reservoir to which the soul returns when the transitory experience of what we call life is finished.

Ibn Rushd's views do not receive much attention or criticism from Muslim scholars, but the Christian scholastics brought two main arguments against this theory, one psychological, the other theological. The psychological objection is that it is entirely subversive of individuality : if the conscious life of each is only part of the conscious life of a universal soul there can be no real *ego* in any one of us ; but there is no fact to which consciousness bears clearer witness than the reality and individuality of the *ego*. This did not touch the possibility that the individual soul might be drawn from a universal soul as its source, nor did it disprove that the individual soul might be reabsorbed again in the universal soul, but in so far as Ibn Rushd's view represented the soul as throughout a part of the universal soul it was argued that this is contrary to experience, which makes it clear that in this present life the *ego* is very distinctly individual. The theological argument was that Ibn Rushd's view denied the immortality of the soul, and so was contrary to the Christian faith. This objection deals more specifically with the reabsorption of the soul of the individual in the universal soul ; such cessation of separate and individual existence, it was argued, meant that the soul as such no longer existed.

As we have already noted, Aristotle gives a rather narrow range to the highest faculty of reason, confining its activity to the perception of abstract ideas ; " as to the things spoken of as abstract (the mind) thinks of them as it would of the being snub-nosed, if by an effort of thought it thinks of it *qua* snub-nosed, not separately, but *qua* hollow, without the flesh in which the hollowness is adherent : so when it thinks of mathematical forms, it thinks of them as separated, though they are not separated " (Aristot. *de anima.* iii. 7, 7-8). Those who followed Alexander Aph. and the neo-Platonists took this " abstract " in a very narrow sense, and in the Arabic commentators these abstractions even become non-substantial beings, as it were disembodied, or rather bodiless, spirits : " in quibusdam libris de Arabico translatis substantiae separatae, quae nos angelos dicimus, intelligentiae vocantur " (S. Thos. Aquin. *Quaest. Disp. de anima.* 16). Can man know these *substantiae separatae* by his natural faculties ? Ibn Rushd says he can : if otherwise nature has acted in vain, for there would be an *intelligibile* without an *intelligens* to understand it ; but Aristotle has shewn (*Polit.* 1, 8, 12) that nature does nothing in vain, so that if there be an *intelligibile* there must be an *intelligens* capable of perceiving it. " The commentator (i.e. Ibn Rushd) says in 2 Met. comm. i. (in fine) that if abstract substances cannot be understood by us then nature has acted in vain, because it made that which is by nature understandable in itself to be not understood by anyone. But nothing is superfluous or in vain in nature. Therefore immaterial substances can be understood by us." (S. Thos. Aquin. *Summa.* 1, 88.)

As the Agent Intellect enters into communication with relative being it has to suffer the conditions of relativity, and so is not equally efficient in all ; it acts on sensible images as form acts on matter, yet the Agent Intellect never becomes corruptible as that on which it acts.

These are in outline the points in the teaching of Ibn Rushd, which show the most marked differences from that of his predecessors, and which afterwards provoked most controversy amongst the Latin scholastics.

Ibn Rushd really ends the illustrious line of Arabic Aristotelians. A few Aristotelian scholars followed in Spain, but with the decay of the Muwahhid power these came to an end. Of those later scholars we may mention Muhyi ad-Din b. 'Arabi (d. 638) and 'Abdu l-Haqq b. Sab'im (d. 667). The former of these was primarily a Sufi, and shows a strong inclination towards pantheism. 'Abdu l-Haqq, the last of the Muwahhid circle, was also a Sufi, but at the same time an accurate student of Aristotle. In modern Islam there is no Aristotelian scholarship, save only in logic, where Aristotle has always held his own.

CHAPTER X

THE JEWISH TRANSMITTORS

We have already seen that the Jews took a prominent part in bringing a knowledge of philosophical research from Asia to Spain, and Ibn Jabirul (Avencebrol) takes his place in the line of transmission by which Spanish Islam was brought into contact with these studies. This did not end the participation of the Jews in philosophical work, but their subsequent writers do not form part of the regular series of Aristotelian students influencing the Muslim world, but are rather confined to Jewish circles. Yet they are of an importance wider than merely sectarian interests, for it was by means of Jewish disciples of Ibn Rushd that he was raised to a position of much greater importance than he has ever enjoyed in the Muslim world. Amongst the Jews, indeed, there arose a strong Averroist school, which later on was the chief means of introducing Ibn Rushd's theories to Latin scholasticism. As we shall see later the transmission of philosophy from Arabic to Latin surroundings falls into two stages : in the earlier the Arabic material passes directly, and the works used are those which had attained a leading importance in Islam, but in the later stage the Jews were the intermediaries, and thus the choice of text-books and authorities was largely influenced by an existing Jewish scholasticism.

Ibn Jabirul shows the Aristotelian philosophy introduced to Jewish surroundings, just as Sa'id al-Fayyumi in Mesopotamia shows the entrance of Mu'tazilite discussions amongst the Jews. In fact, all the intellectual experiences of the Muslim community were repeated amongst the Jews. In Islam the Mu'tazilites and the philosophers were followed by the scholastics, who took their final form under al-Ghazali, and so in Judaism also al-Ghazali has his parallel.

The founder of an orthodox Jewish scholasticism was the Spanish Jew, *Jehuda hal-Levi* (d. 540 A.H. = 1145 A.D.), who lived during the Murabit rule and the coming of the Muwahhids. His teaching is known by a work entitled *Sefer ha-Kuzari*, which consists of five essays, supposed to be dialogues between the King of the Chazars and a Jewish visitor to his court. These dialogues discuss various topics of a philosophical and political character. The study of philosophy is commended, but it is pointed out that good conduct is not attained by philosophy, which is occupied with scientific investigations, and many of these have no direct bearing upon the duties of practical life; the best means of promoting right conduct is religion, which is the established tradition of wisdom revealed to men of ancient times. Even in speculative matters a surer guidance is often

furnished by religious tradition than by the speculations of philosophers. God created all things from
nothing ; the attempt to explain the presence of
imperfection and evil in the world by the theory of
the eternity of matter, or by the operation of laws of
nature is futile ; those laws themselves must refer
back to God. The difficulty arising from the mingling
of evil with good in creation is admitted ; the real
solution is unknown, but it must be maintained that
creation was the work of God in spite of the difficulties
which this presents.

As to the nature and attributes of God, the distinction which Sa'id al-Fayyumi tried to make
between the essential and other attributes is untenable. The attributes stated in the Old Testament
may be applied to God because they are revealed,
which is exactly the same teaching as that of al-
Ash'ari and al-Ghazali. These attributes are either
referring to active qualities, or to relative, or to
negative. Those which are active and those which
are relative are used metaphorically; we do not
know their real significance.

The fifth essay is more especially directed against
the philosophers as teaching doctrines subversive of
revelation. In the first place he disapproves the
theory of emanations ; the work of creation was
directly performed by God without any intermediary ;
if there were emanations, why did they stop short at
the lunar sphere ? This refers to the descriptions
given by the Arabic writers who endeavour to explain

the successive emanations from the First Cause as reaching down to different spheres. He opposes also the attempt of the Mutakallimin to reconcile philosophy and theology as tending to undermine the truths of revealed religion, so that he takes a more reactionary position than al-Ghazali. This was inevitable, for Jewish thought had as yet been much less influenced by philosophy than was the case with the Muslims. He objects also to the description of the soul as intellect, more it would appear because common usage confined " intellectual activity " too much to philosophical speculation, and especially he protested against the implication that only souls of philosophers were finally united to the Agent Intellect. The soul of man is a spiritual substance and imperishable ; it does not win immortality by intellectual activity but is necessarily immortal by its own nature. He admits, however, that the passive soul in man is influenced by the Agent Intellect, which he seems to regard as the wisdom of God personified. Generally, therefore, Hal-Levi defined Jewish orthodoxy as against the teachings of the philosophers : he recognises the force of philosophical speculation, but is himself distinctly conservative. God was literally the creator, and no philosophical definition of creation which tended to explain it otherwise than according to traditional belief was permissible. But Hal-Levi does not seem to have had any great influence outside Judaism, and his work rather tends to show how far Jewish thought of the 6th cent. of

the Hijra was out of sympathy with current philosophical speculation, though no longer ignorant of
it.

It was in Spain that the Jews especially
distinguished themselves as physicians, reproducing
and extending the investigations of the Arabic authorities, who were pupils of the Nestorians and Jews in
the first place. The most distinguished of these
Spanish Jews who became leaders in medical science
was *Ibn Zuhr* (d. 595 A.H. = 1199 A.D.), commonly
known to the mediæval West as " Avenzoar." He
was a native of Seville and member of a family of
physicians. Jewish philosophy does not take a
leading place until the appearance of *Abu Imran
Moses b. Maymun b. 'Abdullah* (d. 601 A.H. =1204
A.D.), a contemporary and follower of Ibn Rushd and
the one who did most to establish an Averroist school,
and so passed on his work and influence to Latin
Christendom. He was the son of a pupil of Hal-Levi,
and, it is said, a pupil of one of Ibn Bajja's pupils.
His family retired to Africa to avoid the persecution
of the Muwahhids and settled for a time in Fez, then
removed to Egypt. It was whilst he was at Cairo
that Ibn Maymun, or Maimonides as he is more
commonly called by European writers, first heard
of Ibn Rushd.

His chief work is known as *Dalalat al-Ha'irin*, "the
Guide of the Perplexed," which, like all his other
books, was produced in Arabic; about the time of
his death this work was translated into Hebrew by

Samuel b. Tibbon as *Moreh Nebukin*. The Arabic
text, edited by Munk, was published at Paris (3 vols.)
in 1856-66, and in 1884 an English translation by
Friedländer was published in London. Next to this
in importance is the treatise *Maqalah fi-t-Tawhid*,
a treatise on the unity of God, of which a Hebrew
translation was made in the 14th cent. A.D. His
other works were mainly medical, and include
treatises " on poisons and their antidotes," " on
hæmorrhoids," " on asthma," and a commentary
on Hippocrates.

Maimonides' teaching reproduces the substance of
that already associated with al-Farabi and Ibn Sina
put into a Jewish form. God is the Intellect, the
ens intelligens, and the *intelligibile* : He is the
necessary First Cause and the permanent source. He
is essentially and necessarily one, and attributes cannot
be so used as to imply plurality : only those attributes
which describe activity are admissible, not those
which imply relations between God and the creature.
Like Ibn Rushd he disapproves of the Mutakallimin,
whom he regards as mere opportunists in their
philosophy and without any staple principles, besides
which their method of compromise does not face
fairly the law of causality. The Aristotelian doctrine of the eternity of matter cannot, however, be
admitted ; creation must have been from nothing, as
follows from the law of causality ; that such was
the case cannot be proved, but every contrary
supposition is untenable. All the properties of

matter, the laws of nature, etc., had their beginning
at creation. On the first day God created the beginnings (*reshit*), that is to say the intelligences, from
which proceeded the several spheres, and introduced
movement, so that on this day the whole universe
and all its contents came into existence. On the
succeeding days these contents were disposed in order
and developed ; then on the seventh day God rested,
which means that He ceased from active operation
and laid the universe under the control of natural
laws, which guided it henceforth.

The teaching of Maimonides shows a somewhat
modified form of the system already developed by
al-Farabi and Ibn Sina adapted to Jewish beliefs.
It had a rapid and wide success, spreading through
the greater part of the Jewish community in his own
lifetime. But this success was not without some
opposition—the synagogues of Aragon, Catalonga,
and of Provence, where a very large number of Jews
had sought refuge from the Muwahhids ; the synagogue at Narbonne, on the other hand, defended him.
It was not until the following century, and chiefly
by the efforts of David Kimchi, that Maimonides
was at length generally accepted as the leading doctor
of the Jewish church.

Although Maimonides was known to the Latin
scholastics, it was not his work nor that of any other
Jewish teacher which really made the Jews important
to mediæval western thought so much as the work
they did in popularising Ibn Rushd, whom they

called "the soul and intelligence of Aristotle."
Jewish MSS. of Aristotle are rarely found without
Ibn Rushd's commentary, and his paraphrases
very commonly bear the name of Aristotle at their
head. It was as the commentator that he held so
high a position in Jewish thought, and it was as the
final and authoritative commentator that he finally
took his place in Latin scholasticism introduced by
Jewish teachers.

The Muwahhid persecution scattered many of the
Spanish Jews to Africa and to Provence and Lan-
guedoc. Those who took refuge in Africa, like Maimonides, retained the use of the Arabic language,
but Arabic quickly became obsolete amongst those
who had fled north. No doubt the refugees in
Provence found it necessary to use the Provencal
dialect for communication with their Christian neighbours, but that dialect had never yet been used for
scientific or philosophical purposes; in Western
Christendom Latin was invariably used for all educational and scholarly purposes, but the refugee Jews
did not feel disposed to adopt a language which had
no traditional associations for them and was altogether
a foreign tongue never as yet employed for Jewish
purposes. Under these circumstances the Jewish
leaders deliberately copied the actual condition
prevailing amongst their Jewish neighbours where
the ancient Latin was in use as a learned language,
whilst its derived dialects were the speech in every-
day use, and so they revived the use of Hebrew as

the medium of teaching and literature. Throughout
Hebrew had retained its place as a liturgical language ;
there had been synagogue liturgies in Greek, but
those belonged to a much earlier period. The revival
of Hebrew produced a neo-Hebrew which does not
preserve a line of historical continuity with the
ancient Hebrew. For some time Hebrew had been
a dead language in the East, and it had never spread
as a living speech to the West. But this artificial
revival, which has more than one parallel in history,
was not so difficult a feat as it sounds at first. The
vernacular speech of the Spanish Jew was Arabic,
and philologically Arabic is very nearly a dialect
if not of Arabic, yet at least of a proto-Arabic, which
shows many close parallels with Hebrew. Of course
at that time the true philological relations were not
understood : influenced by theological prepossessions
the Jew rather tended to regard Arabic as a derivative
of Hebrew ; yet the kinship was obvious, and in the
early translations made from Arabic to Hebrew it is
not uncommon to find that most of the words are
translated in such a way that the same root-form is
used as in the original. Secondly, it was not only
the case that Hebrew " came easily " to those who
knew Arabic, but there had been serious philological
studies by Jehudh Chayyug, David Kimchi, and others
which had emphasized this close kinship, and had
indeed adapted all the rules of Arabic grammar to the
use of Hebrew ; it was therefore possible to compose
and even to speak a tolerable Hebrew by the con-

scious rendering of the Arabic vocabulary into
Hebrew. It is not suggested that the inaugurators
of neo-Hebrew ignored the characteristics of the
classical speech ; in fact they did not do so, but they
were in a position to use Hebrew as though a dialect
differing from Arabic only in detail, and in this
attitude they were more strictly correct than they
supposed. Before long Arabic began to be entirely
discarded, and Hebrew, whose revival flattered
Jewish susceptibilities, was taken up with vigour as a
language of the schools ; how far it came into use in
the home we do not know.

This change necessitated the translation of the
later theological and philosophical writers from Arabic
into Hebrew. Tradition puts the beginning of this
work of translation in the 12th century, but this is
not possibly true. It was not until well into the
13th century that Hebrew translations begin to appear.
The most famous translators were of the family of
Jehuda ben Tibbon, who cannot himself be accepted
as a translator. The first work was done by Samuel
ben Tibbon, who compiled a Hebrew " Opinions of
the Philosophers," which is a catena of passages
from Ibn Rushd and other Muslim *falasifah*. This
production was in general use as a popular manual
until it was replaced by complete translations of the
actual texts, when, of course, such compilations went
out of use. The principal part of the work was done
by Moses ben Tibbon (circ. 1260 A.D.), who translated
most of the commentaries of Ibn Rushd, some portions

of his medical works, and Maimonides' "Guide of the Perplexed." About this time Frederick II. was strongly desirous of introducing the Arabic writers to the knowledge of the West, a matter to which we shall refer again when we come to consider the translation of the Arabic philosophical works into Latin, and so we find him protecting and pensioning Yaqub ben Abba Mari, a son-in-law of Samuel ben Tibbon, at Naples, and this Yaqub employed in preparing a Hebrew translation of Ibn Rushd's commentaries on the Aristotelian Organon.

The thirteenth century A.D. shows us a continuous series of Hebrew scholars either preparing compilations and abridgments or actually translating the full text of the leading Arabic philosophers, and especially of Ibn Rushd. About 1247 Jehuda ben Salomo Cohen, of Toledo, published his Hebrew "Search for Wisdom," an encyclopædia of Aristotelian doctrines mainly based upon the teachings of Ibn Rushd. A little later Shem-Tov b. Yusuf b. Falaquera also reproduced the doctrines of Ibn Rushd in his essays, and later again in the 13th century Gerson b. Salomo compiled "The Door of Heaven," which shows the same influence.

About 1257 Solomon b. Yusuf b. Aiyub, a refugee who had come from Granada to Bèziers, translated the text of Ibn Rushd's commentary on the *de coelo* and *de mundo*, and in the latter part of this century complete translations begin to take the place of abridgments and collections of extracts. About

1284 Zerachia ben Isaac from Barcelona translated Ibn Rushd's commentaries on the *Physics*, the *Mataphysics*, and the treatises *de coelo* and *de mundo*. Rènan has drawn attention to the fact that the same works are translated again and again, sometimes by translators who were very nearly contemporary and lived in the same neighbourhood. Evidently these translations did not quickly enter into wide circulation, and it does not seem that the task of the translator was held in any great esteem ; it was regarded as a purely mechanical work, and not credited with any literary possibilities.

Early in the 14th century Kalonymos b. Kalonymos b. Meir translated Ibn Rushd's commentaries on the *Topica*, *Sophistica*, and *analytica Posteriora* (completed 1314) ; then his commentaries on the *Physica*, *Mataphysics*, *de coelo* and *de mundo*, *de generatione* and *de corruptione*, and the *Meteora* (completed 1317), and followed these by a translation of the *Destruction of the Destruction*. An independent Hebrew translation of this latter work was made about the same time by Kalonymos b. David b. Todros. About 1321 Rabbi Samuel ben Jehuda ben Meshullam at Marseilles prepared Hebrew versions of Ibn Rushd's commentaries on the Nichomachæan Ethics and his paraphrase of the Republic of Plato, which was regarded by the Arabic writers as part of the Aristotelian canon. It is rather interesting to note that somewhere about the same time Juda ben Moses ben Daniel of Rome prepared a Hebrew translation of *de substantia orbis* from the Latin translation which was itself derived from the Arabic. To a great extent the Hebrew and Latin translations were being made contemporaneously but quite independently ; it was not until well into the 14th century that they begin to influence one another. It was during this later stage that so many of the Arabic philosophical works were translated into Latin via Hebrew, and this gave a marked preponderance to Ibn Rushd, the result of the Jewish vogue of his writings ; the earlier translations into Latin from the Arabic rather tend to lay weight on Ibn Sina.

In the course of the 14th century A.D. the Hebrew commentators on Ibn Rushd begin. Chief amongst these was Lavi ben Gerson, of Bagnols, who wrote a commentary on Ibn Rushd's *Ittisal* on the doctrine of the union of the soul with the Agent Intelligence, and on Ibn Rushd's treatise " on the substance of the world." Levi's teaching reproduces the Arabic Aristotelianism much more freely and frankly than was ventured by Maimonides ; he admits the eternity of the world, the primal matter he describes as substance without form, and creation meant only the impress of form on this formless substance.

Contemporary with Levi was Moses of Narbonne, who, between 1340 and 1350, produced commentaries on the same works of Ibn Rushd as had already been treated by Levi, as well as other of the treatises on physical science.

The fourteenth century was the golden age of

Jewish scholasticism and the following century sees it in its decay. Ibn Rushd was still studied and commentaries were still compiled. About 1455 Joseph ben Shem-Tob of Segovia produced a commentary on Aristotle's *Ethics* which he intended to supplement Ibn Rushd, who had not written a commentary on this portion of Aristotle. Elias del Medigo, who taught at Padua towards the end of the 15th century, is regarded by Rènan as the last great Jewish Averroist. He wrote a commentary on the *de substantia orbis* in 1485, and also published annotations on Averroes.

The 16th century shows the final decay of Jewish Averroism. In 1560 an abridgment of the logic of Averroes was published at Riva di Trento, and this has remained a standard work amongst Jews, but outside logic Averroes was beginning to fall into disrepute. Rabbi Moses Almosnino (circ. 1538) uses al-Ghazali's work against the philosophers to oppose Ibn Rushd, and evidences occur of an interest in Plato by those who despised Aristotle as a relic of the dark ages. The later Jewish philosophers such as Spinoza are not in touch with the mediæval tradition, whose continuity is severed towards the end of the 16th century; later work shows the influence of post-renascence non-Jewish thought.

CHAPTER XI

INFLUENCE OF THE ARABIC PHILOSOPHERS ON LATIN SCHOLASTICISM

We have now followed the way in which Hellenistic philosophy was passed from the Greeks to the Syrians, from the Syrians to the Arabic-speaking Muslims, and was by the Muslims carried from Asia to the far West. We have now to consider the way in which it was handed on from these Arabic-speaking people to the Latins. The first contact of the Latins with the philosophy of the Muslims was in Spain, as might be expected. At that time, that is to say during the Middle Ages, we can rightly describe the Western parts of Europe as " Latin," since Latin was used not only in the services of the church but as a means of teaching and as a means of intercourse between the educated ; it does not imply that the vernacular speech in all the western lands was of Latin origin, and of course makes no suggestion of a " Latin race " ; it refers only to a cultural group, and we are employing the term " Latin " only to denote those who shared a civilization which may fairly be described as of Latin origin. In Spain this Latin culture was in contact with the Arabic culture of the Muslims. The transmission of Arabic material to Latin is

especially associated with Raymund, who was Archbishop of Toledo from 1130 to 1150 A.D.　Toledo had
become part of the kingdom of Castile in 1085, during
the disordered period just before the Murabit invasion.
It had been captured by Alfonso VI., and he had made
it the capital city of his kingdom, and the Archbishop
of Toledo became the Primate of Spain.　When the
town was taken it was agreed that the citizens should
have freedom to follow their own religion, but the
year after its capture the Christians forcibly seized
the great church, which had been converted into a
congregational mosque about 370 years before, and
restored it to Christian use.　For the most part,
however, the Muslims lived side by side with the
Christians in Toledo, and their presence in the same
city as the king, the royal court, and the Primate
made a considerable impression on their neighbours,
who began to take some interest in the intellectual
life of Islam during the following years.　The Archbishop Raymund desired to make the Arabic philosophy available for Christian use.　At the moment, it
will be remembered, the Muwahhids were established
in Spain, and their bigotry caused a number of the
Jews and Christians to take refuge in the surrounding
countries.

Raymund founded a college of translators at
Toledo, which he put in the charge of the archdeacon
Dominic Gondisalvi, and entrusted it with the duty
of preparing Latin translations of the most important
Arabic works on philosophy and science, and thus

many translations of the Arabic versions of Aristotle and of the commentaries as well as of the abridgments of al-Farabi and Ibn Sina were produced.
The method employed in this college and the method
commonly followed in the Middle Ages was to use the
services of an interpreter, who simply placed the
Latin word over the Arabic words of the original, and
finally the Latinity was revised by the presiding
clerk, the finished translation usually bearing the
name of the revisor.   It was an extremely mechanical
method, and the interpreter was treated as of minor
importance. It seems that the preparation of a
translation was done to order in very much the same
way as the copying of a text, and was not regarded as
more intellectual than the work of transcription.
The revisor did no more than see that the sentences
were grammatical in form : the structure and syntax
was still Arabic, and was often extremely difficult for
the Latin reader to understand, the more so as the
more troublesome words were simply transliterated
from the Arabic.   The interpreters employed in this
college certainly included some Jews ; it is known
that one of them bore the name of John of Seville.
We have very little information as to the circulation
of the translations made at Toledo, but it is certain
that about thirty years afterwards the whole text
of Aristotle's logical Organon was in use in Paris,
and this was not possible so long as the Latin translations were limited to those which had been transmitted by Boethius, John Scotus, and the fragments

of Plato derived through St. Augustine. But this material already in the possession of the West was the foundation of scholasticism, and was developed as far as it would go. Boethius transmitted a Latin version of Porphyry's *Isagoge* and of the *Categories* and *Hermeneutics* of Aristotle, whilst John Scotus translated the Pseudo-Dionysius. The further development of Latin scholasticism came in three stages : first, the introduction of the rest of the text of Aristotle, as well as the scientific works of the whole logical canon, by translation from the Arabic ; then came translations from the Greek following the capture of Constantinople in 1204 ; and thirdly, the introduction of the Arabic commentators.

The first Latin scholastic writer who shows a knowledge of the complete logical Organon was John of Salisbury (d. 1182 A.D.), who was a lecturer at Paris, but it does not appear that the metaphysical and phychological works of Aristotle were in circulation as yet.

By this time Paris had become the centre of scholastic philosophy, which was now beginning to predominate theology. This takes its form, as yet untouched by Arabic methods, in the work of Peter Lombard (d. 1160 A.D.), whose " Sentences," an encyclopædia of the controversies of the time but a mere compilation, remained a popular book down to the 17th century. The methods and form used in the " Sentences " shows the influence of Abelard, and still more of the Decretals of Gratian. It is interesting to note that Peter Lombard possessed and used a newly finished translation of St. John Damascene.

Early in the 13th century we find various controversies at Paris on subjects very like those debated by the Arabic philosophers, but in reality derived from quite independent sources. Nothing would seem more suggestive of Arabic influence than discussion of the essential unity of souls, which seems as though it were an echo of Ibn Rushd; but this doctrine had been developed independently from neo-Platonic material in the Celtic church, and, in its main features not at all unlike the teaching of Ibn Rushd, was fairly common in Ireland (cf. Rènan : *Averroes*, 132-133). So we find Ratramnus of Corbey in the 9th century writing against one Macarius in refutation of similar views. Here Arabic influence is out of the question; at the time, indeed, Ibn Rushd was not yet born. So of Simon of Tournay, who was a teacher of theology at Paris about 1200 A.D., we read that " whilst he follows Aristotle too closely, he is by some recent writers accused of heresy " (Henry of Gand : *Lib. de script. eccles. c.* 24 in Fabrisius *Bibliotheca*, 2, p. 121), but this simply means that he carried to an extreme the application of the dialectical method to theology.

More interest attaches to the decrees passed at a synod held at Paris in 1209 and endorsed by the decisions of the Papal Legate in 1215. These measures were provoked by the pantheistic teaching of David of Dinant and Amalric of Bena, who revived the semi-

pantheistic doctrines of John Scotus' *Periphysis*, and
the prohibitions dealing with them cite passages from
Scotus verbatim.   The *Periphysis* itself was condemned by Honorius III. in 1225.   But the decrees
of 1209 also forbade the use of Aristotle's Natural
Philosophy and the " commenta," whilst the Legate's
orders of 1215 allowed the logical works of the old
and new translations where perhaps the " new
translations " refers to the " new " translations made
from the Arabic as contrasted with the " old "
versions of Boethius, though it is just possible that
some version direct from the Greek was in circulation and known as the " new translations," and also
forbade the reading of the Metaphysics, Natural
Philosophy, etc., all material which had become
accessible through the Arabic.

In 1215 Frederick II. became Emperor, and in
1231 he began to reorganize the kingdom of Sicily.
Both in Sicily and in the course of his crusading
expeditions in the East Frederick had been brought
into close contact with the Muslims and was greatly
attracted to them.   He adopted oriental costume and
many Arabic customs and manners, but, most important of all, he was a great admirer of the Arabic
philosophers, whose works he was able to read in the
original, as he was familiar with German, French,
Italian, Latin, Greek, and Arabic.   Contemporary
historians represent him as a free-thinker, who regarded
all religions as equally worthless, and attributed to
him the statement that the world had suffered from

three great imposters, Moses, Christ, and Muhammad.
This opinion of Frederick is expressed in passionate
words by Gregory IX. in the encyclical letter " ad
omnes principes et prelatos terrae " (in Mansi.
xxiii. 79), where he compares the Emperor to the blas-
pheming beast of Apocalypse xiii., but Frederick in
reply likened the Pope to the beast described in Apoc.
vi., " the great dragon which reduced the whole world,"
and professed a perfectly orthodox attitude towards
Moses, Christ, and Muhammad.   It is quite probable,
as Rènan (*Averroes*, p. 293) supposes, that the views
ascribed to Frederick really are based on a professed
sympathy towards the Arabic philosophers, who
regarded all religions as equally tolerable for the
uninstructed multitude, and commonly illustrated
their remarks by citing the " three laws " which were
best known to them.   In 1224 Frederick founded a
university at Naples, and made it an academy for the
purpose of introducing Arabic science to the western
world, and there various translations were made
from Arabic into Latin and into Hebrew.   By his
encouragement Michael Scot visited Toledo about
1217 and translated Ibn Rushd's commentaries on
Aristotle's *de coelo et de mundo*, as well as the first part
of the *de anima*.   It seems probable also that he was
the translator of commentaries on the *Meteora*, *Parva
Naturalia*, *de substantia orbis*, *Physics*, and *de generatione et de corruptione*.   Ibn Sina's commentaries
were in general circulation before this, so that they
were very probably the " commentaries " referred

to in the Paris decree of 1209, but we do not know who
was responsible for their rendering into Latin, save
that they almost certainly proceeded from the college
at Toledo.   The introduction of Ibn Rushd, not of
great repute amongst the Muslims, bears evidence to
the weight of Jewish influence in Sicily and in the
new academy at Naples. We know that Michael
Scot was assisted by a Jew named Andrew.

Another translator of this period was a German
Hermann who was in Toledo about 1256, after
Frederick's death.   He translated the abridgment
of the Rhetoric made by al-Farabi, Ibn Rushd's
abridgment of the Poetics, and other less known
works of Aristotle. Hermann's translations were
described by Roger Bacon as barbarous and hardly
intelligible ; he transliterated the names so as to
show even the tanwin in Ibn Rosd*in*, abi Nasr*in*, etc.

By the middle of the 13th century nearly all the
philosophical works of Ibn Rushd were translated
into Latin, except the commentary on the Organon,
which came a little later, and the *Destruction of the
Destruction*, which was not rendered into Latin until
the Jew Calonymos did so in 1328.   Some of his
medical works also were translated in the 13th
century, namely, the *Colliget*, as it was called, and the
treatise *de formatione ;* others were translated from
the Hebrew into Latin early in the following century.

The first evidence of the general circulation of
ideas taken from Averroes (Ibn Rushd) is associated
with William of Auvergne, who was Bishop of Paris,

and these show a considerable amount of inaccuracy in detail. In 1240 William published censures against certain opinions, which he states to be derived from the Arabic philosophers; amongst these he expresses his disapproval of the doctrine of the First Intelligence, an emanation from God, as being the agent of creation, a doctrine common to all the philosophers, but which he attributes specifically to al-Ghazali; he objects also to the teaching that the world is eternal, which he attributes correctly to Aristotle and Ibn Sina, but mentions Averroes as an orthodox defender of the truth; he further condemns the doctrine of the unity of intellects, which most incorrectly he attributes to Aristotle, and also refers to al-Farabi as maintaining this heresy; throughout he cites Averroes as a sounder teacher who tends to correct these ideas, but his description of the doctrine of the unity of intellects reproduces the features which are distinctive of Averroes. The arguments he uses against this latter doctrine are, on the whole, very much the same as those employed a little later by Albertus Magnus and St. Thomas, viz., that the doctrine undermines the reality of the individual personality, and is inconsistent with the observed facts of diversity of intelligence in different persons. He cites Abubacer (Ibn Bajja) as a commentator on Aristotle's *Physics*, but in fact this was a book on which Ibn Bajja did not write a commentary, and the substance of the citation agrees with the teaching of Averroes. At that time evidently the position was that Aristotle and the Arabic commentators generally were regarded with suspicion save in the treatment of logic, the one exception being Averroes, who was considered to be perfectly orthodox. So strange a perversion of the facts could only be due to Jewish influence, for the Jews at that time were devoted adherents of Averroes.

When the friars began to take their place in the work of the universities we note two striking changes : (i.) the friars cut loose entirely from the timid policy of conservatism and begin to make free use of all the works of Aristotle and of the Arabic commentators, and also make efforts to procure newer and more correct translations of the Aristotelian text from the original Greek ; under this leadership the universities gradually became more modern and enterprising in their scientific work, though not without evidence of strong opposition in certain quarters. (ii.) As a natural corollary a more correct appreciation was made of the tendencies of the several commentators.

The leader in these newer studies was the Franciscan Alexander Hales (d. 1245), who was the first to make free use of Aristotle outside the logical Organon. His *Summa*, which was left unfinished and continued by the Franciscan William of Melitona, was based on the *Sentences* of Peter Lombard, and serves as a commentary to it. Peter Lombard, however, had not quoted Aristotle at all, whilst Alexander uses the metaphysical and scientific works as well as the logic.

From this time forth the Franciscans begin to use the Arabic commentators.

The more accurate study of Aristotle in mediæval scholasticism begins with Albertus Magnus (1206-1280), the Dominican friar who first really perceived the importance of careful and critical versions of the text, and thus introduced a strictly scientific standard of method. He studied at Padua, a daughter university of Bologna, but became a Dominican in 1223. His methods were followed and developed by his pupil, St. Thomas Aquinas (d. 1274), who arranged his work on the lines already indicated in Albertus' commentary on Aristotle's *Politics*, lines which became the regulation method in Latin scholastic writers, and he was at pains to get new translations made directly from the Greek, which was now freely accessible ; a new translation direct from the Greek was made by William de Moerbeka at the request of St. Thomas. But there is a significant change from the time when Albertus delivered his lectures : in the work of Albertus the commentator chiefly used was Ibn Sina, but in that of St. Thomas there is a free use of Averroes (Ibn Rushd), although St. Thomas shows that he is perfectly well aware of the peculiar doctrines held by this latter philosopher, and guards himself carefully from them.

St. Thomas frequently enters into controversy with the Arabic commentators, and especially attacks the doctrines (i.) that there was a primal indefinite matter to which form was given at creation (cf.

Summa. lae quaes. 66, art. 2) ; (ii.) that there were successive series of emanations, a doctrine which had now assumed an astrological character ; (iii.) that the Agent Intellect was the intermediary in creation (cf. Summa. 1, 45, 5 ; 47, 1 ; 90, 1) ; (iv.) that creation *ex nihilo* is impossible ; (v.) that there is not a special providence ruling and directing the world ; and (vi.) most of all, the doctrine of the unity of intellects, a doctrine which, as he shows, is not to be found in Aristotle, Alexander of Aphrodisias, Avicenna, or Ghazali, but is a speculative theory of Averroes alone, at least in the form then becoming popular as pampsychism. All these objections were essentially the same as had been already brought forward by the orthodox scholastics of Islam, and undoubtedly al-Ghazali is used in refuting them. According to St. Thomas, the doctrine of pampsychism is entirely subversive of human personality and of the separate individuality of the *ego*, to which our own consciousness bears witness. God creates the soul for each child as it is born ; it is no emanation, but has a separate and distinct personality. As a corollary he denies the *ittisal* or final " union," which involves the reabsorption of the soul in its source.

It is worth noting that St. Thomas received his education before joining the Dominican order in the university of Naples, which had been founded by Frederick II. and was a centre of interest in the Arabic philosophers, and this probably goes far to

account for his more accurate appreciation of their
teaching. Unquestionably St. Thomas Aquinas
must be regarded as the prince of the Latin scholastics,
for it is he who first draws freely upon metaphysics
and psychology and co-ordinates them with theology
—the psychological analysis given in the *Secunda
secundae* of the Summa is one of the best products
of the Latin scholastics—and also he was the first to
appreciate correctly the difficulties of translation and
insist on an accurate rendering as essential to an
understanding of Aristotle. For the most part, as
we have noted, the mediæval scholars undervalued
the translator's task and were content with a hack
interpreter, and saw no reason for applying themselves to the study of the original test, a view in
which the Arabic philosophers shared. Incidentally
St. Thomas was the first who makes free use of all
the Arabic commentators and shows that he is fully
aware of their defects. Undoubtedly he regarded
Averroes as the best exponent of the Aristotelian
text and the supreme master in logic, but heretical
in his metaphysics and psychology.

About 1256 Averroes' teaching about the unity of
intelligences was sufficiently widespread at Paris to
induce Albertus to write his treatise " On the unity
of the intellect against the Averroists," a treatise
which he afterwards inserted in his Summa. In
1269 certain propositions from Averroes were formally condemned. At this time his works were well
known, and there was a distinct party at Paris which

had adopted his views and which we may describe as a semi-Judaistic party. This time both Albertus and St. Thomas published treatises against the doctrine of the unity of intelligences.

Again in 1277 various Averroist theses were condemned at Paris, for the most part emanating from the Franciscans, who, as Bacon notes (opus Tert. 23), were strongly inclined towards Averroes both at Paris and in England, a condition which prevailed until the great Franciscan doctor Duns Scotus (d. 1308) took a definitely anti-Averroist line. Still, even in the 14th century, when Averroism was practically dead at Paris, it still retained its hold amongst the Franciscans in the English " nation."

The Dominicans were less favourably disposed towards the Arabic writers, at least after the time of Albertus, and show a much more careful estimate of their work. This was no doubt due to the fact that they had a house of Arabic studies in Spain, and were actually engaged in controversy with the Muslims. As a rule a careful distinction is drawn between Averroes the commentator, who is treated with great respect as an exponent of the text of Aristotle, and Averroes the philosopher, who is regarded as heretical. It seems as though there was a deliberate policy to secure Aristotle by sacrificing the Arabic commentators. Very characteristic of the work of the Dominicans was the *Pugio Fidei adversum Mauros et Judaeos* of Raymund Martini, who lived in Aragon and Provence ; he was familiar with Hebrew, and freely uses the Hebrew translations of the Arabic philosophers. His arguments are largely borrowed from al-Ghazali's *Destruction of the Philosophers*. It is curious to note that, in his anxiety to defend Aristotle, he accuses Averroes of borrowing the doctrine of the unity of intelligences from Plato, and in a sense there was an element of truth in this, for the Averroist doctrine was ultimately derived from neo-Platonic sources. Raymund also cites the medical teaching of Averroes at a date earlier than any Latin version, and here again shows familiarity with the Hebrew translations.

John Baconthorp (d. 1346), the provincial of the English Carmelites and " doctor " of the Carmelite order, tends to palliate the heretical tendencies of Averroes' teaching, and was called by his contemporaries " the prince of Averroists," a title which was apparently regarded as a compliment.

Amongst the Augustinian friars Giles of Rome in his *de Erroribus Philosophorum* was an opponent of the teaching of Averroes, especially attacking the doctrine of the unity of souls and the union or *ittisal*, but Paul of Venice (d. 1429), of the same order, shows a tendency favourable to Averroism in his *Summa*.

The 13th century had generally used Ibn Sina (Avicenna) as a commentator on Aristotle, but in the 14th century the general tendency was to prefer Averroes, who was regarded as the leading exponent of the Aristotelian text even by those who disapproved his teaching.

The University of Montpelier as a centre of medical
studies might be expected to use the Arabic authorities,
but this university, though traditionally founded by
Arabic physicians driven out of Spain, was re-founded
as a distinctly ecclesiastical institution in the 13th
century, and became the home of Greek medical
studies based on Galen and Hippocrates, though
probably the earlier texts in use were translated
from the Arabic versions. To this more wholesome
Greek character the university remained faithful,
and there was always a tendency at Montpelier to
regard the Arabic use of talismans and astrology in
medicine as heretical. It was not until the beginning
of the 14th century that the Arabic medical writers
began to be used there at all, and they remained in
quite a secondary rank. In 1304 Averroes' *Canones
de medicinis laxativis* was translated from the Hebrew,
and in 1340 we find that i. and iv. of the *Canons*
of Avicenna are included in the official syllabus set
for candidates for medical degrees, and from this
time forward the lectures include courses on the Arabic
physicians. In 1567 the Arabic medical works were
definitely struck off the list of books required for
examination in the schools at the petition of the
students, but occasional lectures on the *Canons* of
Avicenna were given down to 1607.

The real home of Averroism was the University
of Bologna, with its sister University of Padua, and
from these two centres an Averroist influence spread
over all N.E. Italy, including Venice and Ferrara,

and so continued until the 17th century. It was a precursor of the rationalism and anti-church feeling of the renascence, perhaps assisted by Venetian contact with the East. At Bologna Arabic influence was predominant in medicine ; already in the later 13th century the medical course centres in the *Canon* of Avicenna and the medical treatises of Averroes, with the result that astrology became a regular subject of study, and degrees were granted in it. Most of the physicians of Bologna and Padua were astrologers, and were generally regarded as free-thinkers and heretics. Bologna had at one time enjoyed the favour of Frederick II., and he had presented the University with copies of the Latin translations prepared by his order from Arabic and Greek.

The " Great Commentary " was firmly established at Padua, and in 1334 the Servite friar Urbano de Bologna published a commentary on the commentary of Averroes, which was printed in 1492 by order of the general of the Servites. But it is Gaetano of Tiena (d. 1465), a canon of the cathedral at Padua, who is generally regarded as the founder of Paduan Averroism. He was less bold in his statements than the Augustinian Paul of Venice, but still quite definitely an Averroist in his teaching as to the Agent Intellect and the unity of souls, etc. He seems to have had a great popularity, as many copies of his lectures survive. This Averroist cult in Padua held good through the greater part of the 15th century.

Towards the end of the century, however, the reaction begins, and comes from two distinct sources. On one side Pomponat lectured at Padua on the *de anima*, but interprets it by the aid of Alexander of Aphrodisias and discards Averroes, setting forth his doctrines in the form of essays instead of the time-honoured commentary on the Aristotelian text. From this time (circ. 1495) the university of Padua was divided into two factions, the Averroists and the Alexandrians. Pomponat was at the same time a representative of more distinctly rationalist theories, towards which the Italian mind was then tending. It was not that Alexander was more difficult to reconcile with the Christian faith than Averroes, but that those whose scepticism was inclined to be more freely expressed took advantage of these new methods of interpretation to give free vent to their own opinions. Quite independent of these Alexandrians were the humanists proper, who objected most to the barbarous Latinity of the text-books in general use, and especially to the terminology employed in the translations made from the Arabic commentators. Representative of these was Thomæus, who about 1497 began to lecture at Padua on the Greek text of Aristotle, and to treat it very largely as a study of the Greek language and literature.

Philosophical controversy at this time was centred chiefly in the psychological problems connected with the nature of the soul, and especially with its separate existence and the prospects of immortality. This indeed was perceived to be a crucial problem of religion and was very keenly debated. In the early years of the 16th century the controversy became even more prominent, until the Lateran Council of 1512 tried to check such discussions and passed a a formal condemnation, which, however, was powerless to restrain the debates. It is to be noticed that these discussions did not arise from any philo-pagan attitude of the renascence, although they favoured that attitude, but from the topics suggested by the study of the Arabic philosophers in N.E. Italy, and had their beginning in the problem as to whether the soul at death could continue an individual existence or was reabsorbed in the source, the reservoir of life, whether Agent Intellect or universal soul.

Officially the University of Padua continued to maintain a moderate Averroism. In 1472 the editio princeps of Averroes' commentaries was published at Padua. Then in 1495-7 Niphus produced a fuller and more complete edition. Through the next half-century a series of essays, discussions, and analyses of Averroes were produced almost continuously, and in 1552-3 appeared the great edition of Averroes' commentaries, with marginal notes by Zimara. In the course of the 16th century, also, Padua produced a new translation of Averroes from the Hebrew. The last of the Averroist succession was Cæsar Cremonini (d. 1631), who, however, shows strong leanings towards Alexandrianism. By this time the study of the Arabic philosophers in Europe was confined to the medical writers and to the commentaries of Averroes.

Outside Padua and Bologna Averroes retained his position as the principal exponent of Aristotle to the end of the 15th century. In the ordinances of Louis XI. (1473) it is laid down that the masters at Paris are to teach Aristotle, and to use as commentaries Averroes, Albertus Magnus, Thomas Aquinas, and similar writers instead of William of Ockham and others of his school, which is no more than saying that the official attitude is to be realist and not nominalist.

With the 16th century the study of the Arabic commentators on Aristotle fell into disrepute outside Padua and its circle, but for a century more the Arabic medical writers had a limited range of influence in the European universities.

The actual line of transmission in and after the 15th century lay in the passage of the anti-ecclesiastical spirit developed in North East Italy under the influence of the Arabic philosophers to the Italian renascence. The arrival of Greek scholars after the fall of Constantinople and the resultant interest developed in archæological research diverted attention into a new direction, but this should not disguise the fact that the pro-Arabic element in scholastic days was the direct parent of the philopagan element in the renascence, at least in Southern Europe. In northern lands it was the archæological side which assumed greater importance and was brought to bear upon theological subjects.

CONCLUDING PARAGRAPH

We have now traced the transmission of a particular type of Hellenistic culture through the Syrian Church, the Zoroastrians of Persia, and the pagans of Harran to the Islamic community, where it was rather compromised by the patronage of those whom the official Muslim teachers decided to regard as heretics. In spite of this censure it has left a very distinct and enduring impression on Muslim theology and on popular beliefs. After a chequered career in the East it passed over to the Western Muslim community in Spain, where it had a very specialised development, which finally made a deeper impression on Christian and Jewish thought than on that of the Muslims themselves, and attained its final evolution in North-East Italy, where, as an anti-ecclesiastical influence, it prepared the way for the Renascence. But this main line of development is not really the most important; all along that line it was branching off on one side or another, and its richest fruits must be sought in these side issues, in the scholasticism which, in Islam, in Judaism, and in Christianity, was a reaction from its teaching, and in the medical, chemical, and other scientific studies of the Middle Ages, which largely owed their inspiration to its influence. It is the most romantic history of culture drift which is known to us in detail.

CHRONOLOGICAL TABLE

Years from the death of the Prophet Muhammad to the fall of the Muwahhid dynasty in Spain.

A.H.	A.D.	MUSLIM YEAR BEGINS.	LEADING EVENTS.
11	632	Mar. 29	d. of Muhammad.
12	633	,, 18	⌊Abu Bakr Khalif.
13	634	,, 7	Umar Khalif.
14	635	Feb. 25	
15	636	,, 14	
16	637	,, 2	
17	638	Jan. 23	Syria and Mesopotamia
18	639	,, 12	⌊conquered.
19	640	,, 2	
20	640	Dec. 21	Egypt conquered.
21	641	,, 10	Persia conquered.
22	642	Nov. 30	
23	643	,, 19	Uthman Khalif.
24	644	,, 7	
25	645	Oct. 28	
26	646	,, 18	
27	647	,, 7	
28	648	Sept. 25	
29	649	,, 14	

A.H.	A.D.	MUSLIM YEAR BEGINS.	LEADING EVENTS.
30	650	Sept. 4	
31	651	Aug. 24	
32	652	,, 12	
33	653	,, 2	
34	654	July 22	
35	655	,, 11	'Ali Khalif.
36	656	June 30	
37	657	,, 19	
38	658	,, 9	
39	659	May 29	
40	660	,, 17	
41	661	,, 7	Mu'awiya I. Khalif :
42	662	Apr. 26	[*Umayyads.*
43	663	,, 15	
44	664	,, 4	
45	665	Mar. 24	
46	666	,, 13	
47	667	,, 3	
48	668	Feb. 20	
49	669	,, 9	Al-Hasan died. (2nd
50	670	Jan. 29	[Imam.)
51	671	,, 18	
52	672	,, 8	
53	672	Dec. 27	
54	673	,, 16	
55	674	,, 6	
56	675	Nov. 25	

A.H.	A.D.	MUSLIM YEAR BEGINS.	LEADING EVENTS.
57	676	Nov. 14	
58	677	,, 3	
59	678	Oct. 23	
60	679	,, 13	*Yazid* Khalif.
61	680	,, 1	Karbela and d. of al-
62	681	Sept. 20	[Husayn.
63	682	,, 10	[*Marwan* Khalif.
64	683	Aug. 30	*Mu'awiya* II. Khalif :
65	684	,, 18	*Abdu l-Malik* Khalif.
66	685	,, 8	
67	686	July 28	
68	687	,, 18	
69	688	,, 6	
70	689	June 25	
71	690	,, 15	
72	691	,, 4	
73	692	May 23	
74	693	,, 13	
75	694	,, 2	
76	695	Apr. 21	
77	696	,, 10	
78	697	Mar. 30	
79	698	,, 20	
80	699	,, 9	
81	700	Feb. 26	
82	701	,, 15	
83	702	,, 4	

A.H.	A.D.	MUSLIM YEAR BEGINS.	LEADING EVENTS.
84	703	Jan. 24	
85	704	,, 14	
86	705	,, 2	*al-Walid* Khalif.
87	705	Dec. 23	
88	706	,, 12	
89	707	,, 1	
90	708	Nov. 20	
91	709	,, 9	
92	710	Oct. 29	
93	711	,, 19	
94	712	,, 7	
95	713	Sept. 26	
96	714	,, 16	*Sulayman* Khalif.
97	715	,, 5	
98	716	Aug. 25	
99	717	,, 14	*Umar II*. Khalif.
100	718	,, 3	
101	719	July 24	*Yazif II*. Khalif.
102	720	,, 12	
103	721	,, 1	
104	722	June 21	
105	723	,, 10	
106	724	May 29	Hisham Khalif.
107	725	,, 19	
108	726	,, 8	
109	727	Apr. 28	
110	728	,, 16	

A.H.	A.D.	MUSLIM YEAR BEGINS.	LEADING EVENTS.
111	729	Apr. 5	
112	730	Mar. 26	
113	731	„ 15	
114	732	„ 3	
115	733	Feb. 21	
116	734	„ 10	
117	735	Jan. 31	
118	736	„ 20	
119	737	„ 8	
120	737	Dec. 29	
121	738	„ 18	
122	739	„ 7	
123	740	Nov. 26	
124	741	„ 15	
125	742	„ 4	
126	743	Oct. 25	Al-Walid II. Khalif.
127	744	„ 15	Yazid III.—Ibrahim Khalifs.
128	745	„ 3	Marwan II. Khalif.
129	746	Sept. 22	
130	747	„ 11	
131	748	Aug. 31	
132	749	„ 20	End of Umayyad dyn.—
133	750	„ 9	⌊As-Saffah Khalif.
134	751	July 30	
135	752	„ 18	
136	753	„ 7	Al-Mansur Khalif.

A.H.	A.D.	MUSLIM YEAR BEGINS.	LEADING EVENTS.
137	754	June 27	
138	755	,, 16	Umayyads established
139	756	,, 5	⌊at Cordova.
140	757	May 25	Ibn al-Muqaffa' killed.
141	758	,, 14	
142	759	,, 4	
143	760	Apr. 22	
144	761	,, 11	
145	762	,, 1	Baghdad founded.
146	763	Mar. 21	
147	764	,, 10	
148	765	Feb. 27	Imam Ja'far as-Sadiq
149	766	,, 16	⌊died.
150	767	,, 6	
151	768	Jan. 26	
152	769	,, 14	
153	770	,, 4	
154	770	Dec. 24	
155	771	,, 13	
156	772	,, 2	
157	773	Nov. 21	
158	774	,, 11	Al-Mahdi Khalif.
159	775	Oct. 31	
160	776	,, 19	
161	777	,, 9	
162	778	Sept. 28	
163	779	,, 17	

A.H.	A.D.	MUSLIM YEAR BEGINS.	LEADING EVENTS.
164	780	Sept. 6	
165	781	Aug. 26	
166	782	,, 15	
167	783	,, 5	
168	784	July 24	
169	785	,, 14	Al-Hadi Khalif.
170	786	,, 3	Harunu r-Rashid
171	787	June 22	⌊Khalif.
172	788	,, 11	(Idrisids estab. in
173	789	May 31	⌊Morocco.)
174	790	,, 20	
175	791	,, 10	
176	792	Apr. 28	
177	793	,, 18	
178	794	,, 7	
179	795	Mar. 27	
180	796	,, 16	
181	797	,, 5	
182	798	Feb. 22	
183	799	,, 12	
184	800	,, 1	
185	801	Jan. 20	
186	802	,, 10	
187	802	Dec. 30	Fall of the Barmecides.
188	803	,, 20	
189	804	,, 8	
190	805	Nov. 27	

A.H.	A.D.	MUSLIM YEAR BEGINS.	LEADING EVENTS.
191	806	Nov. 17	
192	807	,, 6	
193	808	Oct. 25	Al-Amin Khalif.
194	809	,, 15	
195	810	,, 4	
196	811	Sept. 23	
197	812	,, 12	
198	813	,, 1	Al-Ma'mun Khalif.
199	814	Aug. 22	
200	815	,, 11	
201	816	July 30	
202	817	,, 20	
203	818	,, 9	
204	819	June 28	Ash-Shaf'i died.
205	820	,, 17	
206	821	,, 6	
207	822	May 27	
208	823	,, 16	
209	824	,, 4	
210	825	Apr. 24	
211	826	,, 13	
212	827	,, 2	Decree that Qur'an was
213	828	Mar. 22	[created.
214	829	,, 11	
215	830	Feb. 28	
216	831	,, 18	[(circ.)
217	832	,, 7	Bayt al-Hikma founded

A.H.	A.D.	MUSLIM YEAR BEGINS.	LEADING EVENTS.
218	833	Jan. 27	Al-Mu'tasim Khalif, [orthodox reaction.
219	834	,, 16	(Capital removed to
220	835	,, 5	[Samarra.)
221	835	Dec. 26	
222	836	,, 14	
223	837	,, 3	
224	838	Nov. 23	
225	839	,, 12	
226	840	Oct. 31	Abu Hudhayl died.
227	841	,, 21	Al-Wasiq Khalif.
228	842	,, 10	
229	843	Sept. 30	
230	844	,, 18	
231	845	,, 7	An-Nazzam died.
232	846	Aug. 28	Al-Mutawakkil Khalif.
233	847	,, 17	
234	848	,, 5	
235	849	July 26	
236	850	,, 15	
237	851	,, 5	
238	852	June 23	
239	853	,, 12	
240	854	,, 2	
241	855	May 22	
242	856	,, 10	
243	857	Apr. 30	

A.H.	A.D.	MUSLIM YEAR BEGINS.	LEADING EVENTS.
244	858	Apr. 19	
245	859	,, 8	
246	860	Mar. 28	
247	861	,, 17	Al-Muntasir Khalif.
248	862	,, 7	Al-Musta'in Khalif.
249	863	Feb. 24	
250	864	,, 13	
251	865	,, 2	
252	866	Jan. 22	Al-Mu'tazz Khalif.
253	867	,, 11	
254	868	Jan. 1	
255	868	Dec. 20	Al-Muhtadi Khalif.
256	869	,, 9	Al-Mu'tamid Khalif [returns to Baghdad.
257	870	Nov. 29	Al-Bukhari died.
258	871	,, 18	
259	872	,, 7	
260	873	Oct. 27	(circ) al-Kindi died.
261	874	,, 16	
262	875	,, 6	
263	876	Sept. 24	
264	877	,, 13	
265	878	,, 3	
266	879	Aug. 23	
267	880	,, 12	
268	881	,, 1	
269	882	July 21	

A.H.	A.D.	Muslim year begins.	Leading events.
270	883	July 11	
271	884	June 29	
272	885	,, 18	
273	886	,, 8	
274	887	May 28	
275	888	,, 16	
276	889	,, 6	
277	890	Apr. 25	
278	891	,, 15	
279	892	,, 3	Mu'tadid Khalif.
280	893	Mar. 23	
281	894	,, 13	
282	895	,, 2	
283	896	Feb. 19	
284	897	,, 8	
285	898	Jan. 28	
286	899	,, 17	
287	900	,, 7	
288	900	Dec. 26	
289	901	,, 16	Al-Muktafi Khalif
290	902	,, 5	
291	903	Nov. 24	
292	904	,, 13	
293	905	,, 2	
294	906	Oct. 22	
295	907	,, 12	Al Muqtadir Khalif.
296	908	Sept. 30	

A.H.	A.D.	MUSLIM YEAR BEGINS.	LEADING EVENTS.
297	909	Sept. 20	Fatimite Khalif at
298	910	,, 9	⌊Kairawan.
299	911	Aug. 28	
300	912	,, 19	Al-Ash'ari professes
301	913	,, 7	⌊orthodoxy.
302	914	July 27	
303	915	,, 17	
304	916	,, 5	
305	917	June 24	
306	918	,, 14	
307	919	,, 3	
308	920	May 23	
309	921	,, 12	
310	922	,, 1	
311	923	Apr. 21	
312	924	,, 9	
313	925	Mar. 29	
314	926	,, 10	
315	927	,, 8	
316	928	Feb. 25	
317	929	,, 14	
318	930	,, 3	
319	931	Jan. 24	
320	932	,, 13	Al-Qahir Khalif.
321	933	,, 1	
322	933	Dec. 22	ar-Razi Khalif.
323	934	,, 11	al-Mataridi d.

A.H.	A.D.	MUSLIM YEAR BEGINS.	LEADING EVENTS.
324	935	Nov. 30	Buwayhids seize Bagh-
325	936	,, 10	[dad.
326	937	,, 8	
327	938	Oct. 28	
328	939	,, 18	
329	940	,, 6	al-Muttaqi Khalif.
330	941	Sept. 26	
331	942	,, 15	
332	943	,, 4	
333	944	Aug. 24	al-Mustakfi Khalif.
334	945	,, 13	Al-Muti' Khalif.
335	946	,, 2	
336	947	July 23	
337	948	,, 11	
338	949	,, 1	
339	950	June 20	al-Farabi d.
340	951	,, 9	
341	952	May 29	
342	953	,, 18	
343	954	,, 7	
344	955	Apr. 27	
345	956	,, 15	
346	957	,, 4	
347	958	Mar. 25	
348	959	,, 14	
349	960	,, 3	
350	961	Feb. 20	

A.H.	A.D.	MUSLIM YEAR BEGINS.	LEADING EVENTS.
351	962	Feb. 9	
352	963	Jan. 30	
353	964	,, 19	
354	965	,, 7	
355	965	Dec. 28	
356	966	,, 17	Fatimites in Egypt :
357	967	,, 7	⌊Cairo founded.
358	968	Nov. 25	
359	969	,, 14	
360	970	,, 4	
361	971	Oct. 24	
362	972	,, 12	
363	973	,, 2	At-Tai' Khalif.
364	974	Sept. 21	
365	975	,, 10	
366	976	Aug. 30	
367	977	,, 19	
368	978	,, 9	
369	979	July 29	
370	980	,, 17	
371	981	,, 7	
372	982	June 26	
373	983	,, 15	
374	984	,, 4	
375	985	May 24	
376	986	,, 13	
377	987	,, 3	

A.H.	A.D.	MUSLIM YEAR BEGINS.	LEADING EVENTS.
378	988	Apr. 21	
379	989	,, 11	
380	990	Mar. 31	Al-Qadir Khalif.
381	991	,, 20	
382	992	,, 9	
383	993	Feb. 26	
384	994	,, 15	
385	995	,, 5	
386	996	Jan. 25	
387	997	,, 14	
388	998	,, 3	Rise of Mahmud of
389	998	Dec. 23	[Ghazna.
390	999	,, 13	
391	1000	,, 1	
392	1001	Nov. 20	
393	1002	,, 10	
394	1003	Oct. 30	
395	1004	,, 18	
396	1005	,, 8	
397	1006	Sept. 27	
398	1007	,, 17	
399	1008	,, 5	
400	1009	Aug. 25	
401	1010	,, 15	
402	1011	,, 4	
403	1012	July 23	
404	1013	,, 13	

A.H.	A.D.	MUSLIM YEAR BEGINS.	LEADING EVENTS.
405	1014	July 2	
406	1015	June 21	
407	1016	,, 10	
408	1017	May 30	
409	1018	,, 20	
410	1019	,, 9	
411	1020	Apr. 27	
412	1021	,, 17	
413	1022	,, 6	
414	1023	Mar. 26	
415	1024	,, 15	
416	1025	,, 4	
417	1026	Feb. 22	
418	1027	,, 11	
419	1028	Jan. 31	
420	1029	,, 20	
421	1030	,, 9	
422	1030	Dec. 29	Al-Qa'im Khalif.
423	1031	,, 19	
424	1032	,, 7	
425	1033	Nov. 26	
426	1034	,, 16	
427	1035	,, 5	
428	1036	Oct. 25	Ibn Sina (Avicenna) d.
429	1037	,, 14	
430	1038	,, 3	
431	1039	Sept. 23	

A.H.	A.D.	MUSLIM YEAR BEGINS.	LEADING EVENTS.
432	1040	Sept. 11	
433	1041	Aug. 31	
434	1042	„ 21	
435	1043	„ 10	
436	1044	July 29	
437	1045	„ 19	
438	1046	„ 8	
439	1047	June 28	
440	1048	„ 16	
441	1049	„ 5	
442	1050	May 26	
443	1051	„ 15	
444	1052	„ 3	
445	1053	Apr. 23	
446	1054	„ 12	
447	1055	„ 2	Saljuk Turks in Bagh-
448	1056	Mar. 21	[dad.
449	1057	„ 10	
450	1058	Feb. 28	
451	1059	„ 17	
452	1060	„ 6	
453	1061	Jan. 26	
454	1062	„ 15	
455	1063	„ 4	Ash'arites tolerated.
456	1063	Dec. 25	
457	1064	„ 13	
458	1065	„ 3	

A.H.	A.D.	MUSLIM YEAR BEGINS.	LEADING EVENTS.
459	1066	Nov. 22	
460	1067	,, 11	
461	1068	Oct. 31	
462	1069	,, 20	
463	1070	,, 9	
464	1071	Sept. 29	
465	1072	,, 17	
466	1073	,, 6	
467	1074	Aug. 27	Al-Muqtadi Khalif.
468	1075	,, 16	
469	1076	,, 5	
470	1077	July 25	
471	1078	,, 14	
472	1079	,, 4	
473	1080	June 22	
474	1081	,, 11	
475	1082	,, 1	
476	1083	May 21	
477	1084	,, 10	
478	1085	Apr. 29	
479	1086	,, 18	
480	1087	,, 8	
481	1088	Mar. 27	
482	1089	,, 16	
483	1090	,, 6	
484	1091	Feb. 23	
485	1092	,, 12	

A.H.	A.D.	MUSLIM YEAR BEGINS.	LEADING EVENTS.
486	1093	Feb. 1	
487	1094	Jan. 21	Al-Musta'dhir Khalif.
488	1095	,, 11	
489	1095	Dec. 31	
490	1096	,, 19	
491	1097	,, 9	
492	1098	Nov. 28	
493	1099	,, 17	
494	1100	,, 6	
495	1101	Oct. 26	
496	1102	,, 15	
497	1103	,, 5	
498	1104	Sept. 23	
499	1105	,, 13	
500	1106	,, 2	
501	1107	Aug. 22	
502	1108	,, 11	
503	1109	July 31	
504	1110	,, 20	
505	1111	,, 10	Al-Ghazali died.
506	1112	June 28	
507	1113	,, 18	
508	1114	,, 7	
509	1115	May 27	
510	1116	,, 16	
511	1117	,, 5	
512	1118	Apr. 24	Al-Mustarshid Khalif.

A.H.	A.D.	MUSLIM YEAR BEGINS.	LEADING EVENTS.
513	1119	Apr. 14	
514	1120	,, 2	
515	1121	Mar. 22	
516	1122	,, 12	
517	1123	,, 1	
518	1124	Feb. 19	
519	1125	,, 7	
520	1126	Jan. 27	
521	1127	,, 17	
522	1128	,, 6	
523	1128	Dec. 25	
524	1129	,, 15	Ibn Tumart the Mahdi
525	1130	,, 4	[died.
526	1131	Nov. 23	
527	1132	,, 12	
528	1133	,, 1	
529	1134	Oct. 22	Ar-Rashid Khalif
530	1135	,, 11	Al-Muktafi II. Khalif.
531	1136	Sept. 29	
532	1137	,, 19	
533	1138	,, 8	Ibn Bajja (Avempace)
534	1139	Aug. 28	[died.
535	1140	,, 17	
536	1141	,, 6	
537	1142	July 27	
538	1143	,, 16	
539	1144	,, 4	

A.H.	A.D.	MUSLIM YEAR BEGINS.	LEADING EVENTS.
540	1145	June 24	Jehuda hal-Levi died.
541	1146	„ 13	
542	1147	„ 2	
543	1148	May 22	
544	1149	„ 11	
545	1150	Apr. 30	
546	1151	„ 20	
547	1152	„ 8	
548	1153	Mar. 29	
549	1154	„ 18	
550	1155	„ 7	
551	1156	Feb. 25	
552	1157	„ 13	
553	1158	„ 2	
554	1159	Jan. 23	
555	1160	„ 12	
556	1160	Dec. 31	
557	1161	„ 21	
558	1162	„ 10	
559	1163	Nov. 30	
560	1164	„ 18	
561	1165	„ 7	
562	1166	Oct. 28	
563	1167	„ 17	
564	1168	„ 5	
565	1169	Sept. 25	

A.H.	A.D.	MUSLIM YEAR BEGINS.	LEADING EVENTS.
566	1170	Sept. 14	Saladin in Egypt : end
567	1171	,, 4	⌊of the Fatimites.
568	1172	Aug. 23	
569	1173	,, 12	
570	1174	,, 2	
571	1175	July 22	
572	1176	,, 10	
573	1177	June 30	
574	1178	,, 19	
575	1179	,, 8	An-Nasir Khalif.
576	1180	May 28	
577	1181	,, 17	
578	1182	,, 7	
579	1183	Apr. 26	
580	1184	,, 14	
581	1185	,, 4	Ibn Tufayl died.
582	1186	Mar. 24	
583	1187	,, 13	
584	1188	,, 2	
585	1189	Feb. 19	
586	1190	,, 8	
587	1191	Jan. 29	
588	1192	,, 18	
589	1193	,, 7	
590	1193	Dec. 27	
591	1194	,, 16	
592	1195	,, 6	

A.H.	A.D.	MUSLIM YEAR BEGINS.	LEADING EVENTS.
593	1196	Nov. 24	
594	1197	,, 13	
595	1198	,, 3	Ibn Rushd (Averroes) d.
596	1199	Oct. 23	
597	1200	,, 12	
598	1201	,, 1	
599	1202	Sept. 20	
600	1203	,, 10	
601	1204	Aug. 29	Maimonides died.
602	1205	,, 18	
603	1206	,, 8	
604	1207	July 28	
605	1208	,, 16	
606	1209	,, 6	
607	1210	June 25	
608	1211	,, 15	
609	1212	,, 3	
610	1213	May 23	
611	1214	,, 13	
612	1215	,, 2	
613	1216	Apr. 20	
614	1217	,, 10	
615	1218	Mar. 30	
616	1219	,, 19	
617	1220	,, 8	
618	1221	Feb. 25	
619	1222	,, 15	

A.H.	A.D.	MUSLIM YEAR BEGINS.	LEADING EVENTS.
620	1223	Feb. 4	
621	1224	Jan. 24	
622	1225	,, 13	Az-Zahir Khalif.
623	1226	,, 2	Al-Mustansir Khalif.
624	1226	Dec. 22	
625	1227	,, 12	
626	1228	Nov. 30	
627	1229	,, 20	
628	1230	,, 9	
629	1231	Oct. 29	
630	1232	,, 18	
631	1233	,, 7	
632	1234	Sept. 26	
633	1235	,, 16	
634	1236	,, 4	
635	1237	Aug. 24	
636	1238	,, 14	
637	1239	,, 3	
638	1240	July 23	Ibn 'Arabi died.
639	1241	,, 12	
640	1242	,, 1	Al-Musta'sim Khalif.
641	1243	June 21	
642	1244	,, 9	
643	1245	May 29	
644	1246	,, 19	
645	1247	,, 8	
646	1248	Apr. 26	

A.H.	A.D.	MUSLIM YEAR BEGINS	LEADING EVENTS
647	1249	Apr. 16	
648	1250	„ 5	
649	1251	Mar. 26	
650	1252	„ 14	
651	1253	„ 3	
652	1254	Feb. 21	
653	1255	„ 10	
654	1256	Jan. 30	
655	1257	„ 19	
656	1258	„ 8	Halagu takes Baghdad :
657	1258	Dec. 29	[end of Khalifate.
658	1259	„ 18	
659	1260	„ 6	
660	1261	Nov. 26	
661	1262	„ 15	
662	1263	„ 4	
663	1264	Oct. 24	
664	1265	„ 13	
665	1266	„ 2	
666	1267	Sept. 22	
667	1268	„ 10	Fall of the Muwahhids.

BIBLIOGRAPHY

* This bibliography gives the most useful works accessible to English readers. It does not include :—

(i) General treatises on philosophy which make incidental reference to Arabic writers. Nor—

(ii) Published editions of Arabic texts. For these refer— Brockelmann : *Geschichte des Arabischen Litteratur*, 2 vols. Weimar, 1898–1902. (Some errors and defects, but an indispensable work of its kind.)

Also Supplements, I. 1937, Leiden,
II. 1938.

And small later supplement, 1939.

Arnold, T. W. *Preaching of Islam*. London, 1913.

Baumstark, A. *Gesch. der syrischen Literatur*. Bonn, 1922.

van der Bergh. *Die Epitome des Metaphysik der Averroes*. Leiden, 1924.

de Boer, T. J. *Geschichte der Philosophie im Islam*. Stuttgart, 1901. English trs. by Edw. Jones. London, 1903.
(A slight outline, not at all adequate, but there is no better manual.)

Browne, E. G. *Literary History of Persia*, vols. 1, 2. London, 1919, 1920.
(Vol. 1 is a general description of early Muslim life and thought, not specially connected with Persia.)

Carra de Vaux. *Penseurs d'Islam*, vols. 1, 3, 4. Paris, 1921–3.
(Brief but good. The other volumes deal with Arabic science.)

— *Avicenne*. Paris, 1900.

— *Algazali*. Paris, 1902.

Fr. Dieterici, Fr. *Al-Farabi's philos. Abhandlungen herausgegeben*. Leiden, 1890.

Fr. Dieterici, Fr. *Die Philosophie der Araber im X Jahrhund.*, *Chr.* Leipzig, 1861–79.

Duval, R. *La Litterature Syriaque.* Paris, 1907.

Encyclopædia of Islam. Leiden (in progress).

Flugel, G. *al-Kindi gennant " der Philosoph. der Araber ".* Leipzig, 1857.

Gauthier, L. *Ibn Thofail, Hayy ben Yaqdhan,* text and French trs. Alger, 1900.

Goldziher, I. *Muhammedanische Studien.* 2 vols. Halle, 1889–90.

Haskins, C. H. *Studies in the History of Mediæval Science.* Cambridge (Harvard), 1934.

Horten, M. *Die Metaphysik des Averroes nach dem arabischen, übers. und ekläutert, Abhand. zur Philosoph. u. ihre Geschicht.* Halle, xxxvi. 1912.

— *Das Buch der Ringsteine Farabis mit dem Kommentar des Emir Isma'il el-Hoseini.* Münster, 1906.

Krehl. *Beitrage zur Characteristik der Lehre vom Glauben in Islam.* Leipzig, 1877.

von Kremer. *A. Culturgeschichte des Orients unter den Chalifen.* 2 vols. Wien, 1875–7.

— *Muhammedanische Studien.* 2 vols. Halle, 1889–90.

Labourt, J. *Le Christianisme dans l'empire Perse.* Paris, 1904.

Lammens, H. *Le Berceau d'Islam.* Rome, 1914.

— *Études sur le régne du Calife Omaiyade Mo'awia,* 1er. Paris, 1902.

— *Le Califat de Yazid,* 1er. Beyrouth, 1921.

Lane-Poole, S. *Studies in a Mosque.* 2nd ed. London, 1893.

MacDonald, D. B. *Development of Muslim Theology, Jurisprudence and Constitutional Theory.* London, 1903.

Malouf, L. *Traités inédits d'anciens philosophes arabes.* Beyrouth, 1911.

Mehren, M. A. *Exposé de la réforme de l'Islamisme commencée au 3e siècle de l'Hegire par Abou-l-Hasan Ali el-Ash'ari.* 3rd International Congress of Orientalists, vol. 2.

Merx, A. *Idee u. Grundlinien einer allgemeinen Geschichte der Mystik.* Heidelberg, 1893.

Müller, M. J. *Philosophie und Theologie des Averroes.* Text,
München, 1859. German trs., München, 1875.

Nicholson, R. *Literary History of the Arabs.* Cambridge,
1930.

Palacios, M. A. *Algazel, dogmatica, moral, ascetica.* Zaragoza,
1901.

Patten, W. M. *Ahmad ibn Hanbal and the Mihna.* London,
1897.

Renan, E. *Averroes et l'Averroisme* (3rd ed.). Paris, 1861.

Spitta, W. *Zur Gesch. Abu l-Hasan al-Ash'ari's.* Leipzig,
1876.

INDEX

A CATALOG OF SELECTED DOVER
BOOKS IN ALL FIELDS OF INTEREST

CONCERNING THE SPIRITUAL IN ART, Wassily Kandinsky. Pioneering work by father of abstract art. Thoughts on color theory, nature of art. Analysis of earlier masters. 12 illustrations. 80pp. of text. 5⅜ x 8½. 23411-8

ANIMALS: 1,419 Copyright-Free Illustrations of Mammals, Birds, Fish, Insects, etc., Jim Harter (ed.). Clear wood engravings present, in extremely lifelike poses, over 1,000 species of animals. One of the most extensive pictorial sourcebooks of its kind. Captions. Index. 284pp. 9 x 12. 23766-4

CELTIC ART: The Methods of Construction, George Bain. Simple geometric techniques for making Celtic interlacements, spirals, Kells-type initials, animals, humans, etc. Over 500 illustrations. 160pp. 9 x 12. (Available in U.S. only.) 22923-8

AN ATLAS OF ANATOMY FOR ARTISTS, Fritz Schider. Most thorough reference work on art anatomy in the world. Hundreds of illustrations, including selections from works by Vesalius, Leonardo, Goya, Ingres, Michelangelo, others. 593 illustrations. 192pp. 7⅛ x 10¼. 20241-0

CELTIC HAND STROKE-BY-STROKE (Irish Half-Uncial from "The Book of Kells"): An Arthur Baker Calligraphy Manual, Arthur Baker. Complete guide to creating each letter of the alphabet in distinctive Celtic manner. Covers hand position, strokes, pens, inks, paper, more. Illustrated. 48pp. 8¼ x 11. 24336-2

EASY ORIGAMI, John Montroll. Charming collection of 32 projects (hat, cup, pelican, piano, swan, many more) specially designed for the novice origami hobbyist. Clearly illustrated easy-to-follow instructions insure that even beginning papercrafters will achieve successful results. 48pp. 8¼ x 11. 27298-2

THE COMPLETE BOOK OF BIRDHOUSE CONSTRUCTION FOR WOOD-WORKERS, Scott D. Campbell. Detailed instructions, illustrations, tables. Also data on bird habitat and instinct patterns. Bibliography. 3 tables. 63 illustrations in 15 figures. 48pp. 5¼ x 8½. 24407-5

BLOOMINGDALE'S ILLUSTRATED 1886 CATALOG: Fashions, Dry Goods and Housewares, Bloomingdale Brothers. Famed merchants' extremely rare catalog depicting about 1,700 products: clothing, housewares, firearms, dry goods, jewelry, more. Invaluable for dating, identifying vintage items. Also, copyright-free graphics for artists, designers. Co-published with Henry Ford Museum & Greenfield Village. 160pp. 8¼ x 11. 25780-0

HISTORIC COSTUME IN PICTURES, Braun & Schneider. Over 1,450 costumed figures in clearly detailed engravings–from dawn of civilization to end of 19th century. Captions. Many folk costumes. 256pp. 8⅜ x 11¾. 23150-X

STICKLEY CRAFTSMAN FURNITURE CATALOGS, Gustav Stickley and L. & J. G. Stickley. Beautiful, functional furniture in two authentic catalogs from 1910. 594 illustrations, including 277 photos, show settles, rockers, armchairs, reclining chairs, bookcases, desks, tables. 183pp. 6½ x 9¼. 23838-5

AMERICAN LOCOMOTIVES IN HISTORIC PHOTOGRAPHS: 1858 to 1949, Ron Ziel (ed.). A rare collection of 126 meticulously detailed official photographs, called "builder portraits," of American locomotives that majestically chronicle the rise of steam locomotive power in America. Introduction. Detailed captions. xi+ 129pp. 9 x 12. 27393-8

AMERICA'S LIGHTHOUSES: An Illustrated History, Francis Ross Holland, Jr. Delightfully written, profusely illustrated fact-filled survey of over 200 American lighthouses since 1716. History, anecdotes, technological advances, more. 240pp. 8 x 10¾. 25576-X

TOWARDS A NEW ARCHITECTURE, Le Corbusier. Pioneering manifesto by founder of "International School." Technical and aesthetic theories, views of industry, economics, relation of form to function, "mass-production split" and much more. Profusely illustrated. 320pp. 6⅛ x 9¼. (Available in U.S. only.) 25023-7

HOW THE OTHER HALF LIVES, Jacob Riis. Famous journalistic record, exposing poverty and degradation of New York slums around 1900, by major social reformer. 100 striking and influential photographs. 233pp. 10 x 7⅞. 22012-5

FRUIT KEY AND TWIG KEY TO TREES AND SHRUBS, William M. Harlow. One of the handiest and most widely used identification aids. Fruit key covers 120 deciduous and evergreen species; twig key 160 deciduous species. Easily used. Over 300 photographs. 126pp. 5⅜ x 8½. 20511-8

COMMON BIRD SONGS, Dr. Donald J. Borror. Songs of 60 most common U.S. birds: robins, sparrows, cardinals, bluejays, finches, more–arranged in order of increasing complexity. Up to 9 variations of songs of each species. Cassette and manual 99911-4

ORCHIDS AS HOUSE PLANTS, Rebecca Tyson Northen. Grow cattleyas and many other kinds of orchids–in a window, in a case, or under artificial light. 63 illustrations. 148pp. 5⅜ x 8½. 23261-1

MONSTER MAZES, Dave Phillips. Masterful mazes at four levels of difficulty. Avoid deadly perils and evil creatures to find magical treasures. Solutions for all 32 exciting illustrated puzzles. 48pp. 8¼ x 11. 26005-4

MOZART'S DON GIOVANNI (DOVER OPERA LIBRETTO SERIES), Wolfgang Amadeus Mozart. Introduced and translated by Ellen H. Bleiler. Standard Italian libretto, with complete English translation. Convenient and thoroughly portable–an ideal companion for reading along with a recording or the performance itself. Introduction. List of characters. Plot summary. 121pp. 5¼ x 8½. 24944-1

TECHNICAL MANUAL AND DICTIONARY OF CLASSICAL BALLET, Gail Grant. Defines, explains, comments on steps, movements, poses and concepts. 15-page pictorial section. Basic book for student, viewer. 127pp. 5⅜ x 8½. 21843-0

THE CLARINET AND CLARINET PLAYING, David Pino. Lively, comprehensive work features suggestions about technique, musicianship, and musical interpretation, as well as guidelines for teaching, making your own reeds, and preparing for public performance. Includes an intriguing look at clarinet history. "A godsend," *The Clarinet,* Journal of the International Clarinet Society. Appendixes. 7 illus. 320pp. 5⅜ x 8½. 40270-3

HOLLYWOOD GLAMOR PORTRAITS, John Kobal (ed.). 145 photos from 1926-49. Harlow, Gable, Bogart, Bacall; 94 stars in all. Full background on photographers, technical aspects. 160pp. 8⅜ x 11¼. 23352-9

THE ANNOTATED CASEY AT THE BAT: A Collection of Ballads about the Mighty Casey/Third, Revised Edition, Martin Gardner (ed.). Amusing sequels and parodies of one of America's best-loved poems: Casey's Revenge, Why Casey Whiffed, Casey's Sister at the Bat, others. 256pp. 5⅜ x 8½. 28598-7

THE RAVEN AND OTHER FAVORITE POEMS, Edgar Allan Poe. Over 40 of the author's most memorable poems: "The Bells," "Ulalume," "Israfel," "To Helen," "The Conqueror Worm," "Eldorado," "Annabel Lee," many more. Alphabetic lists of titles and first lines. 64pp. 5$^{3}/_{16}$ x 8¼. 26685-0

PERSONAL MEMOIRS OF U. S. GRANT, Ulysses Simpson Grant. Intelligent, deeply moving firsthand account of Civil War campaigns, considered by many the finest military memoirs ever written. Includes letters, historic photographs, maps and more. 528pp. 6⅛ x 9¼. 28587-1

ANCIENT EGYPTIAN MATERIALS AND INDUSTRIES, A. Lucas and J. Harris. Fascinating, comprehensive, thoroughly documented text describes this ancient civilization's vast resources and the processes that incorporated them in daily life, including the use of animal products, building materials, cosmetics, perfumes and incense, fibers, glazed ware, glass and its manufacture, materials used in the mummification process, and much more. 544pp. 6⅛ x 9¼. (Available in U.S. only.) 40446-3

RUSSIAN STORIES/RUSSKIE RASSKAZY: A Dual-Language Book, edited by Gleb Struve. Twelve tales by such masters as Chekhov, Tolstoy, Dostoevsky, Pushkin, others. Excellent word-for-word English translations on facing pages, plus teaching and study aids, Russian/English vocabulary, biographical/critical introductions, more. 416pp. 5⅜ x 8½. 26244-8

PHILADELPHIA THEN AND NOW: 60 Sites Photographed in the Past and Present, Kenneth Finkel and Susan Oyama. Rare photographs of City Hall, Logan Square, Independence Hall, Betsy Ross House, other landmarks juxtaposed with contemporary views. Captures changing face of historic city. Introduction. Captions. 128pp. 8¼ x 11. 25790-8

AIA ARCHITECTURAL GUIDE TO NASSAU AND SUFFOLK COUNTIES, LONG ISLAND, The American Institute of Architects, Long Island Chapter, and the Society for the Preservation of Long Island Antiquities. Comprehensive, well-researched and generously illustrated volume brings to life over three centuries of Long Island's great architectural heritage. More than 240 photographs with authoritative, extensively detailed captions. 176pp. 8¼ x 11. 26946-9

NORTH AMERICAN INDIAN LIFE: Customs and Traditions of 23 Tribes, Elsie Clews Parsons (ed.). 27 fictionalized essays by noted anthropologists examine religion, customs, government, additional facets of life among the Winnebago, Crow, Zuni, Eskimo, other tribes. 480pp. 6⅛ x 9¼. 27377-6

FRANK LLOYD WRIGHT'S DANA HOUSE, Donald Hoffmann. Pictorial essay of residential masterpiece with over 160 interior and exterior photos, plans, elevations, sketches and studies. 128pp. 9¼ x 10¾.   29120-0

THE MALE AND FEMALE FIGURE IN MOTION: 60 Classic Photographic Sequences, Eadweard Muybridge. 60 true-action photographs of men and women walking, running, climbing, bending, turning, etc., reproduced from rare 19th-century masterpiece. vi + 121pp. 9 x 12.   24745-7

1001 QUESTIONS ANSWERED ABOUT THE SEASHORE, N. J. Berrill and Jacquelyn Berrill. Queries answered about dolphins, sea snails, sponges, starfish, fishes, shore birds, many others. Covers appearance, breeding, growth, feeding, much more. 305pp. 5¼ x 8¼.   23366-9

ATTRACTING BIRDS TO YOUR YARD, William J. Weber. Easy-to-follow guide offers advice on how to attract the greatest diversity of birds: birdhouses, feeders, water and waterers, much more. 96pp. 5³⁄₁₆ x 8¼.   28927-3

MEDICINAL AND OTHER USES OF NORTH AMERICAN PLANTS: A Historical Survey with Special Reference to the Eastern Indian Tribes, Charlotte Erichsen-Brown. Chronological historical citations document 500 years of usage of plants, trees, shrubs native to eastern Canada, northeastern U.S. Also complete identifying information. 343 illustrations. 544pp. 6½ x 9¼.   25951-X

STORYBOOK MAZES, Dave Phillips. 23 stories and mazes on two-page spreads: Wizard of Oz, Treasure Island, Robin Hood, etc. Solutions. 64pp. 8¼ x 11. 23628-5

AMERICAN NEGRO SONGS: 230 Folk Songs and Spirituals, Religious and Secular, John W. Work. This authoritative study traces the African influences of songs sung and played by black Americans at work, in church, and as entertainment. The author discusses the lyric significance of such songs as "Swing Low, Sweet Chariot," "John Henry," and others and offers the words and music for 230 songs. Bibliography. Index of Song Titles. 272pp. 6½ x 9¼.   40271-1

MOVIE-STAR PORTRAITS OF THE FORTIES, John Kobal (ed.). 163 glamor, studio photos of 106 stars of the 1940s: Rita Hayworth, Ava Gardner, Marlon Brando, Clark Gable, many more. 176pp. 8⅜ x 11¼.   23546-7

BENCHLEY LOST AND FOUND, Robert Benchley. Finest humor from early 30s, about pet peeves, child psychologists, post office and others. Mostly unavailable elsewhere. 73 illustrations by Peter Arno and others. 183pp. 5⅜ x 8½.   22410-4

YEKL and THE IMPORTED BRIDEGROOM AND OTHER STORIES OF YIDDISH NEW YORK, Abraham Cahan. Film Hester Street based on *Yekl* (1896). Novel, other stories among first about Jewish immigrants on N.Y.'s East Side. 240pp. 5⅜ x 8½.   22427-9

SELECTED POEMS, Walt Whitman. Generous sampling from *Leaves of Grass*. Twenty-four poems include "I Hear America Singing," "Song of the Open Road," "I Sing the Body Electric," "When Lilacs Last in the Dooryard Bloom'd," "O Captain! My Captain!"–all reprinted from an authoritative edition. Lists of titles and first lines. 128pp. 5³⁄₁₆ x 8¼.   26878-0

THE BEST TALES OF HOFFMANN, E. T. A. Hoffmann. 10 of Hoffmann's most important stories: "Nutcracker and the King of Mice," "The Golden Flowerpot," etc. 458pp. 5⅜ x 8½.   21793-0

FROM FETISH TO GOD IN ANCIENT EGYPT, E. A. Wallis Budge. Rich detailed survey of Egyptian conception of "God" and gods, magic, cult of animals, Osiris, more. Also, superb English translations of hymns and legends. 240 illustrations. 545pp. 5⅜ x 8½.   25803-3

FRENCH STORIES/CONTES FRANÇAIS: A Dual-Language Book, Wallace Fowlie. Ten stories by French masters, Voltaire to Camus: "Micromegas" by Voltaire; "The Atheist's Mass" by Balzac; "Minuet" by de Maupassant; "The Guest" by Camus, six more. Excellent English translations on facing pages. Also French-English vocabulary list, exercises, more. 352pp. 5⅜ x 8½.   26443-2

CHICAGO AT THE TURN OF THE CENTURY IN PHOTOGRAPHS: 122 Historic Views from the Collections of the Chicago Historical Society, Larry A. Viskochil. Rare large-format prints offer detailed views of City Hall, State Street, the Loop, Hull House, Union Station, many other landmarks, circa 1904-1913. Introduction. Captions. Maps. 144pp. 9⅜ x 12¼.   24656-6

OLD BROOKLYN IN EARLY PHOTOGRAPHS, 1865-1929, William Lee Younger. Luna Park, Gravesend race track, construction of Grand Army Plaza, moving of Hotel Brighton, etc. 157 previously unpublished photographs. 165pp. 8⅞ x 11¾.
23587-4

THE MYTHS OF THE NORTH AMERICAN INDIANS, Lewis Spence. Rich anthology of the myths and legends of the Algonquins, Iroquois, Pawnees and Sioux, prefaced by an extensive historical and ethnological commentary. 36 illustrations. 480pp. 5⅜ x 8½.   25967-6

AN ENCYCLOPEDIA OF BATTLES: Accounts of Over 1,560 Battles from 1479 B.C. to the Present, David Eggenberger. Essential details of every major battle in recorded history from the first battle of Megiddo in 1479 B.C. to Grenada in 1984. List of Battle Maps. New Appendix covering the years 1967-1984. Index. 99 illustrations. 544pp. 6½ x 9¼.   24913-1

SAILING ALONE AROUND THE WORLD, Captain Joshua Slocum. First man to sail around the world, alone, in small boat. One of great feats of seamanship told in delightful manner. 67 illustrations. 294pp. 5⅜ x 8½.   20326-3

ANARCHISM AND OTHER ESSAYS, Emma Goldman. Powerful, penetrating, prophetic essays on direct action, role of minorities, prison reform, puritan hypocrisy, violence, etc. 271pp. 5⅜ x 8½.   22484-8

MYTHS OF THE HINDUS AND BUDDHISTS, Ananda K. Coomaraswamy and Sister Nivedita. Great stories of the epics; deeds of Krishna, Shiva, taken from puranas, Vedas, folk tales; etc. 32 illustrations. 400pp. 5⅜ x 8½.   21759-0

THE TRAUMA OF BIRTH, Otto Rank. Rank's controversial thesis that anxiety neurosis is caused by profound psychological trauma which occurs at birth. 256pp. 5⅜ x 8½.   27974-X

A THEOLOGICO-POLITICAL TREATISE, Benedict Spinoza. Also contains unfinished Political Treatise. Great classic on religious liberty, theory of government on common consent. R. Elwes translation. Total of 421pp. 5⅜ x 8½.   20249-6

MY BONDAGE AND MY FREEDOM, Frederick Douglass. Born a slave, Douglass became outspoken force in antislavery movement. The best of Douglass' autobiographies. Graphic description of slave life. 464pp. 5⅜ x 8½. 22457-0

FOLLOWING THE EQUATOR: A Journey Around the World, Mark Twain. Fascinating humorous account of 1897 voyage to Hawaii, Australia, India, New Zealand, etc. Ironic, bemused reports on peoples, customs, climate, flora and fauna, politics, much more. 197 illustrations. 720pp. 5⅜ x 8½. 26113-1

THE PEOPLE CALLED SHAKERS, Edward D. Andrews. Definitive study of Shakers: origins, beliefs, practices, dances, social organization, furniture and crafts, etc. 33 illustrations. 351pp. 5⅜ x 8½. 21081-2

THE MYTHS OF GREECE AND ROME, H. A. Guerber. A classic of mythology, generously illustrated, long prized for its simple, graphic, accurate retelling of the principal myths of Greece and Rome, and for its commentary on their origins and significance. With 64 illustrations by Michelangelo, Raphael, Titian, Rubens, Canova, Bernini and others. 480pp. 5⅜ x 8½. 27584-1

PSYCHOLOGY OF MUSIC, Carl E. Seashore. Classic work discusses music as a medium from psychological viewpoint. Clear treatment of physical acoustics, auditory apparatus, sound perception, development of musical skills, nature of musical feeling, host of other topics. 88 figures. 408pp. 5⅜ x 8½. 21851-1

THE PHILOSOPHY OF HISTORY, Georg W. Hegel. Great classic of Western thought develops concept that history is not chance but rational process, the evolution of freedom. 457pp. 5⅜ x 8½. 20112-0

THE BOOK OF TEA, Kakuzo Okakura. Minor classic of the Orient: entertaining, charming explanation, interpretation of traditional Japanese culture in terms of tea ceremony. 94pp. 5⅜ x 8½. 20070-1

LIFE IN ANCIENT EGYPT, Adolf Erman. Fullest, most thorough, detailed older account with much not in more recent books, domestic life, religion, magic, medicine, commerce, much more. Many illustrations reproduce tomb paintings, carvings, hieroglyphs, etc. 597pp. 5⅜ x 8½. 22632-8

SUNDIALS, Their Theory and Construction, Albert Waugh. Far and away the best, most thorough coverage of ideas, mathematics concerned, types, construction, adjusting anywhere. Simple, nontechnical treatment allows even children to build several of these dials. Over 100 illustrations. 230pp. 5⅜ x 8½. 22947-5

THEORETICAL HYDRODYNAMICS, L. M. Milne-Thomson. Classic exposition of the mathematical theory of fluid motion, applicable to both hydrodynamics and aerodynamics. Over 600 exercises. 768pp. 6⅛ x 9¼. 68970-0

SONGS OF EXPERIENCE: Facsimile Reproduction with 26 Plates in Full Color, William Blake. 26 full-color plates from a rare 1826 edition. Includes "The Tyger," "London," "Holy Thursday," and other poems. Printed text of poems. 48pp. 5¼ x 7. 24636-1

OLD-TIME VIGNETTES IN FULL COLOR, Carol Belanger Grafton (ed.). Over 390 charming, often sentimental illustrations, selected from archives of Victorian graphics–pretty women posing, children playing, food, flowers, kittens and puppies, smiling cherubs, birds and butterflies, much more. All copyright-free. 48pp. 9¼ x 12¼. 27269-9

PERSPECTIVE FOR ARTISTS, Rex Vicat Cole. Depth, perspective of sky and sea, shadows, much more, not usually covered. 391 diagrams, 81 reproductions of drawings and paintings. 279pp. 5⅜ x 8½. 22487-2

DRAWING THE LIVING FIGURE, Joseph Sheppard. Innovative approach to artistic anatomy focuses on specifics of surface anatomy, rather than muscles and bones. Over 170 drawings of live models in front, back and side views, and in widely varying poses. Accompanying diagrams. 177 illustrations. Introduction. Index. 144pp. 8⅜ x11¼. 26723-7

GOTHIC AND OLD ENGLISH ALPHABETS: 100 Complete Fonts, Dan X. Solo. Add power, elegance to posters, signs, other graphics with 100 stunning copyright-free alphabets: Blackstone, Dolbey, Germania, 97 more–including many lower-case, numerals, punctuation marks. 104pp. 8⅛ x 11. 24695-7

HOW TO DO BEADWORK, Mary White. Fundamental book on craft from simple projects to five-bead chains and woven works. 106 illustrations. 142pp. 5⅜ x 8. 20697-1

THE BOOK OF WOOD CARVING, Charles Marshall Sayers. Finest book for beginners discusses fundamentals and offers 34 designs. "Absolutely first rate . . . well thought out and well executed."–E. J. Tangerman. 118pp. 7¾ x 10⅝. 23654-4

ILLUSTRATED CATALOG OF CIVIL WAR MILITARY GOODS: Union Army Weapons, Insignia, Uniform Accessories, and Other Equipment, Schuyler, Hartley, and Graham. Rare, profusely illustrated 1846 catalog includes Union Army uniform and dress regulations, arms and ammunition, coats, insignia, flags, swords, rifles, etc. 226 illustrations. 160pp. 9 x 12. 24939-5

WOMEN'S FASHIONS OF THE EARLY 1900s: An Unabridged Republication of "New York Fashions, 1909," National Cloak & Suit Co. Rare catalog of mail-order fashions documents women's and children's clothing styles shortly after the turn of the century. Captions offer full descriptions, prices. Invaluable resource for fashion, costume historians. Approximately 725 illustrations. 128pp. 8⅜ x 11¼. 27276-1

THE 1912 AND 1915 GUSTAV STICKLEY FURNITURE CATALOGS, Gustav Stickley. With over 200 detailed illustrations and descriptions, these two catalogs are essential reading and reference materials and identification guides for Stickley furniture. Captions cite materials, dimensions and prices. 112pp. 6½ x 9¼. 26676-1

EARLY AMERICAN LOCOMOTIVES, John H. White, Jr. Finest locomotive engravings from early 19th century: historical (1804–74), main-line (after 1870), special, foreign, etc. 147 plates. 142pp. 11⅜ x 8¼. 22772-3

THE TALL SHIPS OF TODAY IN PHOTOGRAPHS, Frank O. Braynard. Lavishly illustrated tribute to nearly 100 majestic contemporary sailing vessels: Amerigo Vespucci, Clearwater, Constitution, Eagle, Mayflower, Sea Cloud, Victory, many more. Authoritative captions provide statistics, background on each ship. 190 black-and-white photographs and illustrations. Introduction. 128pp. 8⅞ x 11¾. 27163-3

LITTLE BOOK OF EARLY AMERICAN CRAFTS AND TRADES, Peter Stockham (ed.). 1807 children's book explains crafts and trades: baker, hatter, cooper, potter, and many others. 23 copperplate illustrations. 140pp. 4⁵/₈ x 6. 23336-7

VICTORIAN FASHIONS AND COSTUMES FROM HARPER'S BAZAR, 1867–1898, Stella Blum (ed.). Day costumes, evening wear, sports clothes, shoes, hats, other accessories in over 1,000 detailed engravings. 320pp. 9⅜ x 12¼. 22990-4

GUSTAV STICKLEY, THE CRAFTSMAN, Mary Ann Smith. Superb study surveys broad scope of Stickley's achievement, especially in architecture. Design philosophy, rise and fall of the Craftsman empire, descriptions and floor plans for many Craftsman houses, more. 86 black-and-white halftones. 31 line illustrations. Introduction 208pp. 6½ x 9¼. 27210-9

THE LONG ISLAND RAIL ROAD IN EARLY PHOTOGRAPHS, Ron Ziel. Over 220 rare photos, informative text document origin (1844) and development of rail service on Long Island. Vintage views of early trains, locomotives, stations, passengers, crews, much more. Captions. 8⅞ x 11¾. 26301-0

VOYAGE OF THE LIBERDADE, Joshua Slocum. Great 19th-century mariner's thrilling, first-hand account of the wreck of his ship off South America, the 35-foot boat he built from the wreckage, and its remarkable voyage home. 128pp. 5⅜ x 8½. 40022-0

TEN BOOKS ON ARCHITECTURE, Vitruvius. The most important book ever written on architecture. Early Roman aesthetics, technology, classical orders, site selection, all other aspects. Morgan translation. 331pp. 5⅜ x 8½. 20645-9

THE HUMAN FIGURE IN MOTION, Eadweard Muybridge. More than 4,500 stopped-action photos, in action series, showing undraped men, women, children jumping, lying down, throwing, sitting, wrestling, carrying, etc. 390pp. 7⅞ x 10⅝. 20204-6 Clothbd.

TREES OF THE EASTERN AND CENTRAL UNITED STATES AND CANADA, William M. Harlow. Best one-volume guide to 140 trees. Full descriptions, woodlore, range, etc. Over 600 illustrations. Handy size. 288pp. 4½ x 6⅜. 20395-6

SONGS OF WESTERN BIRDS, Dr. Donald J. Borror. Complete song and call repertoire of 60 western species, including flycatchers, juncoes, cactus wrens, many more–includes fully illustrated booklet. Cassette and manual 99913-0

GROWING AND USING HERBS AND SPICES, Milo Miloradovich. Versatile handbook provides all the information needed for cultivation and use of all the herbs and spices available in North America. 4 illustrations. Index. Glossary. 236pp. 5⅜ x 8½. 25058-X

BIG BOOK OF MAZES AND LABYRINTHS, Walter Shepherd. 50 mazes and labyrinths in all–classical, solid, ripple, and more–in one great volume. Perfect inexpensive puzzler for clever youngsters. Full solutions. 112pp. 8⅛ x 11. 22951-3

PIANO TUNING, J. Cree Fischer. Clearest, best book for beginner, amateur. Simple repairs, raising dropped notes, tuning by easy method of flattened fifths. No previous skills needed. 4 illustrations. 201pp. 5⅜ x 8½.　23267-0

HINTS TO SINGERS, Lillian Nordica. Selecting the right teacher, developing confidence, overcoming stage fright, and many other important skills receive thoughtful discussion in this indispensible guide, written by a world-famous diva of four decades' experience. 96pp. 5⅜ x 8½.　40094-8

THE COMPLETE NONSENSE OF EDWARD LEAR, Edward Lear. All nonsense limericks, zany alphabets, Owl and Pussycat, songs, nonsense botany, etc., illustrated by Lear. Total of 320pp. 5⅜ x 8½. (Available in U.S. only.)　20167-8

VICTORIAN PARLOUR POETRY: An Annotated Anthology, Michael R. Turner. 117 gems by Longfellow, Tennyson, Browning, many lesser-known poets. "The Village Blacksmith," "Curfew Must Not Ring Tonight," "Only a Baby Small," dozens more, often difficult to find elsewhere. Index of poets, titles, first lines. xxiii + 325pp. 5⅜ x 8¼.　27044-0

DUBLINERS, James Joyce. Fifteen stories offer vivid, tightly focused observations of the lives of Dublin's poorer classes. At least one, "The Dead," is considered a masterpiece. Reprinted complete and unabridged from standard edition. 160pp. 5³⁄₁₆ x 8¼.　26870-5

GREAT WEIRD TALES: 14 Stories by Lovecraft, Blackwood, Machen and Others, S. T. Joshi (ed.). 14 spellbinding tales, including "The Sin Eater," by Fiona McLeod, "The Eye Above the Mantel," by Frank Belknap Long, as well as renowned works by R. H. Barlow, Lord Dunsany, Arthur Machen, W. C. Morrow and eight other masters of the genre. 256pp. 5⅜ x 8½. (Available in U.S. only.)　40436-6

THE BOOK OF THE SACRED MAGIC OF ABRAMELIN THE MAGE, translated by S. MacGregor Mathers. Medieval manuscript of ceremonial magic. Basic document in Aleister Crowley, Golden Dawn groups. 268pp. 5⅜ x 8½.　23211-5

NEW RUSSIAN-ENGLISH AND ENGLISH-RUSSIAN DICTIONARY, M. A. O'Brien. This is a remarkably handy Russian dictionary, containing a surprising amount of information, including over 70,000 entries. 366pp. 4½ x 6⅛.　20208-9

HISTORIC HOMES OF THE AMERICAN PRESIDENTS, Second, Revised Edition, Irvin Haas. A traveler's guide to American Presidential homes, most open to the public, depicting and describing homes occupied by every American President from George Washington to George Bush. With visiting hours, admission charges, travel routes. 175 photographs. Index. 160pp. 8¼ x 11.　26751-2

NEW YORK IN THE FORTIES, Andreas Feininger. 162 brilliant photographs by the well-known photographer, formerly with *Life* magazine. Commuters, shoppers, Times Square at night, much else from city at its peak. Captions by John von Hartz. 181pp. 9¼ x 10¾.　23585-8

INDIAN SIGN LANGUAGE, William Tomkins. Over 525 signs developed by Sioux and other tribes. Written instructions and diagrams. Also 290 pictographs. 111pp. 6⅛ x 9¼.　22029-X

ANATOMY: A Complete Guide for Artists, Joseph Sheppard. A master of figure drawing shows artists how to render human anatomy convincingly. Over 460 illustrations. 224pp. 8⅜ x 11¼. 27279-6

MEDIEVAL CALLIGRAPHY: Its History and Technique, Marc Drogin. Spirited history, comprehensive instruction manual covers 13 styles (ca. 4th century through 15th). Excellent photographs; directions for duplicating medieval techniques with modern tools. 224pp. 8⅜ x 11¼. 26142-5

DRIED FLOWERS: How to Prepare Them, Sarah Whitlock and Martha Rankin. Complete instructions on how to use silica gel, meal and borax, perlite aggregate, sand and borax, glycerine and water to create attractive permanent flower arrangements. 12 illustrations. 32pp. 5⅜ x 8½. 21802-3

EASY-TO-MAKE BIRD FEEDERS FOR WOODWORKERS, Scott D. Campbell. Detailed, simple-to-use guide for designing, constructing, caring for and using feeders. Text, illustrations for 12 classic and contemporary designs. 96pp. 5⅜ x 8½.
25847-5

SCOTTISH WONDER TALES FROM MYTH AND LEGEND, Donald A. Mackenzie. 16 lively tales tell of giants rumbling down mountainsides, of a magic wand that turns stone pillars into warriors, of gods and goddesses, evil hags, powerful forces and more. 240pp. 5⅜ x 8½. 29677-6

THE HISTORY OF UNDERCLOTHES, C. Willett Cunnington and Phyllis Cunnington. Fascinating, well-documented survey covering six centuries of English undergarments, enhanced with over 100 illustrations: 12th-century laced-up bodice, footed long drawers (1795), 19th-century bustles, 19th-century corsets for men, Victorian "bust improvers," much more. 272pp. 5⅜ x 8¼. 27124-2

ARTS AND CRAFTS FURNITURE: The Complete Brooks Catalog of 1912, Brooks Manufacturing Co. Photos and detailed descriptions of more than 150 now very collectible furniture designs from the Arts and Crafts movement depict davenports, settees, buffets, desks, tables, chairs, bedsteads, dressers and more, all built of solid, quarter-sawed oak. Invaluable for students and enthusiasts of antiques, Americana and the decorative arts. 80pp. 6½ x 9¼. 27471-3

WILBUR AND ORVILLE: A Biography of the Wright Brothers, Fred Howard. Definitive, crisply written study tells the full story of the brothers' lives and work. A vividly written biography, unparalleled in scope and color, that also captures the spirit of an extraordinary era. 560pp. 6⅛ x 9¼. 40297-5

THE ARTS OF THE SAILOR: Knotting, Splicing and Ropework, Hervey Garrett Smith. Indispensable shipboard reference covers tools, basic knots and useful hitches; handsewing and canvas work, more. Over 100 illustrations. Delightful reading for sea lovers. 256pp. 5⅜ x 8½. 26440-8

FRANK LLOYD WRIGHT'S FALLINGWATER: The House and Its History, Second, Revised Edition, Donald Hoffmann. A total revision—both in text and illustrations—of the standard document on Fallingwater, the boldest, most personal architectural statement of Wright's mature years, updated with valuable new material from the recently opened Frank Lloyd Wright Archives. "Fascinating"—*The New York Times*. 116 illustrations. 128pp. 9¼ x 10¾. 27430-6

PHOTOGRAPHIC SKETCHBOOK OF THE CIVIL WAR, Alexander Gardner. 100 photos taken on field during the Civil War. Famous shots of Manassas Harper's Ferry, Lincoln, Richmond, slave pens, etc. 244pp. 10⅝ x 8¼. 22731-6

FIVE ACRES AND INDEPENDENCE, Maurice G. Kains. Great back-to-the-land classic explains basics of self-sufficient farming. The one book to get. 95 illustrations. 397pp. 5⅜ x 8½. 20974-1

SONGS OF EASTERN BIRDS, Dr. Donald J. Borror. Songs and calls of 60 species most common to eastern U.S.: warblers, woodpeckers, flycatchers, thrushes, larks, many more in high-quality recording. Cassette and manual 99912-2

A MODERN HERBAL, Margaret Grieve. Much the fullest, most exact, most useful compilation of herbal material. Gigantic alphabetical encyclopedia, from aconite to zedoary, gives botanical information, medical properties, folklore, economic uses, much else. Indispensable to serious reader. 161 illustrations. 888pp. 6½ x 9¼. 2-vol. set. (Available in U.S. only.) Vol. I: 22798-7
Vol. II: 22799-5

HIDDEN TREASURE MAZE BOOK, Dave Phillips. Solve 34 challenging mazes accompanied by heroic tales of adventure. Evil dragons, people-eating plants, blood-thirsty giants, many more dangerous adversaries lurk at every twist and turn. 34 mazes, stories, solutions. 48pp. 8¼ x 11. 24566-7

LETTERS OF W. A. MOZART, Wolfgang A. Mozart. Remarkable letters show bawdy wit, humor, imagination, musical insights, contemporary musical world; includes some letters from Leopold Mozart. 276pp. 5⅜ x 8½. 22859-2

BASIC PRINCIPLES OF CLASSICAL BALLET, Agrippina Vaganova. Great Russian theoretician, teacher explains methods for teaching classical ballet. 118 illus-trations. 175pp. 5⅜ x 8½. 22036-2

THE JUMPING FROG, Mark Twain. Revenge edition. The original story of The Celebrated Jumping Frog of Calaveras County, a hapless French translation, and Twain's hilarious "retranslation" from the French. 12 illustrations. 66pp. 5⅜ x 8½. 22686-7

BEST REMEMBERED POEMS, Martin Gardner (ed.). The 126 poems in this superb collection of 19th- and 20th-century British and American verse range from Shelley's "To a Skylark" to the impassioned "Renascence" of Edna St. Vincent Millay and to Edward Lear's whimsical "The Owl and the Pussycat." 224pp. 5⅜ x 8½. 27165-X

COMPLETE SONNETS, William Shakespeare. Over 150 exquisite poems deal with love, friendship, the tyranny of time, beauty's evanescence, death and other themes in language of remarkable power, precision and beauty. Glossary of archaic terms. 80pp. 5³⁄₁₆ x 8¼. 26686-9

THE BATTLES THAT CHANGED HISTORY, Fletcher Pratt. Eminent historian profiles 16 crucial conflicts, ancient to modern, that changed the course of civiliza-tion. 352pp. 5⅜ x 8½. 41129-X

THE WIT AND HUMOR OF OSCAR WILDE, Alvin Redman (ed.). More than 1,000 ripostes, paradoxes, wisecracks: Work is the curse of the drinking classes; I can resist everything except temptation; etc. 258pp. 5⅜ x 8½.　　20602-5

SHAKESPEARE LEXICON AND QUOTATION DICTIONARY, Alexander Schmidt. Full definitions, locations, shades of meaning in every word in plays and poems. More than 50,000 exact quotations. 1,485pp. 6½ x 9¼. 2-vol. set.
Vol. 1: 22726-X
Vol. 2: 22727-8

SELECTED POEMS, Emily Dickinson. Over 100 best-known, best-loved poems by one of America's foremost poets, reprinted from authoritative early editions. No comparable edition at this price. Index of first lines. 64pp. 5³⁄₁₆ x 8¼.　　26466-1

THE INSIDIOUS DR. FU-MANCHU, Sax Rohmer. The first of the popular mystery series introduces a pair of English detectives to their archnemesis, the diabolical Dr. Fu-Manchu. Flavorful atmosphere, fast-paced action, and colorful characters enliven this classic of the genre. 208pp. 5³⁄₁₆ x 8¼.　　29898-1

THE MALLEUS MALEFICARUM OF KRAMER AND SPRENGER, translated by Montague Summers. Full text of most important witchhunter's "bible," used by both Catholics and Protestants. 278pp. 6⅝ x 10.　　22802-9

SPANISH STORIES/CUENTOS ESPAÑOLES: A Dual-Language Book, Angel Flores (ed.). Unique format offers 13 great stories in Spanish by Cervantes, Borges, others. Faithful English translations on facing pages. 352pp. 5⅜ x 8½.　　25399-6

GARDEN CITY, LONG ISLAND, IN EARLY PHOTOGRAPHS, 1869–1919, Mildred H. Smith. Handsome treasury of 118 vintage pictures, accompanied by carefully researched captions, document the Garden City Hotel fire (1899), the Vanderbilt Cup Race (1908), the first airmail flight departing from the Nassau Boulevard Aerodrome (1911), and much more. 96pp. 8⅞ x 11¾.　　40669-5

OLD QUEENS, N.Y., IN EARLY PHOTOGRAPHS, Vincent F. Seyfried and William Asadorian. Over 160 rare photographs of Maspeth, Jamaica, Jackson Heights, and other areas. Vintage views of DeWitt Clinton mansion, 1939 World's Fair and more. Captions. 192pp. 8⅞ x 11.　　26358-4

CAPTURED BY THE INDIANS: 15 Firsthand Accounts, 1750-1870, Frederick Drimmer. Astounding true historical accounts of grisly torture, bloody conflicts, relentless pursuits, miraculous escapes and more, by people who lived to tell the tale. 384pp. 5⅜ x 8½.　　24901-8

THE WORLD'S GREAT SPEECHES (Fourth Enlarged Edition), Lewis Copeland, Lawrence W. Lamm, and Stephen J. McKenna. Nearly 300 speeches provide public speakers with a wealth of updated quotes and inspiration—from Pericles' funeral oration and William Jennings Bryan's "Cross of Gold Speech" to Malcolm X's powerful words on the Black Revolution and Earl of Spenser's tribute to his sister, Diana, Princess of Wales. 944pp. 5⅜ x 8⅜.　　40903-1

THE BOOK OF THE SWORD, Sir Richard F. Burton. Great Victorian scholar/adventurer's eloquent, erudite history of the "queen of weapons"–from prehistory to early Roman Empire. Evolution and development of early swords, variations (sabre, broadsword, cutlass, scimitar, etc.), much more. 336pp. 6⅛ x 9¼.
25434-8

AUTOBIOGRAPHY: The Story of My Experiments with Truth, Mohandas K. Gandhi. Boyhood, legal studies, purification, the growth of the Satyagraha (nonviolent protest) movement. Critical, inspiring work of the man responsible for the freedom of India. 480pp. 5⅜ x 8½. (Available in U.S. only.) 24593-4

CELTIC MYTHS AND LEGENDS, T. W. Rolleston. Masterful retelling of Irish and Welsh stories and tales. Cuchulain, King Arthur, Deirdre, the Grail, many more. First paperback edition. 58 full-page illustrations. 512pp. 5⅜ x 8½. 26507-2

THE PRINCIPLES OF PSYCHOLOGY, William James. Famous long course complete, unabridged. Stream of thought, time perception, memory, experimental methods; great work decades ahead of its time. 94 figures. 1,391pp. 5⅜ x 8½. 2-vol. set.
Vol. I: 20381-6 Vol. II: 20382-4

THE WORLD AS WILL AND REPRESENTATION, Arthur Schopenhauer. Definitive English translation of Schopenhauer's life work, correcting more than 1,000 errors, omissions in earlier translations. Translated by E. F. J. Payne. Total of 1,269pp. 5⅜ x 8½. 2-vol. set. Vol. 1: 21761-2 Vol. 2: 21762-0

MAGIC AND MYSTERY IN TIBET, Madame Alexandra David-Neel. Experiences among lamas, magicians, sages, sorcerers, Bonpa wizards. A true psychic discovery. 32 illustrations. 321pp. 5⅜ x 8½. (Available in U.S. only.) 22682-4

THE EGYPTIAN BOOK OF THE DEAD, E. A. Wallis Budge. Complete reproduction of Ani's papyrus, finest ever found. Full hieroglyphic text, interlinear transliteration, word-for-word translation, smooth translation. 533pp. 6½ x 9¼. 21866-X

MATHEMATICS FOR THE NONMATHEMATICIAN, Morris Kline. Detailed, college-level treatment of mathematics in cultural and historical context, with numerous exercises. Recommended Reading Lists. Tables. Numerous figures. 641pp. 5⅜ x 8½.
24823-2

PROBABILISTIC METHODS IN THE THEORY OF STRUCTURES, Isaac Elishakoff. Well-written introduction covers the elements of the theory of probability from two or more random variables, the reliability of such multivariable structures, the theory of random function, Monte Carlo methods of treating problems incapable of exact solution, and more. Examples. 502pp. 5⅜ x 8½. 40691-1

THE RIME OF THE ANCIENT MARINER, Gustave Doré, S. T. Coleridge. Doré's finest work; 34 plates capture moods, subtleties of poem. Flawless full-size reproductions printed on facing pages with authoritative text of poem. "Beautiful. Simply beautiful."–*Publisher's Weekly*. 77pp. 9¼ x 12. 22305-1

NORTH AMERICAN INDIAN DESIGNS FOR ARTISTS AND CRAFTSPEOPLE, Eva Wilson. Over 360 authentic copyright-free designs adapted from Navajo blankets, Hopi pottery, Sioux buffalo hides, more. Geometrics, symbolic figures, plant and animal motifs, etc. 128pp. 8⅜ x 11. (Not for sale in the United Kingdom.) 25341-4

SCULPTURE: Principles and Practice, Louis Slobodkin. Step-by-step approach to clay, plaster, metals, stone; classical and modern. 253 drawings, photos. 255pp. 8⅛ x 11.
22960-2

THE INFLUENCE OF SEA POWER UPON HISTORY, 1660–1783, A. T. Mahan. Influential classic of naval history and tactics still used as text in war colleges. First paperback edition. 4 maps. 24 battle plans. 640pp. 5⅜ x 8½. 25509-3

CATALOG OF DOVER BOOKS

THE STORY OF THE TITANIC AS TOLD BY ITS SURVIVORS, Jack Winocour (ed.). What it was really like. Panic, despair, shocking inefficiency, and a little heroism. More thrilling than any fictional account. 26 illustrations. 320pp. 5⅜ x 8½. 20610-6

FAIRY AND FOLK TALES OF THE IRISH PEASANTRY, William Butler Yeats (ed.). Treasury of 64 tales from the twilight world of Celtic myth and legend: "The Soul Cages," "The Kildare Pooka," "King O'Toole and his Goose," many more. Introduction and Notes by W. B. Yeats. 352pp. 5⅜ x 8½. 26941-8

BUDDHIST MAHAYANA TEXTS, E. B. Cowell and others (eds.). Superb, accurate translations of basic documents in Mahayana Buddhism, highly important in history of religions. The Buddha-karita of Asvaghosha, Larger Sukhavativyuha, more. 448pp. 5⅜ x 8½. 25552-2

ONE TWO THREE . . . INFINITY: Facts and Speculations of Science, George Gamow. Great physicist's fascinating, readable overview of contemporary science: number theory, relativity, fourth dimension, entropy, genes, atomic structure, much more. 128 illustrations. Index. 352pp. 5⅜ x 8½. 25664-2

EXPERIMENTATION AND MEASUREMENT, W. J. Youden. Introductory manual explains laws of measurement in simple terms and offers tips for achieving accuracy and minimizing errors. Mathematics of measurement, use of instruments, experimenting with machines. 1994 edition. Foreword. Preface. Introduction. Epilogue. Selected Readings. Glossary. Index. Tables and figures. 128pp. 5⅜ x 8½. 40451-X

DALÍ ON MODERN ART: The Cuckolds of Antiquated Modern Art, Salvador Dalí. Influential painter skewers modern art and its practitioners. Outrageous evaluations of Picasso, Cézanne, Turner, more. 15 renderings of paintings discussed. 44 calligraphic decorations by Dalí. 96pp. 5⅜ x 8½. (Available in U.S. only.) 29220-7

ANTIQUE PLAYING CARDS: A Pictorial History, Henry René D'Allemagne. Over 900 elaborate, decorative images from rare playing cards (14th–20th centuries): Bacchus, death, dancing dogs, hunting scenes, royal coats of arms, players cheating, much more. 96pp. 9¼ x 12¼. 29265-7

MAKING FURNITURE MASTERPIECES: 30 Projects with Measured Drawings, Franklin H. Gottshall. Step-by-step instructions, illustrations for constructing handsome, useful pieces, among them a Sheraton desk, Chippendale chair, Spanish desk, Queen Anne table and a William and Mary dressing mirror. 224pp. 8⅛ x 11¼. 29338-6

THE FOSSIL BOOK: A Record of Prehistoric Life, Patricia V. Rich et al. Profusely illustrated definitive guide covers everything from single-celled organisms and dinosaurs to birds and mammals and the interplay between climate and man. Over 1,500 illustrations. 760pp. 7½ x 10⅛. 29371-8

Paperbound unless otherwise indicated. Available at your book dealer, online at **www.doverpublications.com**, or by writing to Dept. GI, Dover Publications, Inc., 31 East 2nd Street, Mineola, NY 11501. For current price information or for free catalogues (please indicate field of interest), write to Dover Publications or log on to **www.doverpublications.com** and see every Dover book in print. Dover publishes more than 500 books each year on science, elementary and advanced mathematics, biology, music, art, literary history, social sciences, and other areas.